Pershing's Tankers

AUSA Books

Series Editor: Joseph Craig

PERSHING'S TANKERS

Personal Accounts of the AEF Tank Corps in World War I

Edited by
Lawrence M. Kaplan

Foreword by
Dale E. Wilson

UNIVERSITY PRESS OF KENTUCKY

Scholarly publisher for the Commonwealth,
serving Bellarmine University, Berea College, Centre College of Kentucky, Eastern Kentucky University, The Filson Historical Society, Georgetown College, Kentucky Historical Society, Kentucky State University, Morehead State University, Murray State University, Northern Kentucky University, Transylvania University, University of Kentucky, University of Louisville, and Western Kentucky University.

Editorial and Sales Offices: The University Press of Kentucky
663 South Limestone Street, Lexington, Kentucky 40508-4008
www.kentuckypress.com

Library of Congress Cataloging-in-Publication Data

Names: Kaplan, Lawrence M. (Lawrence Martin), 1954- editor. | Wilson, Dale, 1951- writer of foreword.
Title: Pershing's tankers : personal accounts of the AEF Tank Corps in World War I / edited by Lawrence M. Kaplan ; foreword by Dale E. Wilson.
Description: Lexington, Kentucky : University Press of Kentucky, [2018] | Series: AUSA book | Includes index.
Identifiers: LCCN 2018006256| ISBN 9780813176048 (hardcover : alk. paper) | ISBN 9780813176062 (pdf) | ISBN 9780813176055 (epub)
Subjects: LCSH: United States. Army. Tank Corps--History. | World War, — 1914-1918—Europe—Personal narratives, American. | World War, 1914-1918—Europe—Tank warfare.
Classification: LCC D570.9 .P44 2018 | DDC 940.4/1273—dc23

This book is printed on acid-free paper meeting the requirements of the American National Standard for Permanence in Paper for Printed Library Materials.

Manufactured in the United States of America.

Member of the Association of University Presses

Contents

IV. Unofficial Personal Accounts 181

Illustrations

Foreword

Lawrence Kaplan has done readers interested in America's first experience with armored warfare a valuable service by compiling this collection of personal-experience reports by US Army Tank Corps officers and men written immediately after World War I, as well as other primary-source documents that convey the reminiscences of America's first tankers.

The cornerstone of this collection is the narratives American Expeditionary Forces (AEF) Tank Corps commander Brigadier General Samuel D. Rockenbach ordered his officers to write while their experiences were fresh in their minds. Hoping to capture the essence of armored warfare and the important place it had on the modern battlefield, he instructed them to write in the first person and to avoid the dull language characteristic of most after-action reports. Not all of these narratives survived the bureaucratic vagaries of military archives, but enough did to give us an excellent feel for what it was like to plow through German defenses in plodding steeds whose engines created a veritable hell inside their overheated steel walls that proved woefully inadequate against direct hits from enemy artillery pieces.

The editor has been careful to preserve the flavor of the men's accounts while, at the same time, making judicious edits that correct spellings of place-names and clarify some of the military jargon of the era. The reader is thus able to gain fresh insights into this important aspect of the America military experience.

Among those whose accounts are included in this volume are General Rockenbach; Colonel Ira C. Welborn, director of Tank Corps activities in the United States; Colonel George S. Patton Jr., commander of the 304th Tank Brigade; Major Sereno Brett, commander of the 344th Tank Battalion; and a host of captains and lieutenants who commanded companies, led platoons, or served as reconnaissance, maintenance, or staff officers in the light and heavy tank units that fought in the waning months of the war. Their stories reflect the youthful exuberance characteristic of the young men of that era, tempered by the crushing weight of the overwhelming horror of conflict on the battlefields of France in World War I.

Best of all, these accounts are all neatly compiled for readers, sparing them the laborious search the editor made to bring them together in this volume.

Dale E. Wilson
Major, Armor, US Army (Ret.)

Editor's Introduction

The US Army established the Tank Corps in 1918 to help break the deadlock of trench warfare in France in World War I. The army organized the Tank Corps (with components in the United States and France) with British and French cooperation. As plans got under way to train, man, and equip its battalions with American-made tanks, Tank Corps battalions in the American Expeditionary Forces (AEF) were initially equipped with British and French tanks to conduct combat operations. Three of these battalions participated in combat operations during the war. Other battalions in France were being trained and equipped for operations expected to last into 1919, but the war ended unexpectedly on November 11, 1918, before they were ready to be deployed. The 301st Tank Battalion, equipped with British Mark V series heavy tanks and the 326th and 327th light tank battalions (later redesignated the 344th and 345th Tank Battalions), equipped with French Renault tanks, saw limited action over a seven-week period from September 12 to November 1, 1918. The 301st Tank Battalion supported British operations in the Cambrai, St. Quentin sector of the Hindenburg Line, and the 344th and 345th Tank Battalions supported American operations in St. Mihiel and the Meuse-Argonne Offensive.[1]

Shortly after the war ended, on December 4, 1918, Brigadier General Samuel D. Rockenbach, chief of the AEF Tank Corps, issued a memorandum to every Tank Corps officer in France to record their personal experiences in the war to help document the achievements of the Tank Corps. The narratives were to be no longer than one thousand words, containing "all possible local color and human interest" and written in the second person to provide a "vivid, interesting story," not a report.[2]

It is unclear how many officers responded to the memo since the original records no longer exist. The Tank School at Fort George G. Meade, Maryland, subsequently printed a "Compilation of Extracts from Personal Reports of Tank Officers in the World War" that contained a selection of thirty-five personal accounts. Additional accounts also survived in the papers of George S. Patton Jr., at the Library of Congress in Washington, DC, and the papers of Joseph Viner, in the collection of the US Army Armor School at Fort Benning, Georgia. Both Patton and Viner were officers in the AEF Tank Corps. Several infantry officers who served in the Tank Corps during the war also wrote about their personal experiences in papers for the Infantry Officer Advanced Course at Fort Benning, Georgia, in the late 1920s and early 1930s.

It is the purpose of this book to present the human side of Tank Corps operations in World War I, largely through personal accounts, to complement the operational histories that have been written about the Tank Corps. The following personal accounts offer a rare glimpse into the thoughts and experiences of a select few who served with the US Army Tank Corps during World War I. They include commentary from several Tank Corps senior leaders, including General Rockenbach, as well as personal official and unofficial accounts from a variety of soldiers who served in the Tank Corps. General Rockenbach entrusted Colonel George S. Patton Jr., commander of the 304th Tank Brigade, AEF, whose units participated in combat, with collecting the personal-experience accounts from Tank Corps personnel. This volume contains forty-eight official personal-experience reports (including one Infantry Officer Advanced Course paper), twenty-nine unofficial accounts that appeared in the press and other published sources, and six personal letters that George Patton wrote to his wife and father. The personal-experience narratives George Patton collected were never intended for a civilian audience. In a variety of cases, their writers took a somewhat lighthearted view of their experiences rather than writing in a more formal military style. Their narratives vary in size, scope, and depth, and cover a range of topics, including the organizing, training, and equipping of the Tank Corps, as well as its combat operations. In contrast, the Infantry Officer Advanced Course paper, which is longer and includes historical background, was written in a more formal military style. George Patton's personal letters were also never intended for the public, particularly a confession he made to his wife that he assaulted and may have killed an American soldier during a battle for not performing to his satisfaction, an offense that likely would have resulted in a court-martial if investigated.

The following volume includes an edited collection of the Tank Corps personal accounts. Since several personal accounts do not discuss Tank Corps events or operations, these have been excluded from this volume. A number of personal reports contained unintentional misspellings, including proper names and geographic locations. In editing the official narratives, full proper names and titles have been included when possible, abbreviations of military ranks have been written out, misspelled names and unintentional spelling errors—particularly of geographic locations—have been corrected, proper terms for acronyms have been provided when possible, and some style and punctuation changes have been made, including removing paragraph numbers, to standardize the narrative formats.

I

Historical Summary of US Army Tank Corps Operations

When World War I began in August 1914, none of the major belligerents envisioned that the tremendous firepower of modern rapid-fire weapons would contribute to a prolonged period of stabilized warfare on the western front, where defensive firepower predominated and both sides lost the power of maneuver. In trench warfare, a stalemate resulted where each side concentrated great masses of troops and guns on a specific area of the front and made repeated efforts to break through opposing lines that were well protected by dense barbed-wire entanglements. Such actions were very costly, particularly in men, and it became apparent to the Allies, led by Great Britain and France, that some means had to be devised of breaking the stalemate.[1]

Part of the problem leading to the stalemate was the failure of field artillery to enable infantry to maneuver. Earlier, the Russo-Japanese War (1904–5) had demonstrated that infantry could no longer advance under its own firepower against entrenched opponents armed with machine guns without suffering excessive casualties. The general doctrinal solution to counter these conditions called for infantry to be supported by concealed field artillery using observed indirect fire, where a forward observer would relay targeting information back to the guns through some means of communication. The field artillery would then provide timely and responsive fire support to the advancing infantry, which included destroying targets of opportunity such as machine gun nests and enemy artillery batteries. With horse-drawn artillery, this type of fire support put a premium on efficiently destroying targets without wasting large amounts of ammunition and thereby creating resupply problems as the army advanced. The advent of rapid-fire field artillery guns prior to World War I, such as the German Model 1896 77mm gun (Germany's standard divisional field gun during the war) that could fire ten or more rounds per minute, versus its predecessor that could fire one to three rounds per minute, and the French Model 1897 75mm gun (France's standard divisional field gun during the war) that could fire more than twenty rounds per minute, had unforeseen consequences on executing the prewar doctrine. The implications of rapid-fire field artillery were not fully understood by the war's major belligerents, who miscalculated their long-term requirements for artillery ammunition based on its expenditure in the Russo-Japanese War, where there was no rapid-fire field artillery. These miscalculations led both sides to underestimate how much reserve artillery ammunition they needed, and artillery ammunition stockpiles became seriously depleted by the fall of 1914. These ammunition shortfalls soon contributed to a breakdown in artillery support for the infantry, which entrenched itself for defensive purposes along the western front until some means of responsive fire support could once again protect their advance.

By the time industrial production began supplying adequate amounts of artillery ammunition to the belligerents in 1915, the French and British had adjusted to stabilized trench warfare conditions by adopting artillery methods better suited for siege warfare than maneuver warfare. Now, artillery of all types relied largely on preplanned, unobserved, ammunition-intensive barrage fire on designated map coordinates (which destroyed the element of surprise) rather than on the timely and responsive observed indirect fire formerly used in maneuver warfare. This created a situation where advancing infantry could not destroy targets of opportunity, such as machine gun nests, which proliferated on the battlefield, or exploit opportunities for breaking through the enemy's lines and advancing beyond the range of largely static artillery support batteries. Furthermore, by the end of 1915, the French and British had come to believe that the prewar doctrine of observed indirect field artillery was largely obsolete and that preplanned ammunition-intensive barrages were the new norm for modern warfare. In practical terms, however, the infantry still needed some means of responsive fire support that could accompany their advance, and large barrages—which typically preceded an attack by hours or even days—were not the answer.

One solution to breaking the deadlock of trench warfare involved developing new and improved weapons to assist infantry advances. Infantry began adopting tactical mortars in 1915 to cover their advances, but these weapons did not have enough range or firepower to effectively replace field artillery. If infantry could no longer depend on indirect fire support to enable their advance, then devising a new means of direct fire support offered a possible alternative solution.

Both the British and French ultimately found a solution to breaking the deadlock of trench warfare in the development of an armored vehicle that could provide direct fire support to advancing infantry, the tank. In late 1914, the British began developing an armored vehicle to attack machine gun nests that evolved into the large Mark I tank. This was the first armored vehicle capable of traversing immense fields of barbed wire and crossing German trenches. These tanks became operational during the summer of 1916 in the Somme Offensive. In 1914, the French army also began designing an armored vehicle to break through enemy lines, which led to several models, including the small Renault tank, capable of destroying barbed wire and machine gun nests to clear the way for infantry advances. These tanks became operational during the Second Battle of the Marne in 1918.

When the United States entered the war in April 1917, the US Army recognized the necessity of adopting a tank. In determining which type to deploy—the British heavy tank or the French light tank—the army resolved to use both, organized into light and heavy tank battalions, with more of the former than of the latter. The army sent four officers to France to study French tanks and armor tactics. They also began negotiations to purchase some French light tanks as prototypes of an improved American-made version. While these negotiations were under way, the army conducted a comprehensive study of the then-current British tank, the Mark V, both "male" and "female" versions, the former being armed with a six-pounder (57mm) cannon and the latter with .30-caliber Hotchkiss machine guns. The British and Americans subsequently formed a joint commission to develop a new or improved heavy tank, the Mark VIII (see appendix A).

During the fall of 1917, General John J. Pershing, commander of the American Expeditionary Forces (AEF) in France, approved plans for an overseas tank corps, based upon an army to be composed of twenty combat divisions. As originally planned, the AEF Tank Corps was to consist of a headquarters and five heavy and twenty light tank battalions. Later plans increased the heavy battalions to ten. On December 22, 1917, Colonel Samuel D. Rockenbach, a cavalryman attached to General Pershing's headquarters, received an appointment as the chief of the Tank Corps. AEF plans developed for this organization called for a general headquarters, three tank centers (for training and replacement of personnel), two army tank headquarters, and ten brigades. Assembly of the Tank Corps, with an authorized strength of 14,827, began on January 26, 1918.

All AEF Tank Corps units were assigned to the General Headquarters (GHQ), Tank Corps. The GHQ established a light tank school at Langres, France, and an army school center; and it selected officers and men from various organizations in France for transfer to the Tank Corps. Those soldiers initially sent to Langres became members of the 1st Battalion, 1st Light Tank Center, which consisted of a headquarters and three companies, A, B, and C. For specific combat missions, Tank Corps units were attached to armies or to subordinate elements and reverted to GHQ control as directed. An army tank headquarters, designed to function with an army headquarters, consisted of a headquarters and a heavy artillery mobile ordnance repair shop.

Tables of organization and equipment for other Tank Corps organizations were developed in 1918, although shortages of personnel and equipment for their full use prevented conclusive tests during combat. The tables provided for a light battalion of seventy-two light tanks and a heavy battalion of sixty-nine heavy tanks. Both types of battalions had three companies of three platoons each and a battalion headquarters. All platoons were equipped with five tanks. The tank brigade, with a combined total of 225 tanks, consisted of two light battalions, a heavy battalion, a repair and salvage company, and a brigade headquarters. Almost identical to the brigade headquarters was the headquarters of a light or a heavy tank center.

In November 1917, Captain George S. Patton Jr., a cavalryman attached to General Pershing's headquarters, became the first officer to be attached to the AEF Tank Corps. He first took on the task of organizing the light tank school at Langres. He subsequently organized and commanded the 1st Tank Center (redesignated the 302d Tank Center) and the 304th Tank Brigade, which included two light tank battalions that deployed in combat. He also received successive promotions to the rank of colonel by October 1918.

In the United States, the War Department began developing a tank organization similar to the AEF Tank Corps. On February 18, 1918, the War Department authorized a Tank Service in the National Army, a temporary force raised for the duration of the war, under the chief of engineers, and reorganized the 65th Engineers into tank battalions. The Tank Service, under Colonel Harley B. Ferguson, had an authorized strength of 914 officers and 14,746 men, and became a separate branch of the army on March 5. The War Department then revised its initial plans on March 22, after envisioning a greater role for tanks in the war, and created an independent Tank Corps under the command of Colonel Ira C. Welborn, an infantryman. The US Tank Corps had an authorized strength of 925 officers and 13,911 men. The War Department charged Colonel Welborn with organizing, arming, equipping, and training tank units, as well as supervising all tank activities in the United States, including procurement of officers and enlisted men and the establishment and maintenance of tank camps. Neither the Tank Service nor the Tank Corps in the United States had any direct command relationship with the AEF Tank Corps.

Tank units in the AEF and National Army were organized in three separate areas during 1918—in the United States, in England, and in France. Some redundancy occurred in numerical unit designations that required their redesignation to eliminate the duplications. For example, after the 1st Heavy Tank Battalion, Tank Service, sailed for England in March 1918, its designation changed to the 41st Tank Battalion and then, shortly after its arrival in England, to the 301st Tank Battalion, Tank Corps. The organization of the 325th and

326th Tank Battalions in the United States, which deployed to France, also led to the designations of two battalions in France with the same designations being changed in September 1918 to the 344th and 345th Tank Battalions, respectively. Tank units of all types were finally numbered in the 300 series.

The first tank units were organized in February 1918 as elements of the 65th Engineers. The 1st Separate Battalion, Heavy Tank Service, 65th Engineers, and the 1st Battalion and 2d Battalion, Light Tank Service, 65th Engineers, were at Camp Upton, New York, while Company D, 2d Battalion, Heavy Tank Service, 65th Engineers, was at Camp Meade, Maryland. These elements were redesignated during the war as separate battalions, numbered in the 300 series. All tank battalions were numbered 301–346, but those from 309 through 325 were not organized (see appendix B).

The army formed four tank brigades. Originally organized as the 1st, 2d, 3d, and 4th Provisional Tank Brigades, they were redesignated in late 1918 as the 304th through the 307th Tank Brigades, respectively.

The tank centers were also in the 300 series, being numbered from 301 through 314, although the 305th through the 308th and the 312th and 313th were never organized. The first tank centers, established overseas in February and March 1918, were initially designated as the 1st Light Tank Center and the 2d Heavy Tank Center. They, too, were integrated into the 300 series.

Despite a concerted effort to organize and equip tank units as soon as possible, by June 1918, only seven hundred men were in the AEF Tank Corps and about five thousand in the continental US organization. By late July 1918, the combat tank units overseas consisted of two heavy battalion headquarters, three heavy companies, two light battalion headquarters, and six light companies. In the United States they included a heavy battalion headquarters, twelve heavy companies, a light battalion headquarters, and twenty-four light companies (see appendix C). As late as mid-August 1918 no combat tanks had been assigned to any unit of either Tank Corps. In September, two light tank battalions, the 344th and 345th, equipped with French tanks, fought with the US First Army; a battalion of heavy tanks, the 301st, equipped with British tanks, fought with the US 27th and 30th Divisions.

The 344th and 345th light tank battalions belonged to the 304th Tank Brigade, commanded by Colonel Patton, who had supervised their training at the 1st Light Tank Center in Bourg, France. These units, equipped with 144 Renault tanks, were the first American tank battalions to enter combat on September 12, 1918, against the St. Mihiel salient with the First Army (see appendix D). Weighing a little over seven tons, the two-man Renault tank had a maximum speed of six miles per hour and was armed with either a 37mm gun or a .30-caliber Hotchkiss machine gun. For the attack, the 344th was initially assigned to the 1st Division and the 345th to the 42d Division, with sixteen tanks from the 344th and twenty-five from the 345th composing the brigade reserve. Muddy conditions, caused by several days of heavy rain, including the night before the offensive, resulted in a much greater consumption of gasoline than anticipated. Although mud, lack of gas, and mechanical failure caused many tanks to stall in the German trenches, the attack succeeded. After the offensive accomplished its objectives, the two tank battalions withdrew for reorganization to later take part in the Meuse-Argonne Offensive. When the Meuse-Argonne Offensive opened on the morning of September 26, the two light tank battalions, assigned to the 28th and 35th Infantry Divisions and reduced to 123 tanks, led off the attack and took part in the offensive from start to finish (see appendix E).

The 301st heavy tank battalion trained at the British Tank School at Wareham, England, from April until August 1918. In France, the British equipped the battalion with forty-eight Mark V and Mark V Star tanks, and it underwent two weeks of intensive training with the US 27th Infantry Division before going into action with that division opposite the Bellicourt Tunnel, with the village of Bony as its objective on September 29, 1918 (see appendix F). Both the Mark V and the Mark V Star typically had eight-man crews and a maximum speed of approximately four miles per hour. The Mark V Star, weighing thirty-six or thirty-seven tons, depending upon armament, was about five tons heavier than the Mark V. Both were armed with either two six-pounder guns or an additional two machine guns, which were added to the Mark V's usual four machine guns or the Mark V Star's usual five. In its first engagement, the tanks were divided among three US infantry regiments of the 27th Division and the Australian Corps Reserve. Although the attack reached its objective, it was several hours late and considered unsuccessful. Heavy mist and haze made visibility extremely poor, but the failure was attributed mainly to lack of combined tank and infantry training before the operation and a consequent lack of coordination between the two elements as the attack progressed. The battalion also experienced unexpected difficulties when the British neglected to inform them they would be crossing an old British minefield, which resulted in several tanks being disabled by British mines. The battalion lost a total of fifteen tanks to the mines, direct hits by artillery, and mechanical trouble.

On October 8, nineteen tanks of the battalion went into action with the US 30th Infantry Division at Brancourt, where tank-infantry cooperation was excellent, and the tanks earned a large share of the credit for the successful advance. On October 17, the battalion went into action with the US 27th and 30th Divisions at St. Souplet in the La Salle Valley, where the Selle River prevented the tanks from advancing (see appendix G). On October 23, the battalion could muster only a composite company of twelve tanks to support the British at Mormal Forest, but the attack reached its objective (see appendix H). When the armistice ended the war on November 11, the battalion was in a training area behind the lines preparing to take part in an attack scheduled for November 13.

By the time of the armistice, the AEF was critically short of tanks. The War Department's plans for the Tank Corps envisioned equipping its forces with an American-made light tank, based on an improved Renault design, a new American-made Ford light tank, and an improved British Mark V series tank designated the Mark VIII. Unforeseen bureaucratic and production challenges hampered both light and heavy tank production. The first American-made Renault light tanks did not become available in France until after the armistice. Ten of these light tanks arrived in France on November 20, 1918. One prototype Ford light tank was tested in France in October but was judged inferior to the Renault. Ford had a contract to build large numbers of its tank, but only a few were produced before the contract was terminated due to the end of war. No Mark VIII tanks were produced before the end of the war. The Anglo-American facility in France designed to assemble one hundred Mark VIII tanks per day, using British and American parts, was about three weeks away from being completed when construction on it ceased the day of the armistice (see appendix I).

At the end of the war, the strength of the AEF Tank Corps and the National Army Tank Corps reached a total of 1,090 officers and 14,780 enlisted men. Fifty-three percent of the total Tank Corps personnel were in the United States and the remainder either overseas or en route.

II

Tank Corps Senior Leader Commentary

Colonel Ira C. Welborn, Report of the Director of the Tank Corps

The following statement from Colonel Welborn is from "Report of the Director of Tank Corps," Office of the Director of Tank Corps, Washington, DC, September 9, 1918, in *War Department Annual Reports*, vol. 1 (Washington, DC: Government Printing Office, 1919), 1393–95:

On February 18, 1918, the Tank Service of the National Army was authorized and placed under the control of the Chief of Engineers as a branch of that service. For some time previous to that date a general tank project for the United States Army was being formulated under the direction of the commanding general, American Expeditionary Forces, in France, based on the experience gained by the British and French armies in the employment of this new and interesting arm of the service.

To start the organization a regiment of Engineers was begun, which was designated the 65th Engineers. The units of this regiment were created at Camp Lee, PA., Camp Meade, MD., Camp Upton, N.Y., Camp Devens, Mass., and Camp Cody, N.M. With the exception of one battalion of three companies which moved overseas in March, the remaining companies of the 65th Engineers were concentrated at Camp Colt, Gettysburg, PA., during the latter part of March, which place had been selected for general concentration and preliminary training for the tank corps.

Anticipating the rapid growth of this new arm of the service, the Secretary of War, under date of March 6, 1918, directed the organization of the Tank Corps and removed it from under direction of the Chief of Engineers.

Up to this time Col. Harley B. Ferguson of the Engineers, had been in charge of the organization of the Tank Service under the Engineer Corps. On March 9, 1918, he was relieved by Col. Ira C. Welborn, Tank Corps, formerly lieutenant colonel, Infantry, who was appointed and designated Director of the Tank Corps in the United States. A staff was selected and immediate steps taken toward the organization of the Tank Corps.

Col. Samuel D. Rockenbach, Cavalry, attached to the staff of the commanding general, American Expeditionary Forces, and had for some time been formulating the tank project, was appointed chief of the Tank Corps. This officer has since been commissioned in the grade of brigadier general. . . .

The Ordnance Department was charged with the task of tank production and Lt. Col. H. W. Alden, Ordnance Department, assigned in general charge of this undertaking. Since all information relating to tank production is of a strictly secret nature no statements bearing on the subject can be properly made at this time.

On April 15 authority was obtained from the War Department for the enlistment in the Tank Corps of men between the ages of 18 and 40 years, excepting draft registrants, whose voluntary induction for this service was also authorized. Immediately a number of specially selected officers of the Tank Corps were dispatched to various sections of the United States for recruiting duty. They were located at Boston, New York City, Philadelphia, Chicago, Detroit, St. Paul, Kansas City, and Birmingham. From these radial points the adjoining states were reached, and since that date special tours have been made of the south and on the Pacific coast and through the northwestern states. In this manner exceptionally fine types of men were obtained. The appeal of the Tank Corps has been so strong that over 25 percent of the enlisted strength of the corps was obtained through voluntary enlistments of men under and over the limits of the first draft law. The men obtained through voluntary induction came into the service voluntarily and chose the Tank Corps for the reason that they desired to enter a strictly fighting branch of the service. This has resulted in the gathering together of a considerable number of men from nearly every strata of life and has established an excellent esprit de corps. These men came from business and professional life, farm and factory, mill and mine, and the composite type of Tank Corps soldier is representative of the best that typifies American manhood.

Officers of the Tank Corps in the United States have been obtained from various sources. A few transferred from the Regular Army, and a considerable number of second lieutenants were selected from among the qualified candidates at the officers' training camps, while others were transferred from other branches of the service.

Due to the scarcity of officers and the fact that abundant officer material existed among the enlisted men of the Tank Corps, an officers' training school was established at Gettysburg by June 15. A number of candidates qualified out of this school and were commissioned second lieutenants, Tank Corps. Subsequent schools have been held with the result that a large number of highly qualified officers for the grade of second lieutenant had been obtained in this manner.

About July 15, Col. William H. Clapton, Jr., Tank Corps, arrived in the United States with a corps of assistants, both commissioned and noncommissioned, for the purpose of establishing a tank training center. These officers had been in training in England and France in tank training centers for the purpose of returning to the United States and establishing a training center here. Tobyhanna, PA., formerly a field artillery and target range in the mountains of Pennsylvania, was selected for a summer training center and tank units transferred to this camp from Camp Colt at Gettysburg.

Neither of the camps at Gettysburg or Tobyhanna is suitable for winter training. It was necessary, therefore, to select a permanent camp and tank training center where training may be had the year round. After a thorough inspection of many proposed sites, Raleigh, N.C., was selected, and established about three miles from that city. Construction work will soon begin on this camp.

Brigadier General Samuel D. Rockenbach, Congressional Testimony

The following statement from Brigadier General Samuel D. Rockenbach, chief of the AEF Tank Corps, has been compiled and edited from his August 29, 1919, congressional testimony in *Hearings before the Subcommittee No. 5 (Ordnance) of the Select Committee on Expenditures in the War Department,* House of Representatives, Sixty-Sixth Congress, First Session on War Expenditures, Serial 6—Part 1 (Washington, DC: Government Printing Office, 1919), 541–70:

I was assigned to General [John J.] Pershing's staff before his departure for France, accompanied him to France, and then on June 20, 1917, to December 20, 1917, I was in charge of Base Section No. 1 [Services of Supply].[1] I was then ordered to headquarters and appointed Chief of Tank Corps, American Expeditionary Forces (AEF), in January 1918. I got up the Tank Corps and had absolute authority in regard to its personnel and machines and then persuaded the French and British to sell me what we used.

In the American Expeditionary Forces it was purely a merit system. I could get practically no officers from the Regular Army. I was told there were none to spare, and that I could cable for them and get them where I could. I, of course, did get a few, a dozen or more, then we cabled to the United States and requested the corps be raised over here, every officer to be given a grade junior to what we expected him to fill. We put them into our schools in England and in France, and purely according to the merit that they displayed we made them. We literally carried out the motto "Show me and I will shove you." We had youngsters to jump up to high commands right away. For instance, both my brigade commanders, who are very excellent men, have only permanent rank of captain.[2]

We could not adopt the British or French system, which provided for fighting a maximum of three days and then retiring for repairs. The British and French were organized to fight a maximum of three days. To win the war we had to keep up a continuous fight, and that under our commander-in-chief that would be required, so I prepared my companies so the men who fought today, what was left of them, would not fight tomorrow.

Both the British and French recognized that early in 1917; that is, both the British and French military commanders. But they could make very little impression on what you might call the general war council of each nation, and the failure to make an impression which would insure [tank] production was due to the fact that they were producing pretty nearly everything they could.

That was the situation at the first of 1917, but both the British and the French had succeeded in putting a limited number [of tanks] into production. I think the French had gotten authority for a thousand Renault [light tanks] and the British for 500 Mark IV [heavy tanks], which was not very much good, but still they did good fighting. They tried that out off and on during the year of 1917, until the 20th of November 1917, when they [British] made their big attack on Cambrai. At Cambrai they broke 12,000 yards of front and advanced 13,000 yards without firing a shell, with no preliminary bombardment. The saving of that bombardment was estimated to have been worth something like five times what the British tanks cost.

While the British tanks broke through and advanced 13,000 yards, the infantry could not follow them up, they could not go over that No Man's Land with the infantry. They punctured this great rectangle into the Boche [German] line, and on the 28th the Boche started a counterattack from the northeast and from the southeast and hit this wedge that they had punched in there. The north side held, but the south side broke away, so on the third day of December the position of the British Army at Cambrai was worse than it was before the attack. It was an absolutely successful demonstration of the value of tanks, and strategically, it held five German divisions that had started for Italy. Those divisions were brought back, so the thing was a wonderful success and raised the interest in and insured the production of tanks.

When we went into the game the British had some 14 types and the French four. We rejected all but one of the French—the Renault, a [two-man] light tank, which can only cantilever a six-foot ditch. When we went in with the British we would not accept any of their designs. It finally ended up by the meeting coming to an absolute deadlock. I said they had no machine fit to fight with; the best have been aptly described as a deaf, dumb, and blind beast. We then combined on a machine which, in round numbers, was 30 feet long, 30 tons in weight, carried two six-pound guns and six machine guns; would cantilever a 16 foot trench; had flotation of less than a man; but less than nine pounds pressure per square inch on the ground; it of course knocked down all wire it came to and the ordinary European house, which corresponds somewhat to a 50 [foot] × 30 [foot] brick house in the United States. When we could not get the machine gunners out of the second story we rammed the house and went through it, and the house came down, and the machine gunners, of course, came out.

Having decided on the functions, decided on the designs—that we would only take two types and would only take fighting machines—then came up, of course, the question of the production. Neither France nor Great Britain had produced, starting from the design, a tank in less than 19 months, and had not put any usable number in production in less than 18 months, hence you can see the importance of reducing your types of machines down to a minimum. We had the experience of the British and French, and we escaped the numerous types they had, and over there [Europe] we were not bothered by people who had all kinds of theories.

I went over the French and British front and found out what the fighting man wanted, and then we gave the general specifications and started in to make the Mark VIII or Anglo-American tank. The British would not have gone in with us if they had had the material and the manpower to have made a complete machine. We were coming in the last, and no nation had either the material or the manpower and the mechanics with which to produce the tanks in quantities large enough to be of great value. Being able to take advantage of the British experiments, we cut out 14 types of tanks, and saved $23,000,000. That is, in order to get into the tank game up to the point of the French and British development, if we had had the start on it, and assuming we would not have done any better than they did, would have cost $23,000,000, for 14 types of tanks, which were simply death traps.

The British had, when we came in, the best tank, the Mark IV. It was much quicker to modify that tank than to put a new one into production, so they started improving the Mark IV, to make the Mark VIII or Anglo-American tank out of it. I think the first thing they did was to increase the power and make what they called the Mark V. Then they had too much pressure on the ground, and they elongated it and made the Mark V-Star, and then they tried to make the Mark V-Two Star, which, if it had been completed, would have been really the Anglo-American tank.

The Mark IV was filled up with machinery, and unless you were an expert and all the time dodging, you would get put out of commission by getting burned on your own machinery. We insisted, in the first place, on a certain number of pounds per square inch, which they agreed to. We insisted on them being reduced to that of a man; that there should be 10 horsepower per ton weight, which would give us that 30-ton tank that we wanted, with a 300 horsepower engine; that there should be a bulkhead separating the engine room from the gun room, so that there would be no chance of a man getting hurt, and then there were quite a number of minor changes. The Mark IV required four men to drive it. The Mark VIII is as simple to drive as a truck and required only one man. We increased the visibility; we got six machine guns into it, with two six-pounder guns. The gun power and the ammunition carried by that machine, which is handled by an officer and nine men, if operated by artillery and machine gunners, would require 150 men and something like 68 horses, equal to half a battery of field artillery with all its transportation. And there is a thing that is not understood about the tank; one battalion of 49 heavy tanks is equal in gun power to two regiments of field artillery with all its transportation. In addition, it has four wireless signal tanks.

I could not make anybody understand what we were doing. We put in front of the American army at St. Mihiel and in places on the Argonne a gun and a cannon and machine gun power that no army had ever advanced with before.[3] I have tanks that, by counting hits per square foot, we estimate were hit over 3,000 times with rifle bullets and shrapnel fragments.[4] The commander of that tank reported he had not been under any severe fire. You can easily see that when you hit a space 12 [feet] by six [feet]—that is, 72 square feet—a couple of thousand times with bullets, the fire is rather fierce.

It was absolutely impossible, in view of the congested state of our manufactures and production, for us to produce any special armor plate for tanks or special guns for tanks. I knew it would take me a year to put a [57mm] six-pounder, which is a 2.28[-inch] gun, a short gun, into production, so our inter-allied agreement was made with the British with a view to their furnishing what they could furnish quickly and our furnishing what we could furnish quickly.

To produce [the Mark VIII] tank we had to get a 300-horsepower engine already in production. The only engine we could get which was light enough and had the power necessary was the Liberty [aircraft] engine. It is not the motor that we wanted, that is, it was not heavy enough. It was not specially designed to fit into the tank, but, as you understand, it was not possible to get a motor that was not in production, so we had to take what we could get, the nearest engine that would fit the tank. You hear the argument against it that it has for aviation a life of only 200 hours. That is not the case with tanks. For instance, the Aviation Corps counts on doing 100 miles an hour, and for 200 hours that is 20,000 miles. Well, if we can get a tank to run 20,000 miles we will be doing more than the best tank has ever done before.

Before entering into that agreement we cabled the United States, and were informed by the aviation section that they could give us 1,200 Liberty engines by the 1st of June. They fell down on that; they could not produce them. We were going on the assumption that our engines were coming on all right, and it is not up until after the middle of May that I am informed that they cannot produce them. Now, then, they say they will have to reduce on us. They did not say it was a complete fall down. Then, I think in June, we got word that they could not furnish any. I know that I was pretty nearly flabbergasted over it, and a good many of my tank corps wanted to leave me after they had gotten all their training, because we were all anxious to get into the fight.

The promise was made by the aviation section of the Signal Corps. Aviation was not separate then [as an independent branch]. It not only failed to produce engines, but it went out of existence itself. The Aviation Service then started in and told us definitely what they could do.[5] I think that they could handle some 10 or 15 percent of what we required by November. The Ordnance Department then started in on the independent production of the Liberty engine, outside of the Aviation Service. They did have their components ready the 1st of November for a limited number. Of course, the main thing was getting them in production, and getting in shape so as to get them to one place to assemble their parts. Well, I think they expected, and I think it was pretty well founded, that they would have all the American components complete in January 1919, and they expected to make their first shipment by the 1st of February 1919, and I believe that was well founded. The British fell down on their components because their manpower, after the Boche drive in March 1918, was so short that they could not furnish the men in the factories to produce any special parts for tanks.

I got authority from the British to establish a school with them at Camp Wolfe for 3,000 men. Every month, at the end of three months, a thousand men were to go out and a new thousand were to come in. We there used the British tanks for training and, of course, paid our share of the cost.

The Tank Corps of the AEF was based on 20 fighting divisions and 10 replacement divisions. This required the necessary headquarters, training centers, 10 brigades, each consisting of a headquarters, one heavy battalion, two light battalions, and one repair and salvage company.

The summary of this was as follows:

Personnel	21,800
Heavy tanks	730
Light tanks	1,520
Guns, 6-pounder (2.28-inch)	1,400
Equivalent in batteries to	365
Equivalent in regiments to	56
Guns, 37mm	600

Equivalent in batteries to	150
Equivalent in companies	556

On the 20th of August [1918], when General Pershing decided to fight the American army, and gave me the order to fight within 10 days, I did not have a fighting tank. I was then assigned as Chief of the Tank Corps of the First American Army. I got several very influential men, including Mr. [Edward R.] Stettinius, [Jr., Assistant Secretary of War in charge of procurement for the American army] and others, and brought pressure to bear on the French, and on the night of the 30th of August I had two battalions of Americans equipped with 225 tanks. I had 2,000 men trained in heavy tanks in England and about 1,500 trained in the lighter tanks in France.

The British had promised 150 heavies, which it was considered necessary to have to take St. Mihiel without too great losses. They fell down on that and then the French gave me one brigade that they placed absolutely under my command, and that brigade had 225 Renaults. We were in the fight on the 12th of September, but with nothing but fighting machines, so we went ahead with one French brigade and one American. A good deal of our other equipment we could not get, but on the night of the 13th we captured from the Boche all their rolling kitchens and things of that kind.

The country was impassable though for light tanks; it was not designed for that kind of country, and my prediction was fulfilled, and within an hour after we jumped off I had 40 percent ditched, but we got the lead, and we went the farthest north. We got 24 [German] 77mm [field] guns. It was a mile ahead of our farthest north in France, but we did not have infantry with us and we could not hold them. All the Boche in sight threw up their hands and when we turned to the rear some of them had escaped and jumped to their 77 guns, and we got shot in the back very disastrously.

The cry also of every nation was just simply tanks. Well, on [the] 9th of October, the commander-in-chief told me that he would give anything in the AEF for 500 tanks, and on the 10th of October I was authorized to go to Paris and see Mr. Stettinius, and rally anything we had in the AEF, for 100 or 200 tanks. We got into such a state that I actually considered attempting to get taxicabs and putting paulines or tin covers on them and running them in. I had men that were willing to drive them in, and knew the Boche would throw up his hands.

The tank is a counter to the machine gun, and the Renault tank would only cross a six-foot trench. The [British] heavy tank, the cantilever, can cross a 10-foot trench. The [Renault] tank at St. Mihiel was light and we would have saved enormous losses by having 150 British heavy tanks. They did not supply them. As the result of that we were getting a great deal of information, and we found out, with the wire on our front, while damnable, as the posts were rotten, that the French who had sat there and looked at the place for four years, had simply not used mines, and we were more or less hit by it.

Of course, the great feature of the tanks was that we would make a surprise attack after a 31 hours' bombardment, which the high command, and General [Ferdinand] Foch [commander of Allied forces] demanded. We did not have the ammunition for that, but before the advance they insisted we should have this great bombardment. One day of that bombardment, with 2,250 guns, would have fired more ammunition than was fired in the [American] Civil War. We had to have some bombardment, but cut it down to about six hours.

With the British heavies that we were to get, the Fifth Corps, which was attacking almost directly east, was to be covered by a very strong tank force; that is 225, all we could use on their front. On the south angle, the south face of the salient, we were to have about 300. Now, when we dropped out, 150 of the tanks had to be taken away from the front of the Fifth Corps, but the thing turned out much better than everybody expected. On the afternoon of the 12th [of September] I was sent for and told that the French high command had warned General Pershing that if it rained any more the French tanks could not attack, and I still believe he thinks I am a monumental liar, but I told him that as long as the mud was not over two inches deep, it would act as a lubricant for tanks. As a matter of fact, it was better for tanks to run over light mud than to run over sand and dry gravel.

Now, the thing would have been disastrous if it had been as we expected, but you see our bombardment started at 11:30 at night, and for six hours we sat there under the fire of a gun for every 10 yards of that front, and it was absolutely impossible to sleep, and every now and then the Boche would give you gas and you had to have your gas mask on, and after sitting there and contemplating that attack for six hours, everything was so pent up that when you did say go, there was not any stopping it. You see, our own artillery barrage was preceding us by, I think, 300 yards. It was all we could do to hold the men and keep them from running into our barrage.

You cannot today go to St. Mihiel and see how the soldiers got through that wire; you cannot picture where they got through. Instead of the tanks leading, the French applied their tactics, and they followed the infantry. The first American brigade did as we expected, and instead of taking 40 percent of the front line trenches, they got 60 percent over, and they led the way, and on the third day they were up three miles ahead, and across the Hindenburg Line. We had 18 batteries of German 77 guns, and nobody could take them. The machine gun gunners beat it.

It was estimated that a large number of men, I think as high as 30,000, would be lost in taking Mount Sec. We did not lose a man on Mount Sec because of the artillery fire. I was out at twelve o'clock [midnight] and got a place where I could observe a little bit, and Mount Sec just simply commenced to look like a fiery furnace. At daylight it was like a burning haystack. No American troops went up the mountain especially, but we all went around it, so that the losses were not great there, and it was an astounding victory. But it would have been better if we had had the heavy tanks, and it would have been very much better because if we had had them, everybody would have been easy about the thing. It is a terrific responsibility to go into a thing like that when you know you have not got the proper machines. I would like to add another thing on that, that first one thing after another failed us, and there was but one thing to do, to go ahead and do the best we could.

On the 19th day of September, seven days before the Argonne campaign, when every man in the Tank Corps was pretty well exhausted in trying to get up the St. Mihiel, I got a runner right up in the front line, ordering that I go back and submit within 24 hours a plan for a tank attack in the Argonne. The commander-in-chief, on the day that we started the St. Mihiel drive, had already planned his Argonne campaign, and there was not any question in his mind about what we would do, and they did it, but I do not know how; I believe by the act of Providence. You cannot see now how they got through the wire of St. Mihiel; you cannot do it deliberately.

We did not have either sufficient tanks or the proper class of tanks or the proper type of tanks [in the Argonne drive]. The corps ran from right to left—the Third, Fifth, and First. The front of the Third Corps, which was on the left bank of the Meuse [River], was too bad to employ tanks. We decided that there was a very small area in front of the Fifth and the Third and the First that we could use them over. The four years' shelling and the destruction had been such that the plan contemplated that we could not use tanks on the first day; that we would have to follow the infantry on the 26th [of September], when they arrived at a line—Montfaucon and Apremont—on the first day. On the second day the tanks would jump off from that line. The tanks followed up very closely. They were very enthusiastic and kept very close to the infantry; and on ridges, places that you cannot conceive of, the infantry was held up, everything was on the salient going to Montfaucon and going down the Aire [River]. We had to throw the tanks in.

As near as I can estimate, that occurred on the front of both corps about eleven o'clock. At that time the tanks in both situations were hit, both brigade commanders were attacked, and everything forced up to support them; and on the left flank the first American brigade commander got some 300 men up, and when they started over this ridge it was like a rain that was driving horizontally and he was promptly shot, and he and his orderly got into a shell hole on the other side, and the other men kept coming up.

The advance on Montfaucon was pretty nearly the same. The only advantage we had was a compass. We run the tanks like a ship. The men are taught to drive them in the dark, and the only way they keep their direction is by the compass. We encountered every device of the enemy to prevent us from advancing. They mined the country, they inundated it, they made a special antitank gun, and in places they put up miles of concrete columns, six feet square, reinforced with railroad iron three feet in the ground. All we had to do was to run up one of those, turn it over and run over it. It demoralized them so quickly that they did not attempt to fight. I believe that with anything like an adequate tank force, which would have been probably 500 more, although the infantry was green, that we could have shoved that thing ahead that day. The American tanks had been reduced then to 123, and the French had 217.

By the way, at the time this was going on in the Argonne I was fighting the 301st American battalion with the British tanks, equipped with Americans. When I got my heavy battalions trained in England, it was either to lose them, let them go to the artillery or some other branch of the service, or put them into the fight. The British agreed they would equip me if I would let them fight with the British. I told them that was a pretty hard bargain, but at the same time we were over there to win the war and did not care who we fought with; so it was against the Boche; so we put our heavy battalion in and they did magnificent work with the British.

The British front from Arras north is called the graveyard of tanks, but they operated them in a country where they really had no chance to operate. We led the attack of the 30th and 28th divisions with British tanks manned by Americans. We lost three tanks, which were blown up. That heavy American battalion, which fought with the British, got a greater percent of decorations than any unit in the British Tank Corps in the same time.

We had six direct hits, four by 150s [150mm field guns] and two by 77s. They destroyed everything. All we got of the men in those tanks was the identification tag. They were only protected against armor-piercing bullets and shrapnel fragments. Then we got probably 18 glancing hits; they would knock a tank over, and a number of shell struck by the side and in front of us and we went into shell holes.

Most of my men were killed or wounded from getting out and reconnoitering and leading the tanks. I had a lot of fools that wanted to check up their men, and a great many of my officers were either killed or wounded by having the British idea about leading a tank with a stick. You have got to go up and let the men see you get shot at, and if you have not been in action with them you have got that to go through, and then after that it is all over, but it is pretty hard to stop that. I had a peculiar lot of men. I had press correspondents, ministers, and college professors, and the last men you would think of to attempt anything of that kind were the men that wanted to get in a tank and get farthest north. That was the whole cry. Every officer commanding his tank had one ambition in his life, to get farthest north, and you had to threaten him with probably summary punishment if they did not keep the alignment, if they did not keep together. We had enough experience. We got a magnificent team, but it had to be watched pretty carefully. Out of 12 companies, I was operating two. I had 67 percent of those actually fighting killed and wounded, but none of us ever claimed gas as wounded. If you were not gassed within 24 hours you were very lucky.

The essential thing was infantry support. We took the town of Apremont five times on the 28th day of September. We did not have the support. We had not trained with infantry. The tanks could take anything, but they could not hold it, so that it was absolutely essential not only to have an adequate tank force, but it must be trained with the infantry. It is exactly like a football team. If you have got one member on your team that is well trained, and all the members are well trained, but they have not been trained to play ball together, you do not get anywhere. It was the same with us.

We had a few tanks that had the time to train with the infantry and coordinate. All our good work was done with the First Division, and every time a tank got lost I got accustomed to sending over to the First Division to find the tank. They just naturally drifted with the division, they had been trained with it, and we have the highest commendation from [Major] General [Charles P.] Summerall, who commanded the First Division in both the St. Mihiel and Argonne battles.

With the sort [of tanks] that we had at St. Mihiel, and trained divisions, and all the divisions at St. Mihiel had been in the fight before, I do not think we could have [reduced losses]. The country was too bad for tanks, too limited for their use. In the Argonne I think the losses would have been reduced very much, but you must remember that the attacking divisions in the St. Mihiel had to be placed in reserve in the Argonne. The divisions that went into the Argonne were practically green divisions. I mean by that this; they were not untrained divisions, but you put a division into a three days' fight and it will have 50 percent more losses than it will have if you take it out and give it three days of rest and talk the thing over, and then put them back again. The second time you go in you might call it a veteran division. If it has not been in battle, it is green, and there is no telling what it is going to do.

We entered into an inter-allied agreement to produce 1,200 tanks of the Mark VIII type, which is the Anglo-American tank. We got through the discussion on the morning of the 26th of January and that afternoon we went right away to see Mr. Beatty, and Mr. [Winston S.] Churchill [minister of munitions] told me he would arrange, if possible, to get a meeting with Mr. [Arthur J.] Balfour [foreign secretary] at four o'clock, and the treaty was signed about 4:15 [p.m.] on the 26th of January 1918. They were to furnish the guns and armor, and we were to furnish the engine and running gear, so that in order to get an agreement we agreed on the fixed sum of $25,000 per tank, and then each nation was to be credited with what it spent over its share or under its share. Of these tanks the first 600 were to go to the United States, the remaining 600 were to be allocated between France and Great Britain, as they might agree. In addition to that we agreed to put up an inter-allied assembling shop in France [at Chateau Rue, northeast of De Monde], and of course, we made detailed arrangements about keeping the cost, a round sum for the cost of the tank, in connection with the cost of the factory and so on. That is, the Americans were represented in the assembly plant, and the British were represented in the assembly plant, and it would be under American control, and a strict account would be kept of everything that was assembled.

You see, we had nothing but the drawings and the designs, and an officer [Major Herbert W. Alden] of the Ordnance Department started right over. We first had a model made in London, which the fighting men agreed on as the proper thing. We got all the models of the parts and all the designs we could, and the Ordnance officer brought them over here [to the United States], took them to the Ordnance Department, and he was to be in charge of the Tank Division of the Ordnance Department for the production of our parts over here.

Well, it progressed as well as it could except for the exigencies of war. Nobody could foresee the terrible drive the Boche were going to make in March; that reduced the British manpower. There were 278,000 men killed, wounded, and captured in 10 days. The materiel losses in that 25 miles of push that they made through there was the equipment of a splendid army of 500,000 men. There was everything you could think of. There were miles of motor trucks, immense vaults of all kinds of supplies; there were guns there by the thousands; there was nothing that an army needed that they did not take, and the losses in materiel and men of the British Fifth Army were enormous. In 10 days, 20 percent of the entire equipment of the British Army had been wiped out of existence, and as far as they were concerned, 278,000 men is a pretty serious blow to your manpower. The Chief of the British Tank Corps was offered 3,000 men instead of 5,000, and he could not get men for his tank corps, men for his manufactures, and so they could not produce tank armor and tank guns because there were things considered of more importance to be produced first. By the first of June, as the result of the destruction of the British Fifth Army, they could not produce their components.

We did not get the building finished. The building would have been finished on the 1st of December, but we stopped the construction as soon as the assemblies came. I saw it about the 20th of November, and I am not exact as to the percentage of completion, but I should say it was 70 percent completed. The building would have been able to assemble tanks. The thing was enormous. We were going to assemble 100 of the larger tanks a day, and when you want 1,200 tanks, you know, and you want them right away, you have got to have this big assembly capacity.

Our plans were that the great fight—the big offensive—was to come off on the 1st of March 1919. We expected the parts to arrive from England—the British components to arrive from England and the American components from America at about the same time, and we had to assemble quickly and then put out to drill with our American infantry. The Argonne is no example, because we had 47 days there of continuous movement, but taking the average of three periods of three days each, nine days per month, we would have to have 15 percent tanks for replacement. Now, we found that we would want 15 percent of the heavy class alone—that is, if we had 600, 90 tanks more a month. We fully expected—I think the report there was that we would be able to have 1,200 tanks by the first of March 1919, and we fully expected to have them.

I remember we got badly caught, because the armistice was the 11th, and on the 12th, without exception, all purchases in the American Expeditionary Forces were stopped. The British showed that on the 12th of November they had completed 300 components from the Mark VIII tank, and that 150 of these components belonged to the United States, and we took them; had to take them.

[The Renault works at Paris] were very small. They ran up to one battalion a week, 75 tanks. Well, in December [1917] we made an agreement with Renault. You see, the legal part of it was handled direct by army officers. We had good lawyers, good French-Americans that were with the French, good advisers, and we had first to go into his patent rights. It was a commercial concern, and the easiest way to deal with him and get the thing out of the French government was to agree to give him $100,000 for his patent rights. We got then one or two complete Renault tanks, and we put the improvements that we wanted on them. We wanted a self-starter; we wanted a bulkhead separating the engine from the gun room; we wanted a double-case gasoline tank, and some few minor changes. We got that tank and sent it complete, with all its drawings and specifications, to the United States, and asked that a Chinese copy of it be made over here with the changes I have mentioned.[6] I got in February of 1918, 24 French Renault tanks for training.

The [Renault] price at that time I understood was about $5,000, but we had pooled our production under the inter-allied tank committee, which cooperated with the inter-allied munitions committee, and while a round sum was agreed on, nothing was agreed on the basis of cost. They cost the Ordnance Department about $8,000, but that tank, for instance, has a 20 more horsepower engine, and it has a number of improvements on it that the French tank did not have. The first American tank arrived in France on the 20th of November [1918], I heard. I did not see that. I know there were some there; I think there were 10.

What the American Tank Corps did accomplish in getting machines or preparing to get machines could not have been accomplished without the present Chief of Ordnance. [Major] General [Clarence C.] Williams and myself are lifelong friends and we met on the 26th of December 1917, and we adopted our policy in just about half an hour. It was up to the Ordnance Department to get the machines that the fighting men wanted. We were the users and he was the management, and he threw everything that he had to help to assist me. We cut out everybody else. Just as soon as I got out on the French front and the British front and saw what the fighting men wanted, I drew up what I wanted, and the Ordnance Department threw its whole energy into an attempt to get it. The Ordnance Department, due to General Williams, took the Tank Corps under its wing, and I think he was just as keen about producing tanks as he was keen on the other material that was furnished by the Ordnance Department.

The Ordnance Department then was not organized or equipped to go to handling anything new. It could not produce what it already had in production. We had no concern, no manufacturer that could undertake the independent manufacture of the tank. You had to get as good an engine as you could for it, and the result of it is that it is not a satisfactory tank, it is not a tank that is built to be a tank. This is a little harsh, but it is an assemblage of misfits; but that was the best you could do. The whole story was that one manufacturer could not manufacture it, and it required two or three manufacturers. I think they had one company making the engine, for instance, and there were certain other parts made by other people. The track plates have to be of a certain steel that a bullet will fire through and not crack. They had considerable trouble in testing that out, and then the AMC Company—I do not know what that is—finally made a satisfactory track plate. And they had trouble, of course, on the armor. The armor was not satisfactory. Every American-built Renault tank, every plate has the print of a bullet on it, and has been tested by an armor piercing bullet. Every feature about that tank required some special man to make it, one man to make the armor, one the engine, and one the tread, and the sprocket was especially difficult to make, so we have the product of half a dozen different manufacturers in that tank. It was completed in August of 1918. That had to be tried out. That was the first one. That was tried out after it first arrived, after the armistice in November.

Brigadier General Samuel D. Rockenbach, *Infantry Journal* Article

The following remarks are excerpts from Brigadier General Samuel D. Rockenbach, "Tanks and Their Cooperation with Other Arms," *Infantry Journal,* January 1920, 533–45:

The conditions of the World War made necessary secrecy in regard to tanks, consequently, except with the troops employing them, all information given out was misleading. This resulted naturally in general ignorance as to everything pertaining to tanks. . . . The ignorance of our own forces as to tanks caused them to expect the light tanks to cross 12-foot trenches and to do the work of heavy tanks. No one at G.H.Q. [General Headquarters] knew the gun-power we proposed to put in the front line and in front of it. It was 1,460 2.24-inch guns, each weighing with its tank mount 1,482 pounds; 600 37-mm guns; 6,680 machine guns. . . .

Only a few comprehended the great moral effect of tanks. On the 16th of September, 15 tanks were sent east of the Moselle, where by successive feint attacks on the nights of the 17th and 18th they were credited with diverting two German divisions from our front in the Argonne and contributed to the general confusion of the enemy as to our real point of attack.

The commander-in-chief [General John J. Pershing] would not permit the withdrawal of disabled tanks from the Argonne to the repair shops, considering that the bad effect on our own troops would be too great.

On the 10th of October, the chief of the Tank Corps [Brigadier General Samuel D. Rockenbach] was ordered to Paris with authority to give anything in the A.E.F. [American Expeditionary Forces] for 500 tanks (we had the personnel). The situation was ideal for the use of tanks, the Boche was short of artillery and ahead on machine guns. We got 48 more tanks.

On the 16th of October the chief of the Tank Corps recommended the withdrawal of the personnel of the Tank Corps, as out of two battalions, six companies, only enough was left to form one composite company operating 24 tanks. With this nucleus of battle-trained men it was agreed to reorganize and come back within 10 days with two battalions operating 150 tanks. It was decided that the moral effect of the withdrawal on our own troops would be too great, and it was not permitted to take the 24 tanks from the front of the 1st Army. . . .

The subject of tanks early received attention by our G.H.Q. (General Headquarters). The commander-in-chief [General John J. Pershing] arrived in France on the 13th of June 1917. On the 19th of July he ordered a board to investigate the progress made by our allies and submit recommendations for our own service.

The following were the important points of the findings:

a. The tank is considered a factor which is destined to become an important element in this war.
b. There are practically only two models now giving satisfactory results, the 6-ton Renault and the 27–30 ton British Mark VI (not in production and never used), which later was made up as (1) fighting tank and (2) supply tank.
c. Estimate for the machine based on an army of 20 divisions (each division, two brigades): Light tanks, 2,000; heavy tanks, 200; with 15 percent per month for replacement.
d. Tanks must be used in quantities or not at all.
e. A Tank Department, reporting directly to the commander-in-chief, should be organized at once, and a single chief appointed for its direction.

A memorandum of a project for a Combat Tank Service based on a force of 20 fighting and 10 replacement divisions was sent by the commander-in-chief to the War Department on September 23, 1917. It provided for the following:

FRONT	
Division Troops, Light Tank Companies	30
Army Headquarters, Aggregate	2,786
Army Troops, Light Tank Companies	30
Army Troops, Heavy Tank Companies	15
Army Troops, Carrier Companies	5
Army Troops, Artillery Carrier Co's	2
G.H.Q. Aggregate	75
REAR	
Training and Replacement Companies	10
Repair and Salvage Companies	5
Depot Companies	1
Aggregate	14,827

There was nothing provided for a home establishment. There was not enough in the reports furnished to determine what we wanted. The following must be determined:

a. The function of tanks.
b. Types to be produced based on functions and possibility of production.

c. Means of securing designs and production.
d. Organization based on types of tanks adopted and suited to function with the existing organization of the Army.
e. Tactics suited to the special arm tanks, and for cooperation with the other arms.

The means of securing designs and tanks was settled with the Chief of Ordnance [Major General Clarence C. Williams]. The Ordnance Department was to accept the general plan for the machines the Tank Corps wanted and undertake the supply. The supply situation required a minimum number of types.

The Headquarters of the French Tank Corps at its great center in the Forest of Compiègne was visited. The French were using two types, the Schneider and the St. Chamond. Neither were tanks. They were poor artillery carriers, each carrying a 75-mm [field gun] and two machine guns, not designed for cross-country work, and had to be preceded by ground scouts and followed by pioneers. On reaching its firing position the Schneider halted, turned broadside and fired. The St. Chamond was an improvement in having better power and carried its 75 for firing direct to the front. Production of both had been stopped. The Renault, the first land light cruiser, though in manufacture for over a year, had not been produced in usable numbers. The French wanted a heavy tank but would approve of none in production. They were quite bitter against using tanks before they were ready in large numbers. They were firm in the opinion that tanks must be used in masses and as a surprise, or not at all. In the employment tanks were to assist the infantry. The French varied from the idea of infantry accompanying artillery to *artillerie d'assaut* (assault artillery). They must keep up the offensive idea in the employment of tanks. The change in the French idea for the employment of tanks from that of infantry accompanying artillery to *artillerie d'assaut* is considered a proper development from experience. It is not believed that you can make, out of our hasty levies, soldiers who are Jacks of all trades and be able to do any of them well. Our experience is that it is essential to keep up the tank idea of assault and closing with the enemy. This requires merciless handling of the officer or man who does anything but direct firing at distances under 800 yards. The moment the tank goes into the artillery business it loses its idea and has got to increase its personnel for the purpose of observation and special reconnaissance and indirect firing, purely the artilleryman's business. It is believed that it is only by a tank specialist imbued with the assault idea that proper tank work can be accomplished. It is correct that the French used tanks as accompanying artillery, but it should be kept in mind that this was exceptional use. That one arm is capable under emergency of performing the functions of another does not justify the conclusions that "this seems to be a solution of the problem." It is not believed necessary for infantry accompanying artillery to double the weight of the carrier, with the armor-plate necessary for the tank. A modified form of tractor, with an elevated and projecting tread and a body with a steel wedge-shaped nose slightly retired, will enable the accompanying guns to cross all the country that tanks can. If it is thought necessary to protect the gun and carriage, it can be done by a thin, hip-shaped, light-plate cover. The armor on a tank varies from light, where there is little chance of a normal impact, to heavy, where there is a chance of a normal impact.

The French were also decided that they could not maintain the necessary *esprit* (spirit), get proper training and equipment unless they were a distinct combat arm. Tanks could not be operated with much chance of success on over 40 percent of the western front. To permanently attach them as an organic part of each division would require more tanks than they or any nation could produce, hence all divisions were trained with tanks in the rest areas.

Army commanders with their staff, corps and division commanders, followed tanks on foot at their maneuvers and listened to critiques on them in the rain. They then discussed their employment, and the normal was agreed on.

Special transportation arrangements had to be made for bringing tanks to their positions of readiness for battle and, as our artillery has learned, the ammunition, gas and oils had to be maintained by men of the corps.

The third bureau of the War Ministry had a tank division, the head of which was acceptable to the chief of the Tank Corps. The chief of the Tank Corps commanded the Tank Corps and was on the staff of the commander-in-chief and his adviser on tank matters. Tank Corps troops were G.H.Q. troops. Upon recommendation of the chief of the Tank Corps, they would be attached to armies for special situations.

Organization and tactics were subsequently modified in the light of experience had in the war and will be given later. The Renault was approved for our service and two sent over to be copied and manufactured.

A visit was made to British tank headquarters at Bermicourt, France, and to the tank brigade in readiness near the front. The British had gone from armored, or heavy, machine gun battalions to a separate Tank Corps. Influenced by the terrain on their front they advocated only the heavy, long tank. They were equally decided that they had no tank in production that was good. There was little cooperation between the combat Tank Corps and the production department. The heavy tank could not be kept along with the infantry, due to the difficulty of transportation. They belonged to the strategic reserve, and when in a major engagement their use was decided on, they were brought up as close as possible to the front line, preceded the infantry without artillery preparation, and went direct for their objectives in waves, the first going for the enemy's third line, the second for the enemy's second line, and the third for the enemy's first line. Cambrai had demonstrated the practicability of this, but also that without the infantry to follow in sufficient numbers to hold the gain, the total of the result would be nothing. With the British, the general requirements for heavy fighting tanks were agreed upon.

On the 26th of December 1917, a conference with the Chief of Ordnance was held in Paris. It was not feasible for the United States to furnish heavy tanks in one year, all the time we had. We could not produce the engines. To get heavy tanks, we had to pool production. The War Department was cabled and approved the combined project; 1,200 Liberty engines of 300-horsepower by the 1st of June 1918, were promised. A meeting was held with the British Munition Department in London the first week in January 1918, at which we declined to accept any type of British tank in use. The general design of the Anglo-American tank was agreed upon. This was confirmed by treaty agreement on the 20th of January, 1,200 Mark VIII's to be produced, the British furnishing the guns, ammunition, equipment, and armor plate, and the United States the engines and running gear. An assembly plant was to be jointly erected at Chateauroux where the components were to be sent. The first 600 tanks were to go to the American army and the remainder to the British and French as would be agreed to later. The French approved the plan, but would not sign. They subsequently, in July 1918, demanded an equal division.

At the same time arrangements were made for training 3,000 Americans at the British centers in England. An inter-allied tank committee was formed and met in Paris once a month.

Having determined the functions of tanks, the types we wanted, with a chance of getting them and the means of securing them, the organization was revised and sent to the War Department in February 1918. Cable request was forwarded for the personnel to be sent to England for training. All the personnel obtainable in the A.E.F., about 600, was assembled at Bourg, on the south boundary of the staff school territory at Langres, and the Light Tank Center started. Nine Renault tanks were obtained from the French. The few regular officers we could get were sent to the British school in England, then with the British tanks at the front, then to the French centers and the French front, and then to establish a center in the United States. All went with the order to learn all the allies knew, but keep in mind that if we won the war, we would have to improve. From these studies our tactics was evolved. Having no machines, our 301st Battalion was equipped by the British and went into the fight with them in September 1918, incidentally aiding our 27th and 30th divisions. The French sold us 150 Renaults and loaned us one of their brigades for St. Mihiel and the Argonne.

Our organization was modified by the experience gained at St. Mihiel; it was improved in the Argonne. From the 15th to the 30th of October, out of two battalions, six companies of light tanks, we could operate only one. On the 30th of October the personnel of the 2d Brigade was trained and we were prepared to continue the fight with 150 light tanks.

The organization had then been tested by the severest test it could be given and was approved. The tanks only had the opportunity with one of our divisions to get that acquaintance and training which is necessary for success. An extract from a letter of the division commander reads as follows:

> It was a special privilege of the 1st Division to have elements of the Tank Corps in their most difficult operations. The division had learned to appreciate the value of tanks at Soissons, where the French tanks helped us through some very difficult places. The greatest reliance was, therefore, placed upon the tanks in the St. Mihiel advance where tanks presented the only means of destroying wire and machine gun positions that had been developed during the four years' occupancy of the position by the enemy. The performance of the tanks during this advance was brilliant and successful, and the entire division felt the most lively gratitude for the able manner in which every mission had been performed. The same conditions existed on the 4th of October when the 1st Division made that desperate assault with greatly inadequate artillery support against the line of the Montrebeau woods. The manner in which the tanks helped them to open the way to the Exermont ravine elicited the highest praise from all. Again, when the 5th Corps was ordered to advance against the Landres-et-St. Georges position, I eagerly sought and borrowed the small number of tanks in the 1st Corps and utilized them as you have described, feeling that they were indispensable to our success. It was because of these experiences that I appealed to you for the few remaining tanks that you had, to assist our infantry in the great assault of November 1. Here again, although the number was small, I feel that the services of the tanks were of incalculable value.

The local successes gained by a few tanks at St. Mihiel and in the Argonne must not be taken as a basis for conclusions as to their use. Every principle for their employment was violated. . . . What was done was the best possible under the circumstances. For the future we must design and manufacture an improved tank and so organize and train with the infantry as to get the best results.

Tank Staff Control in the First Army

The organization of the Tank Corps of the A.E.F. included a general headquarters for functioning with the General Staff, furnishing a directorate for designing machines and training, and commanding Tank Corps organizations not attached to armies; one or more army Tank Corps headquarters for functioning with the Army Staff and the Chief of the Tank Corps for the operation of the Tank Corps units attached to the Army; Tank Centers for training and replacements, and 10 brigades.

The situation prevented organizing from the top down. The few officers of any service obtainable required two or three months training at British and French tank centers before they were of any use. The American fighting in July, and the delay in our production, stampeded some with the fear that the Tank Corps would not get tanks before the war was over. Consequently the Tank Corps was without an adequate staff and tanks when on the 18th of August the Chief of Tank Corps was ordered to Paris to get tanks and to the 1st Army for temporary duty.

The battle order for St. Mihiel was as follows:

HEADQUARTERS FIRST ARMY,
AMERICAN EXPEDITION FORCES,
FRANCE
5 September 1918

ANNEX NO. 3.
FIELD ORDERS NO. 9.

PLAN OF EMPLOYMENT OF TANKS

1. Based on the general plan, detailed reconnaissance, and the troops to be available, viz.: 1 Regiment French Light Tanks; 1 Groupment and 2 Groups, French Medium Tanks; 1st American Brigade (2 Bns. Light Tanks) and Headquarters 3rd American Brigade; the following allotment of tanks is made:

(a) ALLOTMENT.

(1) The 505th French Regiment (3 battalions) and one groupment to the 1st Corps.

Liaison with the Corps to be maintained by the Chief of Staff, Tank Corps, and Headquarters 3 American Brigades. Detraining Point: BOIS VILLERS-EN-HAYE, BOIS DE LA RAPPE.

(2) The 1st American Brigade (2 Battalions) and 2 French groups to the 4th Corps. Detraining Point: ANSAUVILLE.

(b) HEADQUARTERS TANK CORPS TROOP AT ECROUVES.

By Command of General Pershing:

H. A. DRUM, Chief of Staff.

Official:
S. D. Rockenbach,
Brig. General, U.S.A.,
Chief of Tank Corps.

The experience at St. Mihiel indicated that in future the army order for tanks must prescribe the sectors for their operations. Hence the order for the Argonne reads as follows:

HEADQUARTERS FIRST ARMY,
AMERICAN EXPEDITIONARY FORCES, FRANCE
17 September 1918

ANNEX NO. 3.
TO BATTLE INSTRUCTIONS—OPERATIONS "Z."
PLAN FOR EMPLOYMENT OF TANK CORPS TROOPS
1. The following is the general plan for the employment of tanks:

(a) OPERATION. Tanks to assemble in the FORET de HESSE. On D day they will follow the infantry as soon as the way has been made passable for them, to their position of readiness in the BOIS de MONTFAUCON and near CHEPPY. Thence they will operate in the sectors MANTILLOIS, MONTFAUCON, GESNES, and BAULNY-EXERMONT. On the Hindenburg Line being made passable for them, they should be in the best possible position for exercising their proper functions and will proceed to destroy machine gun nests, strong points and to exploit the success.

(b) ALLOTMENT. The 505th Regiment A.S. Light and two groups St. Chamond to the center (V) Corps to operate in the sectors of the right and center divisions north of the line OERCOURT-OYISY-VERY. The units assigned to the right division will wherever practicable assist the advance of the III Corps.

Detraining point DOMBASLE. Initial supply dump DOMBASLE.

The 504th Regiment (less 1 Bn.) A.S. light, and 1 group St. Chamond to the center (V) Corps to operate in the sector of its left division north of the line CUISY-VERY. Detraining point DOMBASLE-EN-ARGONNE. Initial supply dump DOMBASLE.

The C.O. and Headquarters third American Brigade to the center (V)

Corps for reconnaissance work and liaison of the French Units attached to the Corps.

The First American Brigade, Group Schneider attached, to the left (1) Corps to operate in the sector of its right division north of BAULNY.

Detraining point RECICOURT. Initial supply dump RECICOURT.

(c) TROOPS NECESSARY TO BE ATTACHED. One company of pioneers to the units operating with the center (V) Corps.

Two platoon Pioneers to the units operating with the left (1) Corps.

(d) SUPPLY. The corps to which tank troops are attached will make necessary arrangements to insure gas and oil reaching them.

(e) Headquarters Tank Corps at advance section Army Headquarters.

By Command of General Pershing.

H. A. DRUM, Chief of Staff.

Official:
S. D. Rockenbach,
Brigadier General, U.S.A.,
Chief of Tank Corps.

An examination of the map will show the reason for the allotment. It would be folly to assign tanks to corps or divisions the terrain of whose sectors of operation was impracticable for the employment of tanks.

THE AMERICAN TANK CORPS

The American Tank Corps is based on the following fundamental considerations which must be kept clearly in mind:

1. *The functions of tanks* are to make a path through obstacles for the infantry and protect it from destructive loss from machine guns. The tanks are the counter to the machine gun. Besides its protection it is a conserver of men, mechanically replacing men and brutes.

2. *The Design Is Based on the Functions.*—The tanks must be able to cross a prepared defensive terrain, go anywhere infantry can, have an armament suited to cope with protected machine guns (a cannon and two machine guns), give reasonable protection to its crew, [and have] armor sufficient to stop armor-piercing bullets. They must be used in such numbers that they will present many targets, and the percentage expected to be destroyed by the enemy will still leave enough to accomplish their object.

3. *Production.*—The most serious obstacle to overcome in obtaining a Tank Corps is to produce the tanks in large numbers. Neither Great Britain nor France produced one tank of a special type in less than a year, nor in usable numbers in

less than eighteen months. I am not able to estimate how long it would take us, as we have not built any complete starting from the designing. Hence the types must be few. It is hoped to reduce our two types to one. The light tank can do all that the armored car can, and in addition reach the enemy whether he be in a city or on the battlefield. The light tank is easily put in a truck, and thus gains the necessary speed to be quickly put into its position of readiness for attack.

4. A project for a combat tank corps must be based on the number of fighting units it is proposed to use. The Tank Corps of the A.E.F. was based on 20 fighting divisions and 10 replacement divisions. This would give us the necessary headquarters, training centers, 10 brigades, each consisting of headquarters, one heavy battalion, 2 light battalions, and one repair and salvage company. . . .

III

Official Tank Corps Personal-Experience Reports

302d Tank Center

Colonel George S. Patton Jr., Commander, 304th Tank Brigade

The first experience by this officer in the Tank Corps was November 13th, 1917, when he was sent to the French Tank School at Champlieu, near Compiegne. He and Captain Elgin Braine, Tank Corps, were the first two officers detailed to the Tank Corps and were sent to this school to learn everything possible in connection with the French tanks. At this place every opportunity was given the officers concerned and they made very excellent progress, five of the alterations recommended by them having been adopted by the French tank corps. On leaving Champlieu, Colonel Patton went to Albert and had the pleasure of seeing the last day of the battle of Cambrai, November 30, 1917. On returning to Langres he and Captain Braine collaborated in a report which has been made the basis for the organization of the American Tank Corps.[1]

On December 16th, 1917, Colonel Patton and Captain Braine went to Langres where they reported to the commandant of the army schools for the purpose of establishing a Tank School. The establishment of this school is interesting on account of the smallness of its beginning. For the first month there were no officers available for instructions. Finally 10 temporary second lieutenants, Coast Artillery, reported. As there was no school of tanks and no tanks available, these men were sent to the Infantry Specialists Schools for a course in 37mm guns and to the Automatic Weapons School for a course in machine guns. Two weeks later an additional 18 officers from the same source arrived and were put through the same courses.

In February 1918, Colonel Patton was sent to the replacement division near Tours to select 200 men as a nucleus for the Tank Corps. Thanks to the hearty assistance of [Lieutenant] Colonel [Frederick B.] Hennessey, personnel officer of this division, the men selected were of the most excellent character. They arrived at Langres in February 1918, and were billeted for three days in the town of St.

Geosmes. On February 22nd, the entire personnel, officers and men, moved to the town of Bourg, eight kilometers south of Langres. The only transportation available was one condemned Atlas truck which was obtained through the courtesy of [Major] General [Andre W.] Brewster, Inspector General, and three machine guns borrowed from the Automatic Weapons School. With this very limited material all the men were given a course in gas engines, theoretical, and practical, and in the theory and practice of machine guns.

About the 1st of March some lumber was obtained from G-4 (Supply), GHQ [General Headquarters] and using the men of the Tank Corps for labor, a tank shed was constructed in the Bois sur Marne. About the middle of March 10 Renault tanks arrived. At that time the only officer in the Tank Corps who had ever driven a Renault tank was Colonel Patton. In detraining these tanks, it was necessary for him to drive each tank off the train. The tanks were then lined up along the road and nine men were selected to act as drivers. These men had never seen a tank before but knew something of gas engines as the result of the Atlas truck experience. It is worthy of note that in this first debarkation of tanks by American troops, totally inexperienced as just stated, all tanks arrived at the tank shed two-and-one-half hours after the train had halted at the crossing. This shows the adaptability of the American soldier, for totally inexperienced as they were, they drove the tanks by night, a distance of over two kilometers and loaded them without accident at the designated point. From this time on the instruction became more efficient and all the tanks were worked for a period of 10 hours daily. This work was conducted under the most adverse circumstances as for the first two months no machinery was available except the monkey wrenches and screwdrivers, which came with the tanks.

In April, the first tank maneuver was held in conjunction with the candidate battalion of the Army school. This maneuver was a splendid success and it is believed responsible for convincing a great number of the staff officers who witnessed it of the efficiency of the light tank.

In June, 15 additional Renault tanks were received, making a total of 25, and it was then possible to have company maneuvers. As the days had become very long a schedule was arranged by which general driving instructions were given during each morning, one company maneuver was held from 1:00 p.m. until 6:00 p.m. and a second company maneuver from 6:00 p.m. to 12 midnight. The experience gained in this night work proved invaluable in our later experience in battle.

While more tanks were arriving, additional men and officers were coming in and by the first of August it was possible to organize two tank battalions, each about 15 percent short in personnel and at the same time leaving 25 NCO [noncommissioned officer] instructors for work at the school. The spirit of the men during all this time was most wonderful, for in spite of working six days a week and having inspection on Sunday and in spite of building roads, buildings, sheds, etc., there was not the least complaint; each man and officer doing his very best each moment of the day.

On August 20th, Colonel Patton was directed to report to the commanding general of the 5th Corps, [Major General Charles P. Summerall], to make a preliminary reconnaissance of what eventually proved to be the St. Mihiel offensive. During this reconnaissance an incident occurred which showed the absolute necessity for a tank officer to personally see the ground. The 5th Corps was to operate in the vicinity of Ville-en-Woevre. All the intelligence reports of this section state that the ground was an impassible swamp. We went to various observation posts and all the observers confirmed this statement, yet the evidence of our eyes seemed to belie it. We therefore succeeded in arranging to participate, with the French who held the sector, in a raid. This we did and made a personal inspection of the ground up to the third line of German wire, passing through two lines of wire without opposition. As a result of this it became clear that neither the wire, which had been reported dreadful, nor the ground, which had been reported impassible, were as stated and next day we were able to state our personal knowledge that an attack could be made in this sector. Reconnaissance here was completed and the wires laid to our advance PC [Post of Command], but when everything was ready a change of plan of the higher command required that we cooperate with the 4th instead of the 5th Corps. For this purpose we moved to the Toul front and recommenced our reconnaissance here. Again the advantage of personal observation by the tank commanders was absolutely demonstrated. All reports, even by our own infantry, stated that the ground to the west of the Rupt de Mad was impassible for tanks and the map showed three streams crossing our proposed route. A daylight reconnaissance in No Man's Land proved that these streams were perfectly dry and consequently offered no obstacle to tanks. In this connection it may be interesting to point out that the Madine, a tributary of the Rupt de Mad was also impassible and believing the evidence of the map we laid our plans accordingly. The advance of the 25th proved that the Madine also was no obstacle to the tanks.

"Battle Experience"

When the brigade attacked, on September 12, 1918, the commanding officer, accompanied by his reconnaissance officer and three runners, moved forward to gain touch with the 345th Battalion and the French tanks, which were invisible from the only battle PC available. We arrived near Essey, France, about 10:00 a.m. and passing through the German barrage, which was not heavy, reentered the town. Here we found [Brigadier] General [Douglas] MacArthur and his aide with four or five infantry soldiers. Our party here took about 10 Germans who seemed very anxious to surrender. We then asked General MacArthur if we could move the tanks forward across the bridge at Essey which, contrary to expectation, was found intact. He gave his consent if the bridge was not mined. We walked over the bridge in a most cat-like manner expecting to be blown to heaven any moment, but to our great relief found that the bridge had not been tampered with. We then moved the only three available tanks along the road towards Pannes, two to the east of the road and one to the west, but to our regret two of these tanks ran out of gasoline halfway between Essey and Pannes.

Being very tired Colonel Patton, [First] Lieutenant [Maurice H.] Knowles and one remaining runner mounted on the tank and moved forward towards Pannes. Upon reaching the latter town, the infantry who had been following us, stated that the town was held and they would not enter it. To reassure them we rode into the town on the tank. While this perhaps was good for the infantry, it was certainly not without embarrassment for us as we continually expected to be shot off our precarious perch. At the north end of the town we saw one German and Lieutenant Knowles and Sergeant [Louis F.] Graham, the runner, got off the tank to effect the capture. To their great surprise they found 30 instead of one, but using their pistols they captured the entire crew. The tank continued out of the northern end of the town and advanced across the field. Colonel Patton, who was still sitting on the top of the tank, here had the most horrible experience; he could hear machine gun fire, but could not locate them until, glancing down the left side of the tank about six inches below his hand, he saw the paint flying from the side of the tanks as the result of numerous machine gun bullets striking against the tank. Owing to his heroic desire to make the tank a less enticing target, he leaped from the tank and landed in a shell hole a great distance away. This shell hole, however, was exceedingly small and the Germans took an unpleasant delight in shooting at its upper rim so that the colonel was greatly perturbed at finding himself covered with dirt. His embarrassment was enhanced by the fact that the tank, unaware of this, continued into the field while the infantry, which had passed through the village, had halted about 200 meters behind the colonel. He was in a great state of perplexity, as if he moved backwards and conducted a strategic withdrawal, the infantry would think a tank officer was running away; should he move forward he would become a distinct target of the four machine guns, which he was now able to see about 300 meters in his front. He finally solved the problem by moving sideways until he regained the infantry. During the course of this movement he was repeatedly forced to seek shelter in shell holes. On reaching the infantry he asked them if they could move forward. This they refused to do. He then asked them if they would send a runner to the tank which was cruising about in the field about 500 meters to the front. To this request the heroic infantry made this reply, "Hell no, it ain't my tank." Colonel Patton was then faced with the unfortunate necessity of going for the tank himself. This he did in record time and without accident. When he and the tank returned to the infantry four other tanks had arrived and arranging the five in line they again moved forward against the machine guns.

The infantry did not seem good, but Colonel Patton, being of a generous disposition, decided he would not a second time act as runner so he delegated that honor to [Second] Lieutenant [Darwin T.] Phillips, who had just come up. Lieutenant Phillips successfully withdrew the tanks to the town, but the appearance of five tanks had so disheartened the Germans that they could be seen retreating far below the town of Pannes. The infantry then courageously offered to advance and the tanks for a third time were sent forward. During the course of his third advance the right tank opened fire on an advanced American machine gun which it mistook for a German. The first shell struck just short of the emplacement. Colonel Patton then asked the infantry machine gun officer to apprize it of its error. The machine gun officer replied in the same language as the heroic battalion commander abovementioned and it was necessary for Colonel Patton to again act as runner. This time, however, he did so with less speed since there was very little fire. This third advance of the tanks finally proved successful and the town of Beney was taken by the tanks alone, since, just before reaching it the infantry swerved off to the right. Colonel Patton then, having lost all his runners and his reconnaissance officer, decided to hunt for his left battalion, which was supposed to be at the town of Nonsard; in the course of this hunt moving along the front line of infantry, which at this time, about two o'clock, was digging in. From the result of his walk it certainly appeared that had the Germans counter-attacked at this time, great results from a German point of view would have been attained as the entire infantry line was in a state of extreme disorganization. On reaching the town of Nonsard it was found to be in possession of our infantry, having been taken unaided by Major [Sereno E.] Brett with three tanks; Major Brett having personally killed two German machine gunners in the tower of the church.

The 13th of September was uneventful except that it marked a long struggle to obtain gasoline for the tanks and clearly showed the necessity for having large caterpillar tractors with each tank battalion to carry gasoline across country, since the roads were so congested that it took 32 hours to move two trucks of gasoline 14 kilometers. On the night of the 13th, Major Brett started for the town of Vigneulles with 57 tanks. Colonel Patton rejoined him here on the morning of the 14th at 5:00 a.m. and they proceeded with 50 tanks in the direction of Saint Maurice. Here they arrived about 8:00 a.m. and found a German warehouse partly burned down from which they obtained some gasoline and a large quantity of cigars, hard bread and blankets. They then proceeded towards Woel. When about two kilometers from this town they were informed by [Brigadier] General [Dennis E.] Nolan [Chief of the Intelligence Section of the American Expeditionary Forces, AEF], whom they met in an automobile, that the Germans were just beyond Woel and that Woel itself was held by a patrol of 20 French soldiers.

General Nolan was unable to give any information as to the whereabouts of the 1st Division, which division Major Brett's battalion was seeking. General Nolan was asked if the tanks might attack the Germans west of Woel without infantry. He advised against this and the tanks were hidden in bushes on either side of the road. Patrols were sent out to the north and south to attempt to find American troops and in spite of the fact that these patrols were mounted on stolen horses it was impossible to find any American soldiers; so at twelve o'clock, [Second] Lieutenant [Edwin A.] McCluer with three tanks and five runners was sent out to make a patrol through Woel and to the south. At two o'clock he reported that he was attacked by German infantry, machine guns and artillery and was counter-attacking. Five tanks, under [First] Lieutenant (now Captain) [Gordon M.] Grant, were sent to his assistance. These eight tanks drove the Germans, who amounted to about a company with a battery of 77's and a platoon of machine guns, for a distance of six kilometers through the town of Joinville, situated on the Hindenburg Line.

The country here was ideal for tanks and the results obtained show the tremendous effect which a few tanks may produce against any enemy whose morale is not of the highest order. While the tanks were waiting for the return of the attacking patrol they were shelled with all calibers of German artillery, and two German aeroplanes flew continually over them, indicating their position by the use of tracer bullets. Fortunately no tanks were struck.

The brigade then moved to the Argonne. During the debarkation of the 345th Battalion an interesting incident occurred. When all but four tanks had been debarked the Germans got the range of the station at Clermont and several shells struck near the train; one shell striking the flat car two cars back of the last tank, at the same moment a temporary ramp broke and it appeared that we would lose some tanks before it could be repaired. Thanks, however, to the courage of Captain [William H.] Williams, Tank Corps, this accident was avoided. Captain Williams, using his great strength, pushed the broken ramp to one side and signaled the tanks to move off the train. This they did, dropping off the end of the flat car one after the other, without any accident to the tanks. The laying-up position for the brigade at this point was a little wood in a field about three kilometers north of Clermont. All the American tanks entered this wood under cover of darkness, but one French tank moved past it about 8:00 a.m. and must have been spotted by the Germans. Fearing that this did occur, the American tanks that night moved to another woods and about midnight the woods that they had just evacuated was heavily and accurately shelled by the German artillery. In the approach march of the night of September 25–26th, it was necessary for four companies of tanks to cross the bridge at Neuvilly. Just as the leading tank got there the German barrage opened on this bridge, killing two MP's [Military Police] stationed at this bridge. The tanks were halted and the moment the fire ceased one company was rushed across. The Germans then renewed their firing, but by taking advantage of the intervals which they regularly gave, all tanks crossed the bridge without accident. During the attack in the morning of September 26th the leading tank encountered a German mine field, but thanks to the courtesy of the Germans in leaving up warning signs, the tanks avoided this danger. Later the tanks became stuck in the trenches and after considerable difficulty some infantry were persuaded to help take them across. During the course of this operation Captain [Math L.] English and Colonel Patton chained three tanks together and due to the coolness of the drivers who maneuvered with their doors open, it was possible to get all the tanks across. It is believed that without men of the greatest coolness such a maneuver would have been impossible and the drivers who coolly followed the hand signals of the officers as mentioned, deserve the greatest credit.

Personal experiences of Colonel Patton did not go beyond this point as he was wounded about this time. He, however, knows for a fact that about nine o'clock on that morning three tanks under [Second] Lieutenant [Julian K.] Morrison performed seemingly an impossible task in mounting to the top of Vauquois, where the infantry informed them there were German machine guns. On account of the huge crater at the top of this mountain, their feat was useless, but it shows what tanks driven by good men can do.

The following incidents are reported by officers who witnessed them and the authenticity is vouched for. In one case the tanks were attacking some German machine guns when one of our machine gun tanks jammed its piece about 100 meters from a German gun. The tank crew determined to crush the gun with their track. This they did, but to the credit of the German gunners be it stated that these two men remained at their gun and fired until they were crushed to death by the tank. Their gallant conduct was not useless because owing to it, both members of the tank crew became casualties inasmuch as flying splinters came through the eye slits. Another case: a great pill-box was encountered so situated that a tank could not fire against the embrasure thus completely effacing the fire. Some of the runners of the Tank Corps then came up and dropping some German grenades through the hole killed the crew inside.

G. S. PATTON Jr.,
Colonel, Tank Corps,
Commanding the Brigade.

Second Lieutenant John G. Heming, Headquarters, 302d Tank Center

Having transferred on March 15, 1918, from Base Hospital #15, situated at Chaumont, he commenced his duties as a Private First Class with the Tank Corps. At that time there were two small companies at Bourg, which received training, made possible by their own efforts, for, unassisted by engineers or other units, they constructed the gun-ranges, machine-shops, and tank sheds. Under the guidance and untiring efforts of Colonel George S. Patton, (then Lieutenant Colonel) the corps was trained and disciplined all through the spring and summer months until they were ready and fit for action in September on the St. Mihiel front.

Promoted to the rank of corporal in June, he was assigned as assistant to the transportation officer. This department was responsible for the hauling of hundreds of loads of barracks, lumber, pipe and machinery from such places as Langres, Dijon, and Is-sur-Tille. All was used in the construction of the present Camp Chamberlin.[2]

Owing to the shortage of men in Bourg after the first brigade had left to go into action at St. Mihiel, he acted as dispatch rider between this center and brigade headquarters at Ecrouves, and on several occasions proceeded to the battalions in action.

In the Argonne drive, which commenced in the early morning of September 28, 1918, the Tank Corps had its first real opportunity to distinguish itself and did so admirably. Beset by countless machine guns, snipers, hidden light field-guns, which had been brought up close to the lines, mines placed with extreme cunning, and a thick blanket of fog on the first day, which might have proven disastrous, they fought their way through all these obstacles for over two weeks, tired, exhausted perhaps, never giving up.

On the morning of the attack, he was one of the 10 runners in the reconnaissance party which accompanied Colonel Patton and two other officers. They came upon several companies of tanks (having started out from the advanced PC after the barrage had lifted), which had gained their first objective with very little resistance. The fog was so dense that it was impossible to discern objects at 100 feet. Desultory firing was heard in the distance, but it was difficult to judge how far off owing to the condition of the atmosphere. The runners continued onward with the commanding officer until they reached an enemy narrow-gauge railway about 500 yards south of Cheppy where they waited for the tanks. Presently several snipers opened up on the party from the flanks. The colonel sent out Private Joseph T. Angelo on the left and the writer on the right in order to give the alarm if any attempt was made to advance on or cut off the small group. By this time the machine guns commenced firing bursts and as there was scarcely any natural cover, the order was given to retire to a knoll about 100 yards to the rear. This retirement was made with some difficulty owing to the lifting fog which made them a seemingly easy target. It was affected, however, with injuries to no one. For about two hours the enemy swept the knoll with machine guns and laid down a barrage of heavy artillery, with a gas shell here and there. Meanwhile, a runner had been sent to the rear through this fire for a platoon of tanks to put out the machine gun nests. Great difficulty was experienced in crossing a wide and muddy trench by our tanks. There were about 60 men from the 138th Infantry scattered about in shell holes. They had no officers or leaders. It was imperative that Colonel Patton assume temporary command of this detachment because they exhibited no intentions of following the tanks in the attack. Everyone went over the top of the knoll in the face of the fire about 20 yards in rear of the tanks. The colonel was shot in the thigh during the action and Private [Joseph P.] Angelo fearlessly went to his side, dressed the wound, and made him as comfortable as possible. It was not feasible to remove him then for the fire was too intense. Later, during somewhat of a lull, three enlisted men and the writer carried him on a stretcher three kilometers when they were relieved by several members of an ambulance company. During the days following this, the writer continued his duties as runner in the vicinity of Varennes, Baulny, and Charpentry under fire.

On October 4th, he was recalled to Bourg to accept a commission as second lieutenant in the Tank Corps, and assigned to duty as transportation officer, remaining in this capacity until his reassignment to Company B, 329th Battalion, 302d Brigade. This company has completed the course of training and was recently commended on its high standard of efficiency, bearing in classes and drills.

Private First Class Joseph T. Angelo, Headquarters, 302d Tank Center

On the morning of 26 September 1918, Colonel Patton and his party, consisting of two officers and 12 enlisted men, left the brigade PC and followed the tank tracks in a northern direction, finally coming to a place where there were five French tanks (four heavy and one light). Colonel Patton ordered the party to halt and rest. In a few minutes the French tanks started to advance. Then the colonel ordered me to a spot where I could see the road and report if the enemy was coming. I saw two Germans on the other side of the road and opened fire on them. Immediately they opened fire on us with machine guns. We then fell back to the reverse side of the small hill. As we reached this position we saw, standing, a few French and American tanks. The position of these tanks was under heavy shell fire, also the area was being swept by machine guns. The colonel ordered me back with a message to the CO [Commanding Officer] of tanks, ordering them to spread. I delivered the order to Captain [Math L.] English, but the tanks did not spread. Then Colonel Patton came back to the position of the tanks and asked Captain English what the trouble was. Captain English answered that a place would have to be built across the trenches in order to get tanks over. At this point I informed Captain English that a bridge was being built further down the trench by French soldiers. Then Colonel Patton took command, organized a labor squad and built a bridge across the trench where tanks could pass. Colonel Patton stood erect, in the open while directing this work, and was exposed to heavy shell fire as well as machine gun fire which was sweeping the area.

In a few minutes the tanks began to move forward over the hill where small groups of infantry had taken cover in shell craters. The colonel asked an infantry sergeant if there were any of his officers present, to which he answered, "no." The sergeant then asked Colonel Patton what they should do; he replied, "follow me," to which they consented and followed. As we reached to the top of the hill machine guns opened fire. There was one tank with us. I looked to the right and saw an infantryman fall to the left and another fall. We were then about 50 feet above the hillside. About this time Colonel Patton was hit by a machine gun bullet. I asked if he had been hit and he answered, "yes." I then asked him to come into a shell hole, but he said, "come on, the boys will follow." He became weak from loss of blood and was compelled to stop in a shell hole further on, at which place I dressed his wound. Sergeant Shimitz came forward and Colonel Patton gave him a message for Major [Sereno E.] Brett, stating that he, Major Brett, was in command of the tanks. Machine guns were still playing about us. There were about four tanks on our left not moving. Sergeant Shimitz came back and reported that the message had been sent. The colonel then ordered him to go and spread the tanks before they drew artillery fire. He got them all started, but one, and as he was leaving this tank it ran into a mine which exploded. A tank from the rear appeared on the scene at this time. I jumped from the shell crater, hailed the driver and pointed out a machine gun nest on the right and one on the left, telling him to put them out as the colonel was wounded and could not be moved because of them. The tank put them out. At this time two sergeants came from the rear and helped to carry the colonel back. We secured a stretcher and carried him to the rear.

First Lieutenant Paul S. Edwards, Headquarters, 302d Tank Center

On the morning of September 26th, 1918, at H +1 hour of the attack by the First Army Corps, Lieutenant Colonel George S. Patton Jr., moved forward from this PC at corps headquarters with his brigade staff, which consisted of one officer, myself and 12 enlisted men. We advanced along the right of the Neuvilly-Varennes road following the tank tracks.

There was a very heavy fog—so thick that visibility for more than a hundred yards was very poor. As we moved forward, over and past our first line trenches, we came upon our reserve tanks, which were slowly moving forward. We also overtook the French group who are having some difficulty with the larger tanks in negotiating the muddy terrain. We met several groups of disorganized infantry who were moving about trying to locate their commands. As we moved forward these troops were gathered together by Lieutenant Colonel Patton and we continued on.

Advancing to a point about one kilometer east of Varennes and within sight of Cheppy (we couldn't see Cheppy at the time due to the fog) we halted near a narrow gauge track where Lieutenant Colonel Patton decided to send a message. Groups of troops, disorganized infantry, were coming back, others were wandering forward, through the fog which was beginning to lift. None of these troops had officers with them and were ordered by Lieutenant Colonel Patton to spread out and stand fast as intermittent machine gun fire had started. As we came to the track some large French tanks were there and we stopped near them. They soon pushed forward and the enemy machine gun fire became more intense and we then retired behind the railroad cut and the enemy artillery commenced to range on our area.

Lieutenant Colonel Patton immediately withdrew to a position on the slope of the hill about 150 yards south of the railroad and dispatched a runner and later an officer to tell our reserve tanks to move forward. The fire became more intense and an enemy plane came over, flying low, in the now almost clear morning and began to direct the artillery fire on our position and on the tanks coming up. Then Lieutenant Colonel Patton, seeing a small group of tanks below us and to the rear, sent me to have five of them move up to where we laid and attack the machine guns which were now covering the entire area. Most of the fire was evidently coming from an entrenched position about 150 yards in front of us and it was afterwards learned that 25 machine gun nests were along the edge of the slope leading up to Cheppy, some 400 yards or more in front of us.

The tanks endeavored to climb over the trenches and the first one got stuck. We commenced to dig in the sides of the trenches and under the direction of Lieutenant Colonel Patton, who had come to this position, we succeeded in getting five tanks over. During this work an intense machine gun fire swept the area and the artillery was being regulated by an enemy plane which made frequent trips over us. There were a great many casualties at this point.

As the tanks moved forward Lieutenant Colonel Patton gathered the groups of troops who were with us and advanced to the slope of our former position on the hill. Just as the last tank went over the hill Lieutenant Colonel Patton stood up and waving his cane shouted, "Let's go get them, who's with me,"—all sprang forward through the hell of machine gun fire. They had advanced but about 50 yards when a tremendous mine blew up and the artillery began a terrific barrage—Sergeant Shimitz came back saying that, "Lieutenant Colonel Patton was wounded and wanted no one to come near him, but that he wanted Major Brett to be notified and take command of the brigade."

The tanks had silenced the machine gun fire and we were now having only erratic shelling as the enemy artillery seemed to be ranging on the tanks. Lieutenant Colonel Patton was moved to the rear on a stretcher and I reported to Major Brett, whom I found about 2:00 p.m. As near as I can judge Lieutenant Colonel Patton was wounded about 11:30 a.m.

Captain Maurice H. Knowles, Reconnaissance Officer (RO), Headquarters, 302d Tank Center

There are two people, the brigade commander and the brigade reconnaissance officer, who are the first to know where an attack is going to take place and its general magnitude. They view the entire preparation for a longer time with greater perspective than the remainder of the tank brigade personnel. These two people are the first on the ground in the area of impending attack, studying the terrain, and any dispositions, etc., to determine whether the enemy area lends itself to the employment of tanks or not.

After learning the general infantry plan from the chief of staff of the First Army, we went to the immediate front and found the sector held by the French. The French helped us in every matter possible and gave all available information, furnished guides, etc. A stream in the center of "No Man's Land" paralleling the two front lines was of considerable interest to us as the information at hand left some doubt as to whether tanks could cross it or not. The second night after our arrival the two of us left all means of identification in our lines and joined about 40 French soldiers on a night raid. We came to the stream and pushed a cane into all parts of the area and found that tanks could cross it. The party discovered two wires running between the lines and these were cut, coiled up and brought back. On our return, we heard a shrill human whistle come out of the darkness, which one of the French soldiers immediately answered. Our interpreter told us it was a Boche raiding party. We changed our course, going directly away from the source of the whistle and evidently the Boche did this only in the other direction.

After every detail of the reconnaissance preliminary to the bringing in of the tanks had been attended to, we were ordered to the other side of the salient.

Here we found Americans holding the sector. Our reconnaissance was carefully made, attending to every detail, and as before, observing the enemy and studying the enemy area for at least two hours every day. Here again it was necessary to go into "No Man's Land" to see a stream, a bridge and to examine, take dimensions of the old abandoned trenches. This was done in broad daylight after notifying our troops where we were going to avoid being sniped from the rear. It was safe for it to do this in broad daylight due to the fact that scores of raiding parties went out every night and movement was slow and cautious on account of the countless Very lights both sides shot up.

First Lieutenant Donald C. Wilson, Salvage and Repair Company, 302d Tank Center

Since my transfer to the Tank Corps about seven months ago it has been my ill fortune or good fortune as the case may be, to be in the noncombatant minority of the brigade to which I was assigned. And prior to my assignment, upon the completion of the suitability test at the Army tank schools, I held the much talked of detail as mess officer.

However, associated with a repair and salvage organization and its work in the two shows in which the Tank Corps was cast, my days have been eventful to a greater or lesser degree. Our work at the center included the usual routine which established itself in the year when the first ten tanks began to need mechanical repairs. My introduction to the company came through the foreman mechanic, who took me over the shop, explaining the different details to me and finally leaving me on one of them, the dirtiest and greasiest of the lot, to find out how little I knew about transmissions. Those were dirty days, those of apprenticeship, dirty but interesting, and when finally I rated a clean fatigue suit, and the more lately arrived mechanics began to ask me some embarrassing questions about the construction and nomenclature of the iron horses, our long hoped for orders came for active service. My company commander phoned to me in a hospital in Langres, where my prune supper was prejudicing me against the doctor who was to take out my tonsils the next morning.

Our spare parts and limited equipment were loaded into trucks the next day and at two o'clock in the afternoon the truck train left. My job in the moving up was with the remaining personnel of the company who boarded the train which took the first load of tanks on the same day. After the usual joys of loading tanks at night, on French cars, our journey northward was uneventful. Upon arrival at the St. Mihiel country, however, we got on the wrong spur and went up almost to the line in the wrong place. While awaiting another night for a change, I found my company truck train and we immediately joined the kitchen.

The preparations during the last few days before D-day were full of much work and worry. Twenty-four hours of mud and chainless trucks on slimy, crowded roads, was my first impression of real war. Since then the officers and soldiers of the lines of communications have rated much higher in my estimation. On D-day, after we had reached Beaumont with our train, we spent 36 hours of war-making, but two kilometers on the road.

After our final camp site was reached, we found that we were not stranded with nothing to do. My job included the reconnaissance of the battle area for stranded tanks, and later, was detailed to the work of salvage. Mud was the worst enemy of the tanks in the St. Mihiel show. Not mud in the radiators, nor in the carburetors, but sticky, soggy, awful mud in which the tanks wallowed belly deep. The wonderful artillery preparation stirring up the surface and powdering the clods, assisted Dame Nature in making odds against the tanks in their first chance as part of Uncle Sam's offensive force.

No serious misfortune, mechanically, happened to the tanks. The different jobs of pulling them out of the mud and out of the rivers were greatly interesting. The tactics for the extrication of each mired tank were entirely different and hours of uninteresting monotony did not enter. In fact the morale was higher when we had finished our work and the material was again loaded for transport to another front than when we entered the sector.

In the move to the new front, my responsibility was that of the brigade truck again. I rode a solo motorcycle for 12 hours that day, and when we finally got all the trucks into the "Quarry" near Clermont, after another wonderful, sloppy afternoon, I again pledged my appreciation of the men on the line of communication.

Just on the day of the opening of the Argonne fight, I drew a gentle diversion in the way of an order to proceed to Bourg, for some spare parts which were needed, and after all night I reported back in time to take an advance detail to Varennes, where we worked on some dozen tanks during that day. The sound of occasional stray bigger things [artillery] came only close enough to practice us in the art of "ducking." We were joined the next morning by the rest of the company, and the reconnaissance for disabled tanks occupied a space of a few days.

This reconnaissance, in the Argonne and thereabouts, was entirely different than that in the preceding [St. Mihiel] show. My work took me generally on a motorcycle to all the towns famous in the stories of the battle, and it was in this work that I got my thrills of the fight. I didn't get to shoot at a Boche, but had the experience of having him shoot at me, which I imagine is almost as exciting. Aside from the common bombardment by whizz-bangs [German 77mm artillery projectiles], gas shells and the larger ones with less frequency, one of my rides stands out in my memory. I was on my way to Charpentry taking some necessities to one of the battalion repair units, and had just made the hill out of Varennes to the point where the road camouflage began. This road had been well camouflaged by Fritz, and though there had been a good deal of strafing there in the past few days, I felt safe when I entered the screens. The Hun had direct observation over about three kilometers of that road and had both the Argonne woods. A whizz-bang lit a little behind me and I opened the throttle just a little. About that time another exploded about 40 yards ahead of me. I wondered at that and closed my throttle a little. That ride, over some three kilometers, was my most thrilling experience. When one hears machine gun bullets he is unable to guess whether they are 10 feet over his head or 10 yards, (It's best for a man undoubtedly, to assume that the former is true.). But one can see whizz-bangs when they are as close to one as to throw dirt in your eye. I am sure that he was shooting at me, for I was the only one on the road, and they followed me. It may have been that he was strafing the entire road at the same time, but I think not. I fooled with the throttle a few moments until without my knowing it, I had turned it open. I never was a speed maniac, but that was one time in my life when I appreciated it.

I had barely passed Fritz's line of sight and was slowing down gradually when one of his gas shells burst in the road just ahead of me. I couldn't stop so I had to go through it, but held my breath for some time afterwards. (I was used to holding my breath by that time.) It only made me cough, slightly, but two days later I was evacuated with the Flu.

Experiences have been related about beautiful nurses and lovely white sheets, but I missed them. I became so tired of the hospital in two days—besides I heard that my company commander had been taken ill—that I went AWOL [Absent Without Leave] from an evacuation hospital when I was about to be loaded on a French Red Cross train, caught a returning ambulance, and reported to my company. My recovery did not come so quickly, however, for it was several days before I was able to last a full day working, as I did on my details, with the soldiers in the unditching, salvaging transport of the tanks.

The remaining time in the sector was spent in reclaiming tanks, which Fritz had left strewn in various stages of disability, including some very few which he destroyed entirely. A number of the worst were stripped where they "fell" on the field of honor and only certain parts were worth salvaging. Others were repaired so that they could be run into the park at Varennes, and still others were towed in. In two cases, where the treads were stuck, we loaded the tanks into trucks and got them home that way. This loading with the treads stuck was an interesting operation. We remodeled a big shell hole for the hind wheels of the truck, and let the rear end of the bed down to the ground level. Then with skids and cable around the tank, the other two tanks, one on each side of the truck, pulled the cripple into position where it was made fast. The truck then, of course, had to be pulled out of the shell hole.

The disabled tanks were found to be in irregular groups in nearly every case, and it was usually possible to get one, two or three of the groups running so that these could be used in unditching and towing the total disability cases. We found them in every conceivable predicament, just plain lack of gasoline, in rivers, mine craters and trenches and even shot almost to pieces. One particularly had been the recipient of no less than six direct hits by 77's or 88's and the remaining mass was burned to a char. Another had gotten in the way of a big shell, and from the front of the turret forward and down to the ground, not so much as a belt could be found.

All in all, I can't say that I regret having been in a salvage organization, for my work at the front was very interesting and instructive as well. I will be unable to tell glowing accounts of meeting Fritz and showing him, but I conscientiously feel that I have done my bit in bringing about the present situation. Now that it is over, I am impatiently awaiting the order to embark. Here's luck to our Army of Occupation.

Captain Elgin E. Braine, Headquarters, 302d Tank Center

When with the 6th Field Artillery, Battery D, 1st Division, I received orders to report to Captain [George S.] Patton [Jr.] in connection with the investigation of tank work. Reported to Captain Patton at Champlieu, First Branch Tank Training Center, becoming acquainted with the machines, organization and details connected with this work. Then reported back to GHQ to Colonel [LeRoy] Eltinge, who was then in charge, and with Captain Patton helped to make up the first report on light tanks from which the Tank Corps was organized.

After this report had been submitted, [I] was ordered to Paris to report to Colonel Groom, who has been chief ordnance officer on tank work. Upon telegraphic instructions, was ordered to London for conference with Colonel [Herbert W.] Alden, who was investigating heavy tank work. This conference was to acquaint him with light tank facts preparatory to his returning to the United States.

There were 21 suggested changes to be made of this small tank, all of which were adopted by the French government. These were discussed by Colonel Alden, who stated that he would see that they were incorporated in the machines to be made in the United States, as far as possible. To facilitate this matter a cable was sent governing the major points. I then reported back to GHQ, reporting to [Brigadier] General [Samuel D.] Rockenbach, who had since been put in command of the Tank Corps.

I then reported to Colonel Patton at Langres, care of army schools, where he was then stationed, then went to Martigny-les-Bains, the Second Branch Tank Park, on a second inspection trip with General Rockenbach and Colonel Patton. I then returned from same to work with General Rockenbach, helping to secure an office, rent a house, secure servants, and get a mess started, with many varied experiences owing to my lack of command of the French language. Second Lieutenant [George J.] Crosby reported for duty and was assigned as the general's adjutant. Later on there were 11 lieutenants from the Coast Artillery who reported for duty, whom I took with me to Langres, and reported them to Colonel Patton. Arrangements were made with [Lieutenant] Colonel [Robert J.] Maxey and Colonel [Frank] Parker to take these officers into the 37mm School and Machine Gun School in the main barracks at [Fort de] Peigney. Then, for the next week I went to the station every day to meet an additional number of officers, and finally reported, eight in number, also Coast Artillery lieutenants, all of whom had been regular army sergeants with from seven to 24 years of service. A few of these men were later relieved and sent back to the United States.

An office was secured in the training barracks and arrangements were made with the different schools for the men to take what courses were available. We endeavored to organize a mechanical course, and finally persuaded the Quartermaster Corps to allow us to use a broken-down truck that had been salvaged. Securing a few tools, we started to work to take this truck apart and rebuild same, which was the first equipment ever had by the Tank Corps.

About February 1, 1918, I received orders from the chief of Tank Corps to report to Colonel [James A.] Drain in Paris for duty in connection with the securing of ordnance material for the Tank Corps. I spent some time at the Renault factory, also making up tables of organization for Tank Corps equipment. This consumed about three weeks.

I then received orders to proceed to the United States and report to the Chief of Ordnance in connection with the special machines, and upon completion of these machines to return to my duty in France. I took with me one turret, 37mm tank cannon, and all mounts for both light and heavy tanks, together with all the drawings for same, including drawings for jigs, tools and fixtures, also a letter from Chief of Ordnance, AEF, to Chief of Ordnance, United States, covering the requirements of the Tank Corps.

After many trials, finally got this material on the train and transported same to St. Nazaire, having to convoy it all the way. Upon arriving there, reported to commanding officer for transportation, and was advised that there would be no boats leaving for some time. Thereupon, telegraphed to Colonel Brown, who replied that I had been misinformed. I then found out that there was a boat leaving the following day. This was the SS *Appeles*.[3] Finally got material loaded on this boat.

This ship was an old German freighter which had been interned on the island of Haiti. I was the only passenger, and the freight I had was the only material on board. It even lacked sand for ballast, which they ordinarily required, owing to the lack of sand at that port.

The crew consisted of an old-time sea captain who said he went to sea in the fall of 1874, and no one could tell him how to sail a boat. The first mate was a big Swede who had never been on the Atlantic before. The Chief Engineer was a Scotsman, and the Quartermaster Lieutenant, a second lieutenant, Quartermaster Corps, who kept to his bunk the whole trip. None of the other members of this crew were on speaking terms, and for the whole trip, consisting of 17 days, there never was a word spoken at meals except "Good morning." There was a sign posted in the saloon which read: "This is a place to eat in, not debate, when finished, please vacate."

We left St. Nazaire the morning of the 22nd and steamed down to Verdun Bay, where we were to wait for orders about a convoy. The following night orders were received to sail 23 miles down the coast to meet a convoy, which was coming up from Bordeaux. The skipper absolutely refused to move until he had a pilot and a convoy.

The following morning naval officers came on board and we left that afternoon with a French destroyer and traveled all the way down to Bordeaux, and went into the harbor and stayed there overnight. When coming out we were convoyed the following morning. Just as we were about to pull anchor, we were advised that the channel had been laid full of mines by a submarine, and we would have to wait until the channel was cleared, which was not until late that afternoon. We then steamed out, a convoy of 23 vessels. J. P. Morgan's yacht and some American destroyers convoyed us for 24 hours and we were left to ourselves. We then ran into one storm after another all the way across the Atlantic. One day we only made 20 miles in 24 hours. The lack of ballast and the heavy seas kept the propeller out of the water, and it was impossible to make any speed at all. The morning of the day we left the convoy a submarine was reported to have been sighted, and about daylight guns of this boat started to fire. By the time I got on, I could see absolutely nothing. The rest of our journey was very uneventful, except that we heard many wireless warnings of submarines.

The only other interesting thing was that the stokers and crew went on strike, marched up on the captain's bridge and refused to work unless they got better rations. This was very soon remedied. The usual argument between the skipper and the engineer was that the skipper ordered better time and the engineer refused to run his engines and have them broken down. The weather was very bad, including snow storms.

We finally arrived in New York harbor one morning about the 14th of March, and the Statue of Liberty loomed up in the mist, and we came on deck at Governor's Island, with Staten Island close by. We were supposed to dock that morning. About 8:30 a.m., or a quarter of nine, a tug came and ordered us to haul anchor and steam to Newport News. The skipper advised that he would have to have rations, so he arranged to go ashore.

As I was very anxious to get my material to its destination, I went ashore with the skipper and got permission to land this material in New York. I unloaded the same from the side of the ship onto the tug, later on taking the same down to the Battery. I spent the best part of the day trying to find someplace where I could land this materiel. Every dock that I went to would not take it. Finally, after much running around and telephoning, I got permission to land this on the ordnance dock at Governor's Island. There were many times that this materiel almost landed in the bottom of the bay.

I then telegraphed to the Ordnance officer at Washington, reporting my arrival, and took the train that evening for Washington, spending most of my time trying to find the office of the Chief of Ordnance. Later that afternoon I finally got in touch with the proper people, although the Chief of Ordnance was not in Washington at that time, and I was turned over to Colonel [Lucian B.] Moody of the Engineering Bureau, Motor Equipment Section, Ordnance Department, who in turn got me in touch with Colonel Alden, who had charge of the engineering work on tank construction. He said that they would need this materiel so that they could go ahead and complete the design of their turret, etc.

With an Ordnance lieutenant, I went back to New York. The following morning I secured this materiel from Governor's Island, hired a truck, and transferred same to Pennsylvania Depot. It took the rest of the day to get permission to have this loaded in the baggage car of the fast train to St. Louis, Mo., my destination being Dayton, Ohio. I left there about 2:00 a.m. Saturday morning and reported to Captain [Frank M.] Seig, in charge of the Engineering Office of the Motor Equipment Section of the Ordnance Department at Maxwell Plant No. 2. This was Saturday and they arranged to have this materiel taken up to the plant, but all people working there left and did not return until Monday morning, so I had to sit and wait around until they returned.

It seems that the engineering office in Washington was designing a turret, and also the engineering office at Dayton. It was this confliction of ideas and misunderstanding which was the cause of so many delays after the start. They were told not to make any changes, but to check the drawing and turret of the one they were designing. I then received a telegram to report back to Colonel Moody in Washington at once, and we went over the motor equipment which was suggested and certain changes and recommendations were made by cable to take care of the Tank Corps equipment and vehicles which were supposed to be in production, but found out later, however, that this was not the case.

When I left France, I was advised that cables had been received for 100 light tanks, which would be shipped in April. Later, upon investigation, I found that there was not a line drawn on paper before the first week in January. This information was not discovered until sometime later. My reception at Washington was far from being cordial, and it took considerable time to get acquainted with the people working there. I was told that there would be nothing else for me to do, but I wanted to see that items covered in the letter of introduction were carried out. There seemed to be considerable misunderstanding and lack of cooperation, all the way through.

There was an argument as to which department would have my services, if they decided they were worthwhile. It was a question between the Control Bureau, Administration Bureau, Engineering Division, Motor Equipment Section, Procurement, Production and Supply divisions. I was finally placed under Colonel Moody's orders, and to divide such time as I had to spare with the other departments. There were not more than 12 people working on all tank work, including light and heavy, when I arrived in Washington. There had been no tools ordered, no spare parts ordered, or any of these things. I was not consulted in regard to the question of the gun.

I insisted that the tank gun be put into production, and the standard mount being used by the French, which I had brought over, be made. I was overruled in this matter by Colonel Alden and Colonel [Earl] McFarland, who stated that they could not get into production on these guns in time to meet demand, and they would use the 37mm modified field gun, and they would design a special armor, with a splash proof mark. They said they would also use the Marlin machine gun with a special mask. This design took three-and-a-half months, and upon completion was unsatisfactory. The time lost in learning the different departments of the Ordnance organization, and the number of people who would send you from one person to another before you could get any information, was very discouraging.

Then a trip was planned whereby I should visit the different plants, and I was given many letters of introduction to go over these different plants. After making one or two trips I decided that they were a waste of time and that they were not giving us tanks. The idea seemed to be that I was to be given an impression of what was being done, but I soon found out that little was being done on tank work. Schedules were made showing the production which would be had on tanks, and promises made of many things to bring about this result. Promises made on promises never produced results. I did a considerable amount of kicking, my motto being that the "squeaking wheel gets the grease."

To give some idea of the organization, there were the different sections in the different divisions, such as Motor Equipment, Small Arms, Ammunition, Explosive, Cannon Section, Machine Gun, Automatic Arms, Equipment, Supply, Procurement, Production, etc., all of which had their own engineering and other departments.

I was told about the Ford tractor, the tank which was being very much talked about at the time, there being a great deal of talk about quantity production, etc. I was sent to Detroit and saw this machine, but they were unable to make it run at the time. I later discovered that a cable was sent stating that I had approved of same, which was not so. It was not until sometime later that I saw this machine run, and it did not impress me very favorably. They had two standard Ford motors hooked up by chain, which later developed would not work. They also did not have any tail piece on this machine and when I asked why, they said it was so short it did not need any. The first time it went to cross a trench the machine got over all right, but after it was over it slipped back into the trench. I made several trips to the different plants that had contracts for this machine. This was a very complicated affair.

There were three contractors who had a certain number of machines to build. One company was making all the motors and half the transmission, another company was making the side-parts, track frames, etc., and the third contractor was practically to assemble, procuring motors, transmissions, etc., from the other firms. Besides this, the government arranged the armor plate, tools, magnetos, radiators and other items, which would necessitate a Philadelphia lawyer to keep track of this materiel, together with the constant changes which were occurring, either at the request of the manufacturer so he could secure the proper amount of material, or owing to the mistakes made on the drawings, or owing to the changes which had to be made to meet construction, so that the same would operate. All the work was originally in charge of one officer and some men. When he got this started, he was then transferred to other work, and another officer took charge, so that finally the last man was carrying the load of other people's mistakes, of which there were many, such as drawings, which would never check against assemblies, the assemblies would never check against connected assemblies, so that when they came to put the machines together they found many errors, which caused considerable delay.

They organized production meetings of the manufacturer and contractors, which only resulted in slowing up instead of increasing production, as one manufacturer would see that the other man was not very far ahead, so he could see no occasion for hurry, and so they would delay in getting the work done. The production was also hampered by the fact that this work was controlled by the Ordnance Department in regard to inspection, supply, allocations of material and priority; the tanks having a very poor priority on materiel. For example, one case which I followed up did not have the steel called for some axles. The axle manufacturer said he could not get the steel because he did not have the proper priority. After going to the War Trade Board to secure this priority for the manufacturer, he advised me that he would have to have a priority on billets from the steel mill. The steel mill, in turn, advised that if this priority had been secured they would have to have a priority for billets. The billet people, in turn, needed a priority on coke, the coke manufacturer needed priority on railroad cars, so you can very readily see that with a small number of men following these things results were not very easily obtainable, as this light tank consisted of about 1,200 parts and a total of about 33,000 pieces.

For example, the manufacturer or contractor has an order for a piece of steel for a pin which called for a certain percentage of carbon on the drawing. He advised that he could get a little less carbon steel very readily, which would be just as suitable for this work, and he was advised to go ahead and do so, which meant that the drawing was changed to pass the material. This drawing was on form 434, which was an abortion to prevent quantity production. If the material was not passed by the inspector, the district chief would not okay the account, the man could not receive his money, yet he had authority from the engineering bureau to use this material. This question of inspection was a very serious matter, owing to the delays and misunderstandings, which came up due to conflicting authority.

For example, the chief inspector of a district would advise that he had no authority from the Inspection Division at Washington to deviate from any of the specifications which were covered by the drawings and form 434. As there was, in many cases, deviation, only temporary in some cases as to get production, it would not be policy to change the drawings, and the inspectors would not accept the decisions made at the engineering office in Dayton.

After the manufacturers had gotten started, and had a large quantity of material on hand, an order was issued that all parts must be numbered. This entailed a considerable amount of time to straighten out through the Inspection, Procurement and Production Divisions.

The job of making up the list of spare parts was turned over to me upon which I devoted considerable time, and it was thoroughly understood by all concerned that spare parts would be shipped in proportion to the number of machines shipped. The question of tools and accessories for these machines was also turned over to me, and I was advised that I could specify anything that I thought necessary. I went to Dayton and had a list of tools made up, taking into consideration the size of every nut on the machine for wrenches, the question of grease guns, electric lamps, etc. I was then advised that those would all have to be drawn so that they could be purchased. The draughtsmen were put to work and drawings were made of every tool; with these drawings I went to Washington so as to see that this order was placed immediately. On reviewing these, they informed me that these drawings were not on the proper form, as they were on drawing 313131, which covered the tank, but must be put on the form calling for standard Ordnance tools. This was then done and taken to the Procurement Division. I was then advised that I must use standard Ordnance tools wherever possible. So, I very carefully checked these drawings against standard Ordnance tool drawings, and substituted whenever possible. Again taking these drawings, I sent them to the Procurement Division, who said that they would place the order.

I kept following this matter, and later on was advised that so many of these standard Ordnance tools were out of date that they were out of market, and therefore had to okay the specifications and get the procurement requisition made over again. The procedure, which was followed in this case: the Engineering Division specified the class of material they wished, forwarded the requisition through the regular channels to the Estimate and Requirement Division to figure the estimates and requirements, and then forwarded through channels to the Procurement Division, who issued the procurements, requested the submission of bids, and called for bids from the different manufacturers. The contracts were awarded; they went to the Legal and Finance Divisions for okay, which took from five to six weeks. In the meantime, changes came up, which caused some delay. There were certain items, such as straps, canvas buckets, etc, which were on the list, which came under another department of the Ordnance, which by the time it reached them were being absorbed by the Quartermaster; a joint Purchasing Division for both the Quartermaster and the Ordnance being organized. As they could not agree on a policy to pursue, the orders were held up for three weeks.

Then manufacturers who had accepted orders for a schedule of shipments did not live up to these shipments. Other manufacturers did not want to take the orders for certain amounts and sizes of wrenches, etc., on account of the small order and the trouble involved. Electric hand lanterns, which would have been obtained easily by purchasing any standard lamp, were held up on account of a special lamp designed by the Ordnance, which took trouble and time to have patents and castings made. This gives a good idea of the efforts needed to secure such a small item of tool equipment for tanks.

One rather amusing incident of the delays which occurred were in reference to machine guns. The only machine guns available for tanks were 7,206 Marlin aircraft guns at Fairfield, Ohio, being the property of the Signal Corps. It was decided to have some for tank use, with the putting on of a pistol grip. I was not consulted at all regarding this detail or the modification of these guns, which anyone could easily see would have been inadequate for use in a tank. This order was placed by a memorandum from the Engineering Division, stating the amount needed, and these guns purchased from the Signal Corps, to be forwarded to the Marlin-Rockwell Company to be modified. A cable was received that an early shipment of some of these guns was needed, and I made a special effort to procure this shipment. Some of these guns were shipped to the Marlin people and they commenced work on the same. After having on three different occasions said that they were finished, they were changed at the last minute and they said this could not be done. At last, the final agreement was reached, and they promised 50 guns by a certain date, which they did not live up to; their excuse being that they had to order from the Ordnance Department for this work. Endeavoring to get these guns shipped, the Ordnance Department Supply Division said they could not ship these guns as there was no procurement requisition or purchasing order covering the same.

Interviewing the Supply Division and Procurement Division in connection with this, they stated that no contract had been placed and no agreement as to price could be reached. They said the Requirements Division had figured these 7,000 odd guns as covering a period from 1918 to 1919; so I personally called to see the head of the Requirements Division, persuading him to change it so it would read for 1918.

He said if I could have a letter written from the Engineering Division, he would attend to this, and the Procurement Division advised that they could get this matter straightened out then. I went back to the Engineering Division, signed a letter stating the reasons for this change, and advised the necessity of this being done. This letter was dictated on June 1st. According to the system of the Ordnance Department, the letter could only be signed by the head of the department. This letter was written and I initialed same. I went to the head of the department's assistant, where it should have been countersigned and then sent to him for signature, and then through regular channels to the department. That day I left for Cleveland and Dayton on my work in reference to the state vacuum and speedometer, which I will refer to later. Coming back at the end of 10 days and inquiring if these guns had been shipped, I was advised that they had not been shipped. Tracking the thing down, I found that the Estimate and Requirement Division had never received the letter that I had written. The first day they discovered this letter in their files, but it was dated June 10th! It seemed that during my absence this letter laid on the desk of the assistant of the department and that he had had it rewritten and the date changed. This I took the trouble to call to the attention of the chief of that department, with no results. This was only one of the many instances of the lack of cooperation that I received, at times never even getting telephone calls which came for me, and all mail, personal and otherwise, was opened before I received it, also never being allowed to write any letters or send any communications to France except in a personal way, and then was repeatedly warned against it, as they emphatically informed me that people in France were fully advised as to the progress and situation at all times.

With reference to the speedometer, it was distinctly covered in the requisition that this was to read in kilometers. It was only after they had sent a cable and delayed the manufacture of this instrument that they would acknowledge that I was correct. They finally compromised and had this instrument and odometer to read in kilometers and meters, and the speedometer in miles per hour. I personally made a trip to the factory of the Stewart-Warner people in reference to the vacuum tank in this instrument, and did everything in my power to have them hurry this production, but their excuse was that they had been held up.

I had been traveling back and forth, averaging 22 nights a month on a sleeper, trying to locate something in reference to the Tank Corps in the United States. I finally discovered that Colonel [Ira C.] Welborn was Director of the Tank Corps, and situated in Washington. I wished to call upon him and spoke first to Colonel Moody and [Brigadier] General [John H.] Rice, Chief of Manufacture in the Office of the Chief of Ordnance, to get their permission so as not to have any misunderstanding, and they advised me that I had better not do that, so it was not until some time later that I finally got in touch with his office, and when Colonel [William H.] Clopton [Jr.] arrived was of great assistance to me in having someone to go to and tell my troubles. The lack of sufficient personnel on this work I had questioned from the beginning, and was told repeatedly that other men would be put on this work, and when [Major] General [Clarence C.] Williams, the Chief of Ordnance, arrived things looked much better, and it was thought that there would be a decided improvement. There was a big improvement, but the additional men were slow in coming. I finally went to see General Williams myself, and made a request, and he said they were not allowed any more persons by the War Department. I suggested using Tank Corps men, and he said that would be satisfactory and so informed Colonel Dillett. In the meantime, I had arranged with Colonel Welborn, who said that he would give every assistance possible in the matter.

I arranged to get 25 officers and go down to select these men, but I was sent West and another set of officers from the Ordnance Department sent down and picked out a certain number of men, and I finally believe they did not get the proper men for the job; although there were about 30 men of the Tank Corps working for the Ordnance Department, following up all the loose ends on this job pertaining both to light and heavy tanks.

In connection with this work, I also followed up the Signal Corps, with reference to the wireless apparatus, interphones, splash-proof face guards, steel helmets, and had experiments tried with triplex glass for eye slits, which proved successful. There were five or six interphone manufacturers with whom I took this matter up, and any number of equipment manufacturers on face guards, leather helmets, steel helmets, etc., but it was impossible to get anyone to make a decision on any of these matters.

The situation with reference to the motor vehicles was another one of big interest. It was originally intended to secure all motor transportation from the Ordnance Department, Motor Equipment Section, and to have a standard equipment for the Tank Corps. During this process the Motor Transport Corps was formed, and there was a difference of opinion between them and the Ordnance Department as to just what vehicles each would handle. The argument with reference to the four wheel artillery tractor lasted for three months, the Ordnance maintaining that this was strictly an Ordnance vehicle, they having designed this, some of the four wheel drives, and the French Latil truck. This short-coupled truck was exactly what we originally specified in our requirements. The orders for trailers, etc., were also held up and it was not until a personal investigation that they placed an order for 530 ten-ton trailers to take care of the Tank Corps requirements, although, in the cable sent suggesting a revision of motor equipment, it was stated that all this material was in production.

The instruction book was another item which they promised to have written, but when I went to take this matter up they would detail some men for the job, and when I returned from a trip would find that these men had been transferred to some other work. I finally got hold of one officer, and by the use of long distance telephone, and getting some of the best catalogue writers in the country, I had this work compiled and turned out with the assistance of Lieutenant French within three-and-one-half weeks.

Traveling at that time in the United States, where you had to pay four to four-and-a-half cents per mile and a half cent extra fare for Pullman War Tax, receiving only seven cents per mile in return, hardly compensated for hotel, taxi cab bills, etc., which necessitated some adequate return. All this time, promises were being made and broken in regard to shipments. I finally became acquainted with Captain [Andrew G.] Gardner, Recruiting Officer, New York City, and through him indirectly got in touch with Colonel Drain when he arrived in the United States and he was mainly responsible for consummating something that I had just about started, which was the appointment of a civilian head in charge of tank production: Mr. L. J. Harwords, who organized a large force to take care of this work. About that time, the first two machines were about ready for shipment, and I made arrangements to go back to France. Every effort had been made, heretofore, to keep me here, and up to the last minute they would not let me go, so I went to the Tank Corps office and persuaded Colonel Welborn to issue me an order that I might return. He consented to do this if the order read that I would again return to the United States and carry on my work there. After securing this order I went to Cleveland, got the two machines and personally conveyed them to the port and loaded them. Then, I reported to New York to secure the available transportation to France, being held up at that place for nearly a week, having to have physical examination, passports, special forms and orders, etc.

Having arrived in France, I proceeded immediately to Chaumont and reported to the Chief of Tank Corps, who sent me on an inspection trip to Varennes, where I looked over the machines in the park there and came back to him and reported. I was then sent to the 302nd Tank Center for duty. There, I was told to reorganize the Mechanical School and the Tank Driving School, which was done, and also the Tank Repair Shed and Machine Shop.

I endeavored to get a course of instruction that would fit the men, as companies, to be able to learn about the care and operation of their machines, so that the instruction could be made of use when they were formed into units and secure the proper equipment.

Also organized the Central Stock Room, Salvage Department, Central Gas and Oil Station. In connection with these duties, also took charge of the Motor Transportation Organization.

In endeavoring to keep the matters of the Tank Corps more or less confidential I was forced to decline many invitations and demands to make speeches by the Four Minute Men's Club and other organizations, and also to keep away from the reporters who were endeavoring to obtain information regarding the production of these machines, which would have only been embarrassing and occasioned still more delay. There are many other items that might be added, but as a whole, I say the Tank Corps never had a seat at the table and therefore did not get a fair showing. Being the first member of the Tank Corps, although not a volunteer, I have had at all times a great personal interest. If it is desired, many of the details concerning the work with which I was connected can be more fully described.

326th/344th Tank Battalion

Major Sereno E. Brett, Commander, 344th Tank Battalion

The present commander of the 344th Battalion, Major Sereno E. Brett, arrived in France with the 1st Division as a first lieutenant of infantry. During the early days in the history of the AEF he was assigned to several posts, including the unenviable post of Provost Marshal of St. Nazaire. Later, when the division moved to northern France, he was placed in command of one of the machine gun companies of the 28th Infantry and shortly after received his promotion to the grade of captain. Then began an intensive training which no old 1st Division man shall ever forget. They were truly preparing the division to revive the glorious history of American arms.

During the first part of November, just when the division was expecting to see action, Captain Brett was greatly disappointed by receiving an order from GHQ detailing him as senior instructor in the 37mm section of the Army Infantry Specialists School at Langres. From that time to the first of March, 1918, he labored with young reserve officers, attempting to prove the 37 mm cannon was the most powerful of all weapons.

Early in March the opportunity came to transfer to the Tank Corps and it was eagerly accepted. Then began another period of relentless training and fatigue, ending finally on September 8th, when we started for the front to put on our first "show." During this period Captain Brett held the positions of chief instructor, company commander of old Company B, commanding officer of the old 327th (345th) Battalion and finally commanding officer of the old 326th (344th) Battalion. During this period, Captain Brett graduated from the Army General Staff College, in addition to his other duties. He was appointed major in the Tank Corps on July 14, 1918.

Never will the feeling of pride, when orders first came to proceed to the front, be forgotten. Scarcely any of the officers and men had ever been under fire, but everyone knew that the Tank Corps represented by the two battalions, would make a success. Everyone realized that the two battalions were destined to initiate the history of the American Tank Corps, and all grimly set themselves to an initiation of which the American army and the American people could justly be proud.

Preparations were quickly made and huge difficulties were overcome by the old 326th Battalion, and then came the long to be remembered night of September 11, 1918,—the night before St. Mihiel. The rain was pouring down, the night was intensely dark and the mud knee deep, when the battalion squirmed out of its place of hiding at 9:00 p.m. and its long column began rolling forward to its battle position. The night was terrible, but, somehow, extremely impressive. The sector was absolutely quiet, except for the rain and wind,—long lines of infantry and engineers appeared suddenly out of nothing, slid by and disappeared into the blackness of the night,—artillery and machine gun outfits packed the roads, the drivers cursing their animals and the cannoneers heaving on the wheels. Every animate and mechanical thing seemed to be moving forward. It was truly an impressive sight.

The head of the battalion was just crossing the Rupt de Mad when the first shell from our batteries whined overhead. It was 1.00 a.m. September 12th, and everyone in the battalion realized that the show had finally commenced. The battalion finally got to its battle position, near Xivray-Marvoisin at 2:00 a.m. and then commenced the hardest period of the entire fight,—the three hours wait before they went "over." A few shells from the German "heavies" landed close, but everyone seemed to enjoy the sensation.

Four-thirty, and the column began to move forward to enable it to be in position in front of the infantry at H-hour. Everything went fine until the first enemy trenches were reached. Here it was that the true mettle of the tankers was first tested. The trenches proved difficult to negotiate and the battalion commander, with pride, saw officers and men leading their commands, but of momentarily serious situations on foot. Here it was that he saw captains [Howell P.] Wood, [Harry H.] Semmes and [Math L.] English, standing on the parapet of trenches, under heavy fire directing their companies over difficult ground. It was also in this vicinity that Captain Semmes risked his life to save that of his driver by re-entering his tank and pulling him out when the tank had fallen into a river and was submerged. The difficulty was quickly overcome and the battalion proceeded with the attack. During the first day, the 326th [344th] Battalion took active part in the actions against all objectives and wound up the day by capturing Nonsard.

But, with this exhilarating success of the first day, came disappointment when they learned they progressed so fast that they had run away from their supplies; thereby making it possible to employ only a small group of tanks under the command of First Lieutenant Harry E. Gibbs on the second day of the advance. This small group did very effective work and on the evening of September 13th were far ahead of the infantry without gas and oil. Here again the true tanker's spirit came to the front. Rather than abandon his tanks, Lieutenant Gibbs ordered a defensive position to be organized in Hattonchatel.

The third day of the fight found the entire battalion at Woel, five kilometers in front of the advanced infantry. Patrols under lieutenants [Edwin A.] McCluer and [Gordon M.] Grant were sent out to gain contact with the enemy. The patrol under [Second] Lieutenant McCluer consisted of three tanks and five runners, penetrated as far as Joinville, and put to rout a battalion of enemy troops advancing from that town. A defensive position was maintained by the battalion in the vicinity of Woel all day, and late in the evening orders were received to proceed with all possible haste to the Bois de Thiaucourt. On arriving at the Bois de Thiaucourt, the battalion learned that it was to be entrained for another sector and another fight.

The details of endurance, personal courage and true tank spirit during the fight and in the long hikes and rides to the new sector are too numerous to mention in this work, but they shall long be remembered by the members of the battalion and by those associated with it. The battalion had learned fast on its first fight, so that the details of preparation for the second show were purely routine.

12:30 a.m. September 25th, 1918, saw the 326th Battalion again in battle position near the Cotes de Forimont in the Argonne. 5:30 a.m. and they were again at death grips with the Hun. They soon learned that this was quite a different fight than that at St. Mihiel, and that here the enemy was grimly earnest about keeping what he had.

The entire First Brigade suffered heavily that first day, for at the end we learned that the brigade commander, Colonel G. S. Patton Jr., had been seriously wounded while heroically attempting to rally disorganized infantry—to attack a machine gun nest. Major Brett was then called to command the brigade and he found a number of his tanks destroyed—four out of six of the captains wounded and evacuated—one officer, [Second] Lieutenant Guy [R.] Chamberlin, killed while leading his tanks over a difficult piece of ground on foot, and a great number of enlisted men killed or wounded. A reorganization of the brigade was commenced immediately and Captain [Claude H. Ranulf] Compton, commanding officer of the 345th Battalion, was placed in command of the forward units. The fighting now settled down to a grim contest for position after position. The tanks were in each day and did frightful execution in the enemy ranks. But the fighting began to tell on the brigade, not on its spirit, which was admirable, but on its members. By October 11th, it had become so depleted that a provisional company, operating 24 tanks, was formed. Then came a brief rest for the men until they attacked in support of the 42nd Division on the morning of October 15th against the enemy position between Landres-et-St. Georges and St. Georges. The tanks reached that objective, but the infantry could not follow. From October 16th to November 1st, the men and officers enjoyed a much deserved rest, as there was no fighting of any serious character. On November 1st, the provisional company again supported the advance, this time with the 2nd Division, which led to the final breakthrough and the rapid progress of the American army to the Meuse and Sedan. The last remnants of the 1st Brigade were finally relieved by the 3rd Brigade on November 10, 1918.

During the series of actions in the Argonne, the 321st R&S [Repair and Salvage] Company commanded by [First Lieutenant] J. [Jessie] L. Thompson, rendered signal and conspicuous service in repair and salvage work under the most hazardous circumstances.

If there be any doubt as to the fighting and endurance qualities of the 1st Brigade, the following statement will dispel it.

During the period September 26th to November 10th, the 1st Brigade supported the following divisions: 1st, 2nd, 28th, 42nd, 80th, 82nd, and 91st.

The episodes of bravery in the Argonne are again too numerous to detail. They can easily be found among the official records awarding the many medals and promotions, which were well earned.

And now the armistice has been signed and things are uncertain, but still the old battalion and the old officers and men, desire, more than anything else, to take a place where they are needed and where they may again, if necessary, add to the prestige of American arms.

Second Lieutenant Donald M. Taylor, Headquarters, 344th Tank Battalion

About the rankest thing there is in this man's army is a big buck private or a non-commissioned officer detailed on duty as a runner at the front. And when such a man is on such duty with the Tank Corps, he outranks the German Gott [God] himself. One really cannot appreciate the amount of authority with which a runner considers himself invested until he has held such office with a brand new outfit on its first trip into battle. The writer was one such of the latter variety at the front; in the St. Mihiel sector in the big drive, which started September 12th with a billion dollar barrage, and wound up with a wild rush for souvenirs.

The writer never could understand what should cause any sane man to commence a story such as he read some time ago, with the following words: "T'was a dark and stormy night and the rain it fell in torrents." That is, he never could understand it until the night of September 11, 1918, the year in which Gott deserted his company commander. Now he knows that the writer of these tragic lines must have been the advance agent who booked the night of September 11, 1918, on the St. Mihiel salient.

On the afternoon of the 11th, when it became known in Headquarters Company of the 326th Battalion that the outfit was to go over the next morning, the "Goldbricks" of that organization, numbering 16 in all, including the writer, loudly clamored with apparently honest zeal to be allowed to take part in the picnic. Major Sereno E. Brett, commanding the battalion, had a peculiar habit of taking men at their words. So, that afternoon the entire 16 were equipped with maps of the ground to be taken, given a few necessary instructions and detailed as a unit of runners to follow the major's tank, they were all equipped with the official insignia of the runner (red arm band) so that if at any time during the engagement they should become wearied with the amusement of being shot at, they could depart hastily and boldly for the SOUTH without being picked up by an MP and herded back to the lines.

What with the protection of the red arm bands and the knowledge that the major had strict instructions to keep his tank at least a kilometer behind the lines, it seemed like a nice soft graft with a chance for some excitement and very little danger. In this connection I will say this much for the major; he complied strictly with these instructions right at the start of the fight, leaving his tank at least a kilometer behind the lines as he decided that that means of locomotion was too slow; he hopped out calling "follow me" and beat it for a point about a kilometer ahead of the tanks.

But to return to our beginning, about 6:30 a.m. the tanks left their camouflaged position in the woods and started moving out for the jumping-off place, about five miles up the line. When the procession started it was silent and secret as any inner chamber session of the Masons or XP's. Everybody who spoke at all spoke in whispers. No lights were shown and all were careful to put their feet down gently in the mud holes so as to avoid creating a loud splash. But by the time the outfit had reached the jumping-off place, instructions were being howled back and forth, cigarettes and flashlights were being used to guide the tanks into position, and pistols were being fired to attract attention. Barnum & Bailey's Circus never came into town as well advertised. However, there was that million dollar barrage to deaden these minor sounds, and so it happened half of Jerry's flock were already well on their way to Berlin by the time dawn and H-hour had arrived.

About nine o'clock that night it had commenced raining and it rained such as it had never rained before the flood or since, otherwise Noah would have had the SRO [Standing Room Only] sign hanging out long before he had sublet the contract for 2 by 4's. The writer, being an American of the highly intelligent variety, started out without a raincoat, carried a full pack all night closely following the major's tank and after arriving at the jumping-off place thought to tie it to the tail of the major's tank.

At one o'clock sharp the frequently aforementioned million dollar barrage started. It was rather a disappointment in the way of noise to "our hero" after having read a few of Irvin S. Cobb's and George Patallo's descriptions of a big American barrage. But he was compensated for this disappointment by a sight on the morning of the 12th such as few men and neither of the aforementioned gentlemen can truthfully assert that they have witnessed. He saw with his own eyes an American aviator with an American plane on the front.

Five-thirty a.m. was H-hour. About 5:15 Captain Newell P. Weed approached the writer and conversed with him in the following terms: "Rush like hell down the line and tell my blankety-blank drivers to get their blankety-blank tanks cranked up and ready to start." He performed this little deed. The battalion moved out on time.

From that time on until 7:00 a.m. that day a pandemonium reigned. The American soldier has frequently been heralded in history and fiction as an individual fighter and believe us no one could accuse any member of the 326th [344th] Battalion, Tank Corps, that day of not being a true American. Never before or never since has it been the writer's privilege to witness so much individual fighting at one time. In fact the fighting became so individual in the course of the next half hour or so that it looked as if there were at least six different wars going on instead of only one. However, this can be said about the tanks, they were all and everyone in them working with the one purpose in view and that purpose was to get as far forward as possible, in the shortest time possible and connect with Heinie [Germans] even if they had to get out and walk. And that is what the majority of them did. For the tanks after starting out the night before with no (extra) bidons [cans] of gas on board had only enough left in the morning to run a few kilometers.

The Huns had decided to counter our attack on this front by a strategic retreat and the Renaults were never built for prize winning on a speedway. Nevertheless, with the aid of some good foot work, a good many of the boys did establish liaison with Fritz, as can be proven by the fact that we secured that day, that which the Americans have been fighting for—"Souvenirs," and beaucoup [many] of them.

Immediately, the major's first tank landed in a ditch and stayed there; he hopped out with his pigeon basket and grabbed the next tank in the column. Five minutes more and it was in a ditch and another three minutes and his third tank was tangled up in the ruins of a village. Apparently thoroughly disgusted with the turn affairs had taken, but secretly quite pleased that he could now disregard his colonel's instructions to stay 1,000 meters behind and direct the fighting, he moved up on foot to the head of the column and of course the runners had to follow. The writer brought up the rear. About half way across an open field the major passed by a shell hole and his nostrils caught a peculiar odor. Deciding it was gas, he gave the alarm. The writer got his mask on in less than five minutes, but not much less. If there had been any gas there, the great American public would never have the pleasure of reading this story. He there and then decided to, at the first opportunity, take a train for some good reliable gas-school in the SOS [Services of Supply] and take about three weeks of gas instructions, feeling that he could in this way best protect Uncle Sam's $10,000,000 investment. The major's party traveled rapidly ahead for another 15 minutes or so and then halted while the major made a reconnaissance of the terrain and the state of affairs in Jerry's front line, which consisted of a few machine guns and some 77's that he had been unable to haul away, manned by a few men who didn't know any better than to stay there. The writer was sent back to see if any tanks were coming up. About 200 meters back he found eight tanks commanded by Captain Weed in the leading one. Captain Weed had halted his tank and was apparently arguing with himself as to which was the best of several places to cross a trench. The writer, by right of the red bandanna wound around his right arm, decided for him and led him up to Major Brett as per instructions. The major, having dispatched these tanks and several which followed to various points of the line, again moved forward until we reached a shallow trench. One man in the vicinity had his arm half blown off about this time so the major decided there must be some shrapnel flying about and ordered the detachment down into the trench. A Red Cross stretcher bearer standing thereabouts, a fellow about six feet, six inches, decided that this taking cover was all foolishness. About 30 seconds later he changed his mind quite rapidly and tried to hide behind a clod of dirt about four inches high. This trench stuff grew too monotonous for the major in a short time, so he moved on again.

Shortly, eight reserve tanks, loaned us by the 327th [345th] Battalion, arrived and the CO having decided to take an active part in the picnic, secured himself a second lieutenant for a driver, climbed into the tank and started off to hunt up machine gun nests. We started to follow. The major ordered us to stay where we were as he was going off on a little personal affair. If some brigadier general had happened along about this time we would probably have been awarded the DSM [Distinguished Service Medal] for the promptness with which we obeyed these instructions. We did more than obey them, we moved back 100 meters and crawled into a shell hole, opened up a couple of cans of corn willy [corned beef] and some hard tack and had lunch. The line had moved so far ahead by this time that we feared that before the day was over we would lose our 20 percent increase [in pay] for foreign service.

After dinner we moved up to locate the major. After traveling a couple of kilometers, we reached the brow of a slight rise just out of Nonsard and sat down to watch the waves of doughboys going by, down the hill and into Nonsard. They came past us in squad columns. The first man in the first wave which passed us had his gun slung and was busy with both hands rolling a cigarette. The next man was busily engaged in carrying a head of cabbage in one hand and feeding himself hardtack with the other. The writer was rather shocked and felt almost called upon to admonish these men for such disgraceful behavior in the face of the enemy. However, probably the enemy were too busy to notice this breach of battlefield etiquette—both of them. Sergeant [John J.] McGinty took one, securing a watch and a good German steel razor, and Major Brett shot the other one out of the church steeple in Nonsard where he was busy firing a machine gun. Sergeant McGinty's prisoner was a man of apparently sixty years or so who probably had been too tired to run with the rest. Neither the age, sex, nationality or number of Major Brett's victim could be identified, as the major had made a bull's eye in the center of the target with his little 37mm. We waited on the brow of the hill until the conquering heroes returned to seek a good camouflaged position for the night; we then held a feast of canned tomatoes, corn willy and hard tack to celebrate the victory. The writer was then dispatched to Essey with a message for the colonel. Reaching Essey, he stood at the appointed place to await the arrival of the CO until 6:30. He then decided that the message could be of no real importance, so he found himself a billet and retired for the night. Thus ended the writer's first, last and only day under fire on the battlefields of France.

First Lieutenant Julian K. Morrison, Company A, 344th Tank Battalion

Probably no branch of a modern army affords opportunities for a more varied life than the Tank Corps. As its colors indicate, it is a combination of infantry, artillery and cavalry.[4] Quite a distinctive branch of the service; its officers and men too are distinctive. One can hardly imagine a more distinctive organization than a "Suicide Club." Early in its existence the American Tank Corps acquired this nickname, and it was often called that by the "doughboys" who saw the tankers in action. Some of their escapades will live long in the memories of the men of other organizations who saw them in action. At times it seemed that the men of the Tank Corps were really trying to live up to their colors in that they tried to be infantry, artillery and cavalry at the same time. More than once tankers have been seen in the front line of infantry or even further up than that with a rifle in their hands, which they had picked up on the field. The writer remembers one instance of a cavalry operation carried out by two privates of his platoon. These two privates were advancing on foot with the infantry at St. Mihiel. The action, at that particular point, was not quite exciting enough for them, so they decided to go on a little excursion of their own. They dashed out ahead of the infantry lines and after advancing several hundred meters took cover in a wood. Crawling through the wood they came upon a German orderly in the attempt to get away with two horses, evidently in his care. One of the men dropped the Hun where he stood and together they captured the horses. Two days later these same men carried out a patrol at Woel on their captured horses. As for artillery, the Huns themselves can probably give the best evidence as to the intensity and accurateness of the fire put down by the tank "Artillery."

The writer came to the Tank Corps in search of just the spirit he found when he arrived. He considers himself unusually lucky in that he was among the first officers to be assigned to the Tank Corps. Having grown up with the organization he has an interest and pride in the corps, which he could probably have gotten in no other way. He formed friendships truer and more lasting than any previous ones, and he has been greatly benefited by coming in close daily contact with men of a type as fine as ever came together under any standard.

Looking back now over the months spent in training at the old Tank School at Bourg, France, the writer can recall many pleasant ones interspersed with long days of tedious study. It's a working organization, this Tank Corps, and were it not for the indomitable spirit of its members and the ability not only to make the best of things, but to find pleasure in their work, there might have been a number of AWOL's [Absent Without Leave] not only among the enlisted men, but the officers as well. Every day, some Sundays excepted, a fixed schedule was carried out from daylight to dark and then for the officers' school at night. The writer always got a great deal of encouragement from these lectures, usually given by Colonel Patton. He was made to understand by the colonel that a tank officer was meant to die. His favorite message to his officers was "Go forward, go forward. If your tank breaks down go forward with the infantry. There will be no excuse for your failure in this, and if I find any tank officer behind the front line of infantry I will _____." All tank officers know the rest. The result was that each officer left these lectures with the determination never to fall behind the front line of infantry, no matter what happened. It must be admitted, however, that at times immediately after these lectures it was difficult to keep visions of the Services of Supply out of one's mind. This message of the colonel's was passed on down by the officers to their men with the result that in the St. Mihiel drive tankers could be seen anywhere from one to seven kilometers in front of the infantry. Everyone fought—cooks, company clerks, mess sergeants, runners and mechanics. So closely was the order carried out that the Tank Corps nearly starved for two or three days afterward. Needless to say, before the next fight orders came out to the effect that anyone leaving the post assigned to him would be dealt with by court martial; the courage of the Tank Corps having been sufficiently proved.

One lasting impression the writer has of the Tank Corps is the mystery surrounding it. Every move made was shrouded in mystery. Rumors were always floating around, and of course they always afforded a topic for conversation during the few idle hours. The writer does not remember a week that passed without a rumor that we were going to the front. When the real order to go up really did come everyone had their doubts until it happened. It was an eager outfit that entrained for the first time on September 8, 1918. Little did they know what the next weeks held for them. No matter what was to come, however, their spirit was not to be dampened. They went into the fight at St. Mihiel after having undergone trials and hardships for four days that cannot be described. Without food, except the well-known "iron ration," with little or no sleep for four days, and after having slaved through rain and mud to get their tanks there, they "jumped off" at 5:00 a.m. on September 12th and before the night of that first day had made everyone think that the Tank Corps really was a "Suicide Club." Not that anyone tried to commit suicide, but because they did things which seemed suicidal to undertake.

Such was the life of the Tank Corps right on up to the time hostilities ceased on November 11, 1918. They worked at night moving the tanks from place to place and keeping them in fighting condition and the same men fought the next day. The only thing that ever overcame the terrible handicap under which they labored was their indomitable spirit. No matter how nearly gone their endurance was, they never thought of giving up. One of the most unique scenes it has ever been the privilege of the writer to witness happened near Charpentry during the Argonne-Meuse attack. The fighting had been fierce for nine days, and very few of the men had had any rest to speak of. Most of them were physically unfit for further fighting, but they knew that the next morning, October 4, 1918, they were to attack with the 1st Division. The tanks had been driven into a valley and placed on a reverse slope of a hill, not more than 700 meters from the enemy's lines. Just across on the other slope were the remains of some German barracks. In these barracks some of the men found a German piano. They dragged the piano out and carried it over to the camp. It was just beginning to get dark and all the men gathered around the piano and began to sing back at camp. While they were singing, shells frequently landed not more than a hundred yards away. Infantrymen passing by stopped with wonder at men who could sing with such light hearts when probably the morning would bring their death. This little incident shows the "stuff" the men of the Tank Corps were made of.

Although its life at the front was short, its weight was undoubtedly felt, and had the war continued, the American Tank Corps would have grown upon a firm and secure foundation laid by the two battalions, the 344th and 345th.

First Lieutenant Leslie H. Buckler, Company A, 344th Tank Battalion

I was assigned to Company A, 344th Battalion, Captain [Harry H.] Semmes commanding, and when the company went into action on the morning of September 26th, I was in command of the leading platoon. During the march from the point of readiness to the point of departure the company was in column. Our orders were to remain in column until forced to deploy and to proceed from the point of departure, 50 or 100 meters in rear of the initial line of the barrage, on a course approximately due north and passing through a notch close under the easterly end of Vauquois Hill. Thence we were to proceed northerly and to the west of the Aire River, being prepared to move in support of the companies which had preceded us, but with the primary object of reaching Cheppy and crossing to the east side of the Aire River on the bridge at that town. Thereafter, we were to gain contact with the enemy and operate with the 138th and 140th Infantry regiments, 35th Division.

A detail of engineers under First Lieutenant [Raymond P.] Pennoyer, Company RO [Reconnaissance Officer], preceded the company and prepared for an adequate passage through the lines to within about 50 meters of the east side of Vauquois Hill. As the company passed this point dawn had just broken and the smoke screen was very dense, cutting down the visibility range to about 50–75 meters. Captain Semmes, in the lead, observed five tanks mired directly in our course and signaled to me to halt the company. We made a brief reconnaissance and found a platoon of Company C, 344th Battalion, Second Lieutenant [George M.] Booth in command, stuck in a swamp which appeared to run close up to the steep sides of Vauquois and of the hill to the east and as far ahead as we could see. Captain Semmes then led the column up onto the high ground to the west of our line of advance and we reached the crest in good order. At this point we were again halted by the steep slope and shell torn condition of the trenches terracing the hill. Captain Semmes was wounded by a sniper and I took command after sending the captain and another casualty to the rear with a detail of engineers as bearers (9:30 a.m.).

After a reconnaissance, I determined to return halfway down the hill and try to pick a course on the high ground to the left of the swamp and substantially on the course originally laid out. While carrying out this maneuver, with the help of the platoon sergeants, second lieutenants [Julian K.] Morrison and [Edwin A.] McCluer were sent to reconnoiter the easterly side of the swamp. By 10:30, the column had penetrated to a point which brought the head beyond Vauquois Hill, where it was finally halted by the fact that the northern slope of the hill was too much cut up to follow, and the swamp, torn by unusually large shell holes full of subsurface water ran out in a bay along the north side of Vauquois Hill. During this operation, which took an hour, the smoke cleared up and the tanks were exposed continuously to directed shell fire and to intermittent rifle fire. There were material casualties in the reserves of the infantry engaged in clearing out snipers and observers.

At 10:30 a.m., lieutenants Morrison and McCluer returned and reported that a system of roads running northeasterly would bring us to the highway to Cheppy after a detour of about four kilometers. A course was selected and the tanks reversed and led to the undestroyed end of the road, up which each was sent separately to rendezvous in a wood about one kilometer away. Each tank was chased by shell fire. A mechanic was left in charge of four untracked Company A tanks and two Company C tanks. Twelve Company A tanks and three Company C tanks reached the rendezvous at 12:00 noon. The men were allowed 20 minutes for lunch in filling water bottles while lieutenants Morrison, McCluer and I made a reconnaissance in the hope of finding a cross-country cut off which would reduce the four kilometers by road. We had also run off the crayon tracing map with which we had been provided and succeeded in getting a look at one in the possession of an engineer officer. We proceeded at 12:30 by road, reached the Cheppy highway and arrived at a point 250 meters southerly of the Cheppy bridge at 2:30. During this portion of the march we dropped out three tanks for minor repairs. The length of time was necessitated by the condition of the roads and traffic. The detail of engineers and a tank operated continuously getting horse-drawn vehicles out of our way.

At the point 250 meters south of Cheppy bridge I met Captain [C. H. Ranulf] Compton, 345th Battalion, with about 20 tanks of that battalion and several French tanks. I reported to him stating my course of operations as laid down in orders and was told to wait. He then conferred with a group of US officers and returned stating that I should proceed in accordance with the original plan that would be in support of some French tanks which had just pulled out; that the enemy was at Very. I spent 10 minutes filling up with gas and then crossed the bridge and went out the Very road in column.

Upon coming in sight of Very, the town was being shelled by the enemy; so concluding they were further on, I attempted to cut across the Ran de Clery to save time and exposure to fire on about one kilometer of road. The attempt across the brook failed and we circled about through the town of Very and drew up against the bank along the road beyond the town. I was about to hunt up an infantry PC when I observed the French tanks coming over the hill from Cheppy. The officer in charge stated that he had just received orders to retire to Cheppy for the night as he was useless for an attack so late in the day. He then went back with his outfit.

I then went up the hill above the Ran de Very along the Very-Charpentry road and found a major of infantry holding a line along the military crest. He stated that he was holding on with difficulty; that he had about two companies of infantry composed of representatives of the 138th, 139th and 140th Infantry, and several machine gun sections, and that their casualties had been and were very heavy. I told him that we would remain in the shelter of the foot of the hill for the night, and would be in readiness to operate on the next day when they were reorganized. Two things persuaded me to stay: the road back was being shelled intensely and was under observation; the moral support of the tanks (although practically valueless during the night) was evidently great among all ranks on the hill above us. They had no artillery support and we were the only aid and comfort they had seen. I feared the effect of a withdrawal. Shelter from everything but direct hits was found for the men and the night passed quietly except for visits from infantrymen on special duty with circumstantial reports of counterattacks immediately impending.

The morning of the second day, September 27th, was seen by me in conference with several infantry officers at Very. A message was sent by pigeon reporting action to date. Two messages were sent the preceding day reporting the wounding of Captain Semmes, and the orders of Captain Compton. There were 13 tanks for actions and at 2:00 p.m. they moved out under orders to go into line on the plateau between Very and Charpentry and proceed with the infantry toward the latter place; the tanks were not to go more than 150 meters ahead of the infantry. They were to rendezvous at Very, or if this was impractical, to send a runner there.

Lieutenant Morrison led out with five tanks, followed by Lieutenant McCluer with five tanks. I had one tank, two having broken down at the start. The French tank outfit put in an appearance, pushed by us as we were starting, and went over the hill. A heavy artillery fire opened once and I ordered the two platoons to move out without completing their straightening out movements in the column. The French tanks counter-marched almost immediately and drew a concentrated fire on the road and draw up which it ran. With difficulty traffic was kept clear and 10 tanks got into line. I cannot speak too highly of the conduct of the men on the three broken down tanks which were frequently being hit by shell fragments. Their disappointments on dropping out caused them to work on repairs although literally sprayed with mud. I ordered them undercover.

Lieutenant McCluer returned with his five tanks at about 6:30, reporting that upon the infantry failing to follow he had returned. At about 8:00 p.m., a runner from Lieutenant Morrison reported that he had two tanks. At about midnight, Lieutenant Morrison came in and reported that three tanks had failed to respond to his signal to retire. A party with supplies was sent out and the three tanks of Lieutenant Morrison's platoon got back to Very by daybreak. Two tanks were put out by shell fire, one sergeant being killed.

September 28th was spent fixing tanks, resting the men and conferring with infantry officers. A runner reported a tank PC at Varennes after the arrival of First Lieutenant Gordon Grant who took command by seniority. I went back that night and conferred with Captain Compton.

From this point the operations of the group of tanks at Very is best covered by Lieutenant Grant's report. My own activities were known to him being under his direction. They consisted in going to the rear for conferences at night and attending to the much-needed organization of the outfit. We had no mess sergeant, cooks, first sergeant, or any of the personnel required for administration. A duty sergeant was taken from the platoons and a group of six infantrymen volunteers attached. I went with the Very group to Charpentry where we merged in Captain [Courtney H.] Barnard's group [Company C, 345th Tank Battalion].

On the day that the 1st Division came in and went over to Exermont, I got permission to lead my platoon into action for the first time. We proceeded from the hill on the north side of the draw north of Charpentry to Montfaucon then passing to the left in column and remaining in column until the series of steep ravines crossing our line to Exermont were passed. Almost immediately upon coming in view of Exermont my tank was overturned by running into a dry ditch partly concealed by bushes and smoke. The doors were locked and I was out of action having been rendered unconscious by gasoline fumes.

I recovered sufficiently after being dug out of my tank to return to Charpentry in the afternoon and continued to perform my duties until the Charpentry group under Captain Barnard withdrew to Varennes. I then reported for treatment to the MO (Medical Officer) and was evacuated.

No men who were with the tank units can ever forget the faithfulness with which all ranks performed their duties. No danger and no amount of fatigue made any man hesitate for an instant in the performance of orders and instructions. There were not, however, any acts under my personal observation which transcended conduct in the line of duty as laid down for the Tank Corps. I have seen men who I shall never cease to admire ignore difficulty and danger so completely as to be apparently unconscious of it. For the officers and men that I operated with their conception of duty was to do their utmost.

First Lieutenant Gordon M. Grant, Company A, 344th Tank Battalion

Night of September 26th. Company was in bivouac near Very in support of 35th and 91st Divisions. Many calls for help from infantry commanders, but no concerted plan of action seemed available. After consultation about 3:00 p.m., October 27th, two platoons went forward to support 35th Division in attack—plateau north of Very. Artillery support for infantry very poor and infantry were unable to hold place with tanks. Heavy direct fire from enfilading guns planted in Epinonville and sweeping the plateau kept the infantry back, so the tanks ran ahead quite some distance. The platoon leaders, [second] lieutenants [Edwin A.] McCluer and [Julian K.] Morrison, seeing the situation, withdrew their tanks to the infantry lines as darkness was coming on. Lieutenant McCluer returned with all his tanks; Lieutenant Morrison lost three tanks by direct shell hits.

Tanks again camped at Very in shelter of high number of artillery fire directed against them that failed to register any direct hits. Following day spent in meeting small counterattacks, in patrols by tanks, and in detailed reconnaissance by all officers.

Night of October 28th, Lieutenant McCluer and five tanks were sent to support of Captain [Math L.] English, commanding Company C, in support of attack on Montrebeau Woods by 35th Division. Morning October 29th, whole company together with several tanks of other outfits, moved up to Baulny, acting as reserve for 35th Division. At 5:00 p.m., called upon to meet counterattack from north of Montrebeau Woods and directed to hold line Baulny-Eclisfontaine. This was done, tank patrols established to allow infantry to reorganize on new line, and at dark tanks withdrawn to draw southeast of Baulny.

September 30th–October 23rd, spent in minor operations, frontline remaining same; 1st Division took over sector. On night October 3rd, issued combat orders, tanks supporting 1st Division as follows: Company A, 16th Infantry; Company C, 18th Infantry; Companies B and C, (345th) 28–26th Infantry. Direction attack line 200 meters north Baulny-Eclisfontaine; direction attack 120 [degrees] west of north objective line, Fleville Hill 270.

Tanks started at H-hour, overtaking infantry 500 meters from departure at 1,000 meters. Company A swung from support company into frontline, supporting 16th Infantry. Attack moved forward, tanks giving splendid support. First and second objectives reached and infantry, unable to advance, dug in at these lines and tanks were withdrawn at dark. Until withdrawal, tanks assisted 1st Division in local attacks, taking several towns, etc.

First Lieutenant Raymond P. Pennoyer, Company A, 344th Tank Battalion

Report of the Battle of the Argonne

The front to be attacked extended from the Meuse River through the Argonne Forest, a distance of about 30 kilometers, and held by the French up to the night of the 25th September, the Americans holding the second line. On the night of the 25th, the Americans relieved the French with the following divisions from left to right: 91st, 37th, 35th, 28th and 77th. The objective of the first day for the 35th Division was a line extending approximately southwest between Exermont and Baulny, which was the crest of a long slope.

The tanks were with the 28th and 35th Divisions; one company of the two battalions were with the 28th, and two companies from each of the two battalions were with the 35th, whose front extended from the Argonne Forest to one kilometer west of the Bois de Cheppy. I was entirely with Company A, 326th [344th], which operated with the 35th Division.

The French were operating on our extreme left and their barrage started at 1:30 a.m., September 26th, while the Americans' barrage started at 2:30 a.m. The fire was principally directed on Vauquois and the German second line, which was two kilometers in the rear, the German first line being a series of strongly fortified hills. The artillery had been placed extremely far forward; two batteries of 75's being at the edge of the woods, one kilometer south of Vauquois.

The zero hour was 5:30 a.m., September 26th, and at 5:00 a.m. an indirect machine gun barrage was set on Vauquois, and the second line which was lifted at 5:30 a.m., the artillery barrage then becoming a rolling barrage with a rate of 50 meters per minute.

The tanks in the operation consisted of the 326th [344th] and 327th [345th] Battalions of light Renault tanks, 160 in strength. The 327th [345th] acted as a reserve and Company B, 326th [344th] went to the right of the Aire River. The tanks were landed at Clermont four days before the action and the number one position was a wood about nine kilometers from the line. At dark on the 25th, the tanks moved up to a wood three kilometers in rear of the front line and there were filled up with gasoline and oil already placed there. Each tank took one large bidon of gas strapped to its tail. At 4:00 a.m. the tanks moved up to number two position about 500 meters in rear of the front line. One line of trenches were previously leveled by a detail of engineers. This movement was executed in a dense fog without mishap, except mechanical troubles with three tanks.

Company C under Captain Math L. English sent one platoon to the west of Vauquois and two to the east, one being in reserve. Company A, 326th [344th], followed the road to the hill north of Cheppy where they formed line.

I was acting as reconnaissance officer for Company A, 326th [344th], and henceforth this report deals only with that company.

Progress was made with difficulty from the start due to many well-placed and tenaciously held machine guns. The enemy had perfect observation and excellent liaison with the artillery. The country was a series of woods and hills which made the advance slow. Company A did not fight any action during the first day and arrived at Very with 14 tanks. On the second and third day the company had two platoons in action and did good work in silencing machine guns and confusing the enemy infantry in spite of very heavy artillery fire.

On the fourth day the PC was moved to Charpentry where we were brigaded with the 327th [345th] Battalion. Two actions were fought here and the tanks were a great help to the infantry. On the 30th of September the 1st Division relieved the 35th and one company of tanks attacked with them that morning. We were then having much trouble mechanically with the tanks as they had been run to their limit. Progress from here was even more difficult as the tanks had to face artillery fire from a few hundred meters range.

I was not in action in this battle, but acting as company reconnaissance officer. I was with the tanks at all times. On October 5th I received a dose of gas, and on October 7th was sent to the hospital, staying there 17 days.

I did not observe any acts of conspicuous bravery for all the men did their full duty willingly, which means in that battle that all the men deserve the highest praise. The death of Captain [Math L.] English was a severe loss to the Tank Corps as he was a wonderful and brave officer. He was in every action always leading and inspiring his men and always carried out orders to the limit of his ability.

Captain Newell P. Weed, Company B, 344th Tank Battalion

If it hadn't been for that glass of wine one day in Paris, he would have never been in the Tank Corps, but being quite fed up on casual companies and sore on the world in general, he dropped in for a bit of the "imprisoned laughter of the peasant maid," which comes red or white and drives away the blues. At the next table sat a small group of officers and their conversation, which one could not help hearing, was of the prospects of the Tank Corps.

An application followed quickly and soon Lieutenant [Harry H.] Semmes and he reported to "Captain" [George S.] Patton [Jr.] for "test for suitability." It was an examination on gas engines and with the help of a small book on engines, issued by some oil company, they passed the test, neither knowing a magneto from a carburetor.

These days to come were full of hopes (there's an "e" in that word) but a Tank Corps without tanks is quite as exciting as a dance without girls.

Finally they came, and soon augmented by others, great fleets of tanks were tearing up wheat fields and forest to the delight of the French. One who has not passed with the corps through the different stages of its development in France has missed the greatest thing in life, a "show" for the staff college once a week regularly and only the refusal of the War Department to make everyone a general kept us from having one a day.

During this period, this officer, aided and abetted by a "file number" in Washington and "something or other" here, rose from a shave-tail [second lieutenant] to a captaincy and was put in command of "B" Company of the old 326th Battalion.

For some weeks life was "one nomenclature after another" and finally the great day came—a rush to the front for reconnaissance of the place we were to attack, back again to tell the company, another rush to the front for another reconnaissance, and back again. Finally, the whole company moved to the front and were detrained, God knows where, the poor company commander never did find that out; for he went to the place the French said they would detrain, and of course, oh, well what's the use.

The big day was finally set for September 12th, and except for many doubts as to whether the spuds we were told to put on the tracks of the tanks were iron rations or not, and as to whether the tanks which had sunk out of sight in the mud could be gotten out, things were finally reported ready on the evening of September 11th.

"T'was the night before D-day
And all through the mud
Not an engine was missing
Not one was a dud"

The route from Bois de Nauginsard to the point of departure was the darkest one in the world, and with the whole battalion in column it was quite like the game of "snap the whip"; the noise of an intense artillery preparation drowned the noise of our approach, and we soon reached the point of departure. Here, a few minutes were spent in final preparation, and amid shouts of goodbye and good luck and a final handshake with our battalion commander, the first American attack, in which American manned tanks were used, started.

Practically no resistance was met the first day except from fan belts and pulsators, each one accounting for heavy casualties among the tanks. Nonsard was taken that afternoon by a beautiful flanking and frontal attack of tanks and infantry. That evening was spent some half kilometer back of this village where we were visited by our colonel and the general, but neither of them brought any gas that is the kind that can be used in tanks. So, the next day was spent in prayer, prayers that gas would reach us before the Boche reached Berlin. But our prayers were unanswered and it was not until that evening that we went forward to the town of Vigneulles, which we reached sometime after midnight.

After a few hours rest we started forward, reaching the town of St. Maurice, where a halt was called. As it was found our infantry were some miles in our rear, our colonel had joined us and upon consulting his speeches to the staff college, found that we were acting without infantry, and were therefore "a cavalry patrol." Just what the Boche thought no one knows, but he was mighty inquisitive and we had several callers in the shape of avions [airplanes], who feeling honored by our presence, shot off some pyrotechnics and in other ways expressed their delight. That evening we retired and reached the Bois de Thiaucourt.

That evening a further retirement was made to the Bois de la Hazelle, not far from Seicheprey. Here several days were spent overhauling the tanks and locating the ones which had been left in different parts of the battlefield. The aforesaid locating was no easy job and it would have taken a Sherlock Holmes himself to locate some of them.

Word then came that we were to prepare for another battle in the Argonne and cheers greeted the announcement by the general that after this action was over 50 officers and 150 men would be sent back to the States as instructors.

The battalion was entrained that evening with high hopes and wet feet. We were off for what was to be one of the hardest fought battles in the history of the world.

We detrained at Clermont, which was some eight or nine kilometers behind the lines, and spent our first evening in a wood near that place. Major [Sereno E.] Brett had a hunch next day and moved us. It was well he did, for the Boche let down [an artillery attack] about eleven o'clock the next morning and cleaned out our former nest. Three days was spent in this wood getting everything ready.

On the evening of the 25th this officer and his company set out for the Farm Abancourt, which was our lying in place. About three a.m. we left this point and left for our point of departure, which was some four kilometers away. At five o'clock all was set, and over we went, picking our way through a dense fog. The captain and Sergeant Knight walking ahead of the tanks soon were lost from view, and he sent Sergeant Knight in one direction, and went in another himself, trying to locate the column. After progressing some 200 meters, sought shelter in a friendly trench or it was friendly until its former occupants, the Boche, objected to his incursion by surrounding him and starting him Berlinward. A friendly tank from the 345th, however, stuck its nose through the fog and the Boche dropped their booty and took to their heels.

From there quick progress was made to Varennes under the cover of smoke and fog, and by this time the battle was at its height. Tanks on fire and being put out by direct fire were no uncommon sight and his few brave runners were soon picked off by snipers on the enemy side. No infantry being in sight, the captain and his driver, Corporal [Raul] Veeder, drove back several hundred meters to endeavor to get the infantry. Getting out of his tank to talk to an officer, the captain ran into a shell which bowled him over, but didn't touch him. Corporal Veeder spent the remainder of the day along, alternately driving his tank and firing his gun.

The captain finally got back to Varennes where Privates McFarland, Vestal and McKee were either killed or wounded carrying messages under a most intense machine gun fire. The exceptional acts of bravery done by these men are but an example of the spirit and devotion to duty shown by every man of the company. No mere words can express what these men went through that day, nor can it be contradicted that if at any time during this day the tanks had not held the position that was slowly annihilating them, that the infantry could have barely left its own front line, and so the progress of the battle was not as it had been planned. The tanks, by their wonderful work, made it possible for the infantry to cross No Man's Land and give the engineer troops time to rebuild the destroyed bridges and roads, and make the further progress of the battle and ensuing day possible.

The captain and Corporal Babcock ran into a gassed area which made them both casualties and prevented their further participation in the greatest of all battles, "The Battle of the Liberation," which began on the 26th day of September and ended by the complete defeat of the Hun and his acceptance of the armistice terms on November 11, 1918.

Captain Harry G. Borland, Reconnaissance Officer, Company B, 344th Tank Battalion

In the next few days, Special Order #1, 1st Tank Center, was written up, appointing the writer as supply officer, and again trouble commenced. As time progressed, the 1st Tank Center gradually took shape and the great day came, February 15, 1918, when our first enlisted personnel reached Langres, and the still greater day, March 21, 1918, when our first 10 tanks reached us and were uploaded without a hitch. The writer has had a great respect for Colonel [George S.] Patton's bravery ever since that night when the colonel, then a major, crawled into the first tank and started it down the ramp, none of us knowing what was going to happen; whether it was going to kick over, catch fire, blow up or what. But, however, nothing happened. All the tanks came off okay, and then began the daily grind of training, and the writer's grind of getting supplies, including food, clothing, tools, gasoline, oils and a thousand and one things needed.

In May, much to the writer's joy, he was relieved as supply officer, and assigned to B Company, 326th Battalion, as first lieutenant and was ordered to go to the Center each day to the various schools, tank driving, oiling and washing, gas engines, 37mm guns, pistol, visibility signaling, grenade throwing and lastly reconnaissance and then away to the Gas School. After this came a couple of months of training the company until September 1st, when the battalion was ordered to the field.

On September 4th, the writer was ordered to pack his stuff and report to Colonel [Joseph W.] Viner at Center headquarters, who sent him with a motorcycle and a truck up to the Toul Sector, to report to Colonel Patton. There, he was instructed to take the motorcycle and report to the town of Nancy and reconnaissance work, which he did the next morning; his first trip to the front line, and the first morning up where, along with Major [Sereno E.] Brett, captains [Howell P.] Wood, [Harry H.] Semmes and [Maurice H.] Knowles, managed to get out in No Man's Land, and ate lunch and finished off with some apples and plums, which we picked from trees out there.[5] None of the bunch were molested because "Fritzy" must have thought they were a harmless bunch of maniacs.

While at this front, the reconnaissance officers made three complete plans before the right one was taken and after all plans were completed and routes marked out, from unloading points to points of readiness, the unloading point would be changed. On September 6th we were notified that the tanks for our respective battalions would be in that evening, so away we went to our unloading point, to wait for the train and wait we did until next morning—no tanks. As soon as daylight got strong enough for the roads to be seen, the writer started on a hunt for the tanks and ended up at brigade headquarters, bursting in upon the colonel as he was eating his breakfast. The colonel started action at once and after having breakfast, the writer again started out, going back and caught up with the colonel near the point where we were supposed to have unloaded. A few quick words and off again to the French tanks with [Second] Lieutenant [Guy R.] Chamberlin as a liaison officer, and a "hurry up" return. On the road back was met by Lieutenant Theodore J. Sledge and directed to go to Boucq as the tanks were there. Reached Boucq and found one train of tanks there ready to unload 9 kilometers from the point of readiness. A long night hike and fortunately the next day was foggy and there was no visibility from the air or from Mont Sec, so we moved on with the main body of tanks through the woods.

There was considerable delay with engine trouble and broken fan belts, so that tanks kept falling out and as they all had to be guided, it became necessary for the RO's to make several trips to finally get all the tanks together in the worst mud hole in the world. A reconnaissance officer picked the spot, but he did not reckon on three days' rain. However, on the 11th, Major Brett gave [First] Lieutenant [John W.] Castles [Jr.] a special mission and the writer started with him on a flying reconnaissance trip, which they returned from at 7:00 p.m., and at 8:30 p.m., started with the five tanks through a heavy downpour of rain and a half foot of mud under foot. No lights were allowed, but the quick reconnaissance of the afternoon was enough.

The tanks were led across country to our trenches and these were crossed okay. From there on the writer led the line getting direction from a luminous pocket compass and with a wonderful piece of luck came out within a hundred yards of where we were aiming at. Previous orders were for the writer to report to the brigade commander after getting Lieutenant Castles to his jumping-off point, so away he went in the direction of Beaumont, where he was supposed to find the colonel and from there attempted to follow in the colonel's trail.

About 5:00 p.m., the writer reached the point where Major Brett was laying up for the night and in a few minutes along came the colonel. He said let's go back to Beaumont, and back he started with the writer coming a close second, dead tired and with sore feet. Beaumont was reached at about 7:00 p.m. and the writer stretched out on a wire bunk, then became dead to the world immediately. The colonel got ready to go and left, leaving word for the writer to meet him at Essey, at 5:00 a.m., the next day. The writer managed to get seven hours' sleep, first since the 8th, then off again hiking to Essey, where a PC was established.

Captain Edmund N. Hobart came up and took charge and during the rest of the offensive all the writer did was to hang around the office, with one exception, when he took a truck train of supplies forward to Major Brett's battalion, which he found about six miles in advance of the infantry. He arrived there okay. Nothing happened on the way, only was bombed by enemy aeroplanes and sprayed with shrapnel, one man being wounded.

On September 18th hurry-up orders were given for the whole staff to report back to brigade headquarters at once, which they did with two trucks and two Dodge cars. On arrival there, received orders to proceed to headquarters, First Army, and from there to Recicourt, from which place the preliminary reconnaissance for the Argonne offensive was made.

On September 31st, the tanks arrived and the writer was detailed as RO, 344th Battalion, where he reported the same morning, picked out a beautiful PC and established the major there, but as the major did not like the looks of the place, changed again in the afternoon. The next few days were taken up in preparing maps, reconnoitering the ground and endeavoring to show the different company RO's where their zone of action would be.

On the morning of the 26th of September, when the drive started, Major Brett, with his staff, including the writer, started forward in a heavy fog. In about two hours they found themselves up with the leading tanks and as afterwards proved, with the leading infantry, under heavy artillery and machine gun fire. Everyone soon decided that it was not a healthy place to be and started for a sheltered position, working on the basis of Major Brett's previous knowledge of Boche artillery fire, which for once proved wrong, thereby very nearly causing the demise of the writer, as a shell passed between the major and the writer at about the waist line and exploded a few feet in front of him. No one hurt and they finally reached a sheltered ravine at which place the major was notified that he was in command of the brigade, the colonel having been wounded while trying to lead a dozen men armed with pigeon baskets and message books against about a million machine guns. From this time on nothing of any importance happened to the writer. He remained with Major Brett during the rest of the drive, taking over Lieutenant Sledge's job, as Adjutant, when Lieutenant Sledge became sick. Proceeded there—to write numerous orders regardless of authority, sending men and officers here, there and everywhere on this and that mission, which in more settled times would have got him into "beaucoup" [much] trouble. Finally, on November 10th, he returned to Bourg, having gone through two offensives and had had nothing more serious happen to him than to become a home for cooties, fleas, etc., and to have grown a healthy dislike for all sorts of canned "Willy."

First Lieutenant David M. Bowes, Company B, 344th Tank Battalion

While the first pitifully few American soldiers at the Marne and Chateau Thierry were just beginning to make the victoriously sweeping march of the Huns toward Paris hesitate, while at Cantigny and Belleau Wood, American blood commenced pouring out the grim balance and the Huns' onswelling tide was turned back, never again to menace the peace of the world; my order, two months delayed, reached me. After months of weary city streets, draughtings and motor cars, I am back again where the nights are split with the crash and roar of hate, where men's differences forever are being put to the sacrifice, where life's vital answer is being debated night and day in red-dipped, lead-vomiting thunder.

And so, late in July, as the increasingly great weight of the pressure from the "men from home" began to cause the Hun great command a few sleepless nights, and Paris to breathe again, I came to the tanks for training.

I didn't, like most Americans, take too quickly to the guns, and anyway, the engineer stamp was too strong, so I was detailed to course after course in reconnaissance, which consisted largely in putting red and blue lines on clear maps and drawing a few comic dance programs and posters. My assignment to a company as a reconnaissance officer was such a surprise to the commanding officer that I was thoughtfully left to continue on my comic-picture drawing way until the rumors of a move became so insistent that at an inquiry of the captain, I found I had just time to catch a truck to the already established camp. I had been left out of the calculations entirely. My first company duty, long unused infantry drill, made its way into the order of things. The new tanks were already being "tuned up," out in the long rows where they were picketed like iron horses, and which were never a lessening source of delight to me.

And the men in these last days—it is of the men that I have the most remembrances, their devotion, their keenness and perception, it is to them that the success in the days to come were to be fully due—they fell to their tasks with a will. It was the first time that they had each had something that each could feel was his own, and that rivalry that each might be better than his fellows.

I won't forget that first train after the weeks of expectant waiting for its final appearance. Even the rain could not dampen the ardor of these men, men chosen from all the forces in France to lead into battle the first tanks of the American breed. Mud, mud and mud, loading the tanks on the train, and then two days later, still mud into which they lumbered from the train. A march a night, and a foggy drippy day, which perhaps saved us from Boche observation, and we settled down to live under a little piece of camouflage in a crease in the mud between the tread of the tanks, with modern conveniences, running water and Boche gas.

"D" night it rained the blackest, wettest, muddiest night I have ever seen. I fell down once and cursed—at that I didn't much care, it was all the same, wallowing, slipping and squirming up to our position of waiting. We were in position by midnight, when, as though the very elements were synchronized, the heavens miraculously cleared, the stars came out clear and bright to see the show, the air became perfectly still as before a storm. It broke. Far to the west a gun spoke. Behind one answered. Then at the signal, like hounds unleashed, the southern skies leaped forth over the crest into the Hun wire.

Five hours later I followed that rush with barrels of gas and boxes of rations. And rush it was. Hour after hour I followed breathlessly, only catching up late at night with the headlong advance. Day and day followed alike, until the generals said "enough." When the Hun command heard it, he had several days march back to resume contact.

Two weeks later the tanks again crouched, sheltered in the friendly trees of the Argonne, waiting again the same word, a word that was to shock finally the last props under the trembling throne of imperialism.

The days that followed were breathless, weary, racking days. The tanks jumped off into a leaden wall, staggered, braced, and plunged forward, fell back for the infantry, then staggered on again. The infantry was having hard going of it. It was in these days that the spirit that prevailed back in the pup tent days was to show itself. Day after day the battle raged and day after day these men went forth in weakening, doubtful tanks, only to repeat the slow, terrible surge northward, and night after night they crawled slowly back to refill and groom the iron monsters for a further effort, stumbling off finally for an instant's relief in a water-logged, reeking dugout from which they were to be almost instantly snatched up by some unfeeling officer to beat once more the Hun's terrible reveille. To us who watched the unfailing, untiring energy of the men, vying with one another in greater sacrifice, the courageous, unfaltering facing of the severest trials, the generous conduct of the men is our kindest memory of these days. No individual heroism can be recorded; what they did was simple, a whole-hearted offering of their all to the cause. To those who have come back after those terrible days and nights, when they looked without flinching full into the face of horror, to those who left only after their last measure had been given, and to those who lie there where their tanks bore them to immortal glory, no special credit will be given nor do they seek it, but I, who saw them, know who it was that wrote the glorious history of the Tank Corps in miles of wooded waste, which they wrested from the desperate defenders. To have officered among such who needed no officers, was indeed my privilege.

Second Lieutenant Stephen L. Conrey, Company B, 344th Tank Battalion

According to attack orders [for the Argonne] from the First Army Corps, Company B, 344th Tank Battalion, attacked with the 28th Division, supported by Company A, 345th Tank Battalion. The attack began at 5:30 a.m. [September 26th].

The first obstacle we encountered was heavy barbed wire in front of the German trenches. The tanks could not cross the trenches and we were held up sometime while the engineers and our men were filling in the trenches. We again caught the infantry nearly a kilometer farther, just about the time the fog and smoke lifted.

I changed tanks three times before getting in contact with the enemy. I took Sergeant Oslund's, who had come back wounded, and went in search of machine guns in the right edge of the Argonne that were holding our flank. Three tanks followed me and we spent the afternoon trying to get at them; and while we could not see our results, we drove them back and the infantry were able to advance a few hundred yards behind us.

I had two men wounded and two tanks ditched. About four o'clock our artillery began to bombard the sector and after pulling out the ditched tanks, I withdrew and joined the remainder of our company tanks who were rallying and returned to Boureuilles.

Six tanks were in shape the next morning and I left with four more repaired by about noon. I passed through Varennes, where I lost one tank with a broken track, and found our machine gun troops held up with fire from the woods a kilometer farther. I patrolled the woods to Montblainville, losing one tank with mechanical trouble and one with direct artillery hits. I met the other platoon at Montblainville and after dark we returned to Varennes to gas up.

I left Varennes at 5:00 a.m., September 28th, in charge of five tanks under [First] Lieutenant [Thomas C.] Brown [Company A, 345th Tank Battalion] and joined the attack north of Montblainville. We were unable to accomplish anything on the plateau and we worked up the ravine into Apremont which we worked three times before the infantry got the town. I returned to Montblainville after dark. I took part in no further attacks.

Second Lieutenant Donald M. Call, Company B, 344th Tank Battalion

The writer left the United States of America June 30th, 1917, as a member of the Volunteer Ambulance Section, organized by the City Club of New York, of which he is a member. The section went to Paris by way of Liverpool and London, where it was reorganized as Section 32 of the American Field Service, serving with the French army. After a week in a training camp, the section was sent to the front and permanently attached to the 37th Division of the French Army.

In October, the 37th Division went into the trenches north of Verdun. At this time things were pretty lively at Verdun, and the roads were under fire practically all of the time. Every member of the ambulance section worked day and night for five weeks, and when they were finally relieved, everyone was pretty much all in, and the section had lost several cars. The division then moved back to Bar du Luc for a short rest.

About this time the US Army took control of the American Field Service, calling it the US Army Ambulance Service [USAAS], with the French Army. Recruiting officers soon came to each section and the members were given an opportunity of enlisting in the army or leaving the ambulance service. The writer signed up as a private and continued working with the section.

After a rest of two weeks, the 37th Division again went to the Verdun front, but this time more to the west, near Hill 344. After a few days preparation, a very successful attack was launched which resulted in a considerable advance in the French lines. The wounded came in pretty fast, and the little "flivvers" of Section 32 were kept very busy for a few days. For his work during this attack, the writer was later awarded the Croix de Guerre [Cross of War], with divisional citation. Shortly after the attack, the division moved back to the Vosges, for a long rest, where Section 32 settled down to a weary cold winter. They had now become section 344 of the USAAS.

Late in January, the division again went to the front, this time in the Lorrain sector, near Nomeny, north of Nancy. This was a comparatively quiet sector, and after their trying experiences at Verdun, the members of the American Section found it hard to realize that they were near the front. However, before they left the sector things livened up a bit.

About the middle of March a memo was sent out to all the sections of the USAAS, asking for volunteers for the US Tank Corps. The writer and one of his pals, thinking themselves suited to this sort of work, offered their services and two weeks later were transferred with orders to report to the CO, First Tank Center. It was with some misgivings that they said goodbye to their old friends in the Ambulance Section, as they little knew what was ahead of them. When they arrived about April 1st at Bourg; near Langres, they found things rather discouraging. The Tank Corps was just beginning to take shape and there were many hardships to go through before things really became organized. There were ten little French tanks and most of the time was spent cleaning and repairing them.

After five months of training with courses of instruction in machine guns, 37mm [guns], pistol, rifle, tank driving, gas engine, signaling, mapping, visibility and various other subjects, two battalions were equipped with the Renault light tanks and sent up by rail to the St. Mihiel sector. This was the first experience of the US Tank Corps, and they naturally made many mistakes. From the railhead to the point of departure was a long and difficult run. The roads were terrible and the weather worse; nothing but mud and rain. The night before the attack the writer slept under his tank in a muddy hole with water, mud and oil dripping down his neck. It made him long for his little "flivver" and a nice, warm, dry bed. The next night, shortly after dark, the tanks started up towards the front line trenches. It was a black, rainy night, and navigation was extremely difficult. All that could be seen was the black mass of the tank ahead looming up against the grey sky. Towards morning the weather improved, and at H-hour the rain had stopped, but the mud was a great handicap.

From the first it was quite evident that the St. Mihiel attack was going to be a great disappointment to the members of the Tank Corps who were anxious to see real fighting. For three days the tanks went forward just as fast as gasoline and oil could be brought to them. In spite of having reached all of their objectives and helping in straightening out the St. Mihiel salient, the Tank Corps hardly felt that they had seen a real battle. They wanted to see some lively fighting and they certainly got what they wanted not long after in the Argonne fight.

In the Argonne, the Tank Corps profited by the mistakes that had been made at St. Mihiel. The attack was launched with much more dexterity. The weather conditions were more favorable and the ground ideal. However, shortly after crossing the French front line trenches a heavy fog fell. This delayed the tanks for about half an hour, while the infantry pushed ahead. When the fog lifted, the tanks soon caught up to the infantry who were encountering strong machine gun resistance. The writer [a corporal], driving one of the tanks, with Captain [John W.] Castles' gunner, was sent over to the edge of the woods, and commenced firing. Hoping to get a more accurate aim with his 37mm gun, Captain Castles ordered the driver to stop the tank. After that he fired three shots, when the tank was hit directly on the left side by a German 77mm shell, disabling it completely. The writer and Captain Castles both got out of the tank, which was still being fired upon. Discovering that they were under machine gun fire, they took to a shell hole. Captain Castles was badly wounded and was evacuated to the rear. The next day, the writer was without a tank, but the third day he drove for Sergeant Phelps who had lost his driver.

During the third day's fighting, their tanks disabled, Sergeant Phelps and the writer were fired upon by an Austrian 88mm [field gun], while they were endeavoring to camouflage the tank. In an effort to escape, both were wounded by shell fragments and taken to the rear. Upon returning to the 302nd Tank

Center the writer was commissioned a second lieutenant in the Tank Corps, and was later awarded the Distinguished Service Cross [and Congressional Medal of Honor].

First Lieutenant Henry C. Jennings, Company C, 344th Tank Battalion

Soon after this officer had fought the "Battle of Biarritz," there was a closed meeting in Colonel [Joseph W.] Viner's office, and he found that he was to be one of a reconnaissance party to leave for the front immediately. Stock went up at once and all considered the party very lucky. Camouflaged in various colors and insignia, the party left and [Second] Lieutenant Guy R. Chamberlin and this officer were deposited below Seicheprey and in the Ansauville sector. This was their first trip to the front, so the pair set out the next morning to see the wonders of war. There was no activity in this sector at that time, so the next three weeks were spent telling lies about our mission, wondering why everything was so quiet, doping out laying-up points and tank routes. The only evidence of war to be seen were two lines of trenches, and an occasional doughboy scattered here and there along our front line, and shells dropping on Dead Man's Curve at regular intervals.

Finally, the tanks were expected. One night was spent in the rain, waiting for the train that never came. Another night and they came rolling in. After much swearing and cussin' they were safely stored away in the Bois de Hazelle to await D-day and H-hour, which was scheduled for the following morning. As was said before, this officer was not assigned, but he anticipated a great time going over with the infantry, following tanks, and perchance the opportunity of getting a berth in the tank of some departed hero, when lo' on the eve of D-day, he was handed the order which blasted his hopes and put the jinx on his experiences at the front. "Lieutenant Henry C. Jennings is hereby detailed to act as liaison officer with the 42nd Division and will report to Division Headquarters immediately," was the way it read. With much misgivings, and many doubts as to what were the duties of a liaison officer, he reported to his post of duty. H-hour arrived, the battle raged, the tanks swept on, the enemy swept back, noble deeds and good work of tanks and tankers were passed on when received. Out of it all, the only experience the liaison officer got was that of a news reporter gleaning news from the bulletins as they came in, also a vague idea of what was expected of a liaison officer. Not very interesting, but very necessary to get the proper cooperation and to keep those in command informed of the operations of their units. Time dragged on, the battle was over and this officer was ordered to the 344th Battalion and was attached to C Company.

Fine! The war was not yet over; there would probably be more fighting and maybe he would get in on the next shift. Then came a few days of pleasant living in pup tents listening to the deeds of his friends and comrades. Of how [Second] Lieutenant [Edwin A.] McCluer with a patrol of three tanks went out nine kilometers, captured Joinville and ran a whole battalion of Huns down the hill, came back and reported that there was some resistance to the north somewhere; of how Captain [Howell P.] Wood shot the hands off the clock in Nonsard and captured the town. These and scores of others that will be told in time.

Then we folded our tents like the Arab and silently stole away to Clermont. The next few days were spent moving from woods to woods just before Fritz decided to shell the one from which we had just moved. Spirits were gay in those days and rumors were rife concerning the coming party. Things were sitting pretty and an erstwhile liaison officer was very self-satisfied. But it was all too good to be true and another order was promulgated from the quarry which took the joy out of life and sent him back on the same old job. The big day came again and all messages were eagerly scanned for tank news, nor was it hard to find, for deeds of the iron cavalry were in evidence on every hand. It soon dawned upon us that this was really a bitter struggle, but everybody knew that there could be but one final result. First came the news that the commander [Colonel George S. Patton Jr.] of the First Brigade was wounded, then that other friends and comrades had paid the supreme sacrifice and were doing their bit for the world, and adding glory to the already glorious record of the Tank Corps.

It was here that the unofficial reports came in of Lieutenant McCluer's bloody campaign. Of how, though wounded and gassed and physically exhausted, he stuck to his job until the doctors finally forced him to be evacuated. How [Second] Lieutenant [David M.] Bowes went out behind the German lines, heated corn willy and coffee, had his lunch and disgustedly reported that the infantry wouldn't follow. Of how [Second] Lieutenant [William C.] Louisell, with three tanks, two of them running on one cylinder under a barrage of two one-pounders [37mm guns] and "General Nolan's orders," set out to ride around the German army and force them to surrender. Many times was the army corps in deadly fear of a counter-attack because our aviators reported that tanks far behind the German lines were seen maneuvering around, when as a matter of fact the Germans didn't have a tank in operation.

But there is always balm in Gilead and fortune smiled on the liaison officer. After all hope had been despaired of, the First Provisional Company, First Brigade, Tank Corps, was formed and the liaison officer was ordered to join this organization. Aside from the fact that there was probably a chance to see some action, to be in the same organization with men who having already fought the fight and done all that could be expected of them were willing to remain at the front and help drive the Hun from his last stand, was a source of great pride to him. He joined the company and there followed a very pleasant stay of three weeks in Exermont. Those were the good old days. The reputation of the tanks in training followed them into the lines and the god of Bacchus was unusually kind to this little bunch of tankers who were expecting daily to receive attack orders. When things would get dull, Fritz would break the monotony by doing up the town with gas and dropping a few HE's [high-explosive shells] uncomfortably close.

After many conferences with generals and near generals, the 2nd Division came in and the attack order was published. Out in the inky blackness the First Provisional Company wended its way and with them went the liaison officer. Finally, he was to have his fling. Over they went at H-hour and although the efficient artillery had almost completely smothered all resistance, the tanks found much work to do in the vicinity of Landres-et-St. Georges and St. Georges. It was here that several hundred Germans were planning to make their getaway when according to their own story, two tanks came along and began throwing "hand grenades" so fast that they decided to Kamerad [surrender] and seek protection with the Marine doughboys. After the first line of resistance was overcome, the advance was much like the St. Mihiel drive. Continuing the advance, the tanks under [Second] Lieutenant [Lloyd F.] Callahan captured an active battery of 77's and machine gun nests and the day closed with the infantry on their final objectives and the tanks just ahead, assisting in the capture of four machine gun nests and 79 Germans.

First Lieutenant Edwin A. McCluer, Company C, 344th Tank Battalion

I feel that my experience in the AEF began with the Saint Mihiel show. Previous to that I had spent nine months overseas in the French artillery schools, in the "rest" sectors of the Vosges, as an instructor at the 331st Tank Center. I was given command of the 1st Platoon of Co. A, 326th Battalion, two weeks before the drive to wipe out the salient started.

My experience of the first day of the show included leading my battalion across the German trenches, Captain [Harry H.] Semmes, my company commander, having lost his tank in a water-filled shell hole, from which tank he dragged his half drowned driver, at the risk of his life. Guiding [a] tank on foot across the trenches and pulling all of the tanks of the platoon out of the positions in which they had become stuck; opening numerous lanes through the enemy wire and thru the dense woods for the infantry; bridging an . . . extra wide and deep trench by collecting duckboards from its bottom; getting [a] tank tangled in overhead wire in the woods and having a bad three minutes breaking loose while our barrage, falling short, burnt around me; putting to flight about a dozen machine gun crews, causing them to abandon material, but without inflicting casualties; getting in a smoke barrage while changing from one sector to another and being nearly blinded by burning ashes coming through the slits; leading [a] tank out of the blinding choking smoke wave, guided by the sound of clanking tanks, finally getting out of gas and going into Nonsard on foot with the tanks as an emergency commander or driver, taking prisoners with the patrol to enter the town, exploring along a house on the outskirts and taking five Boche from its basement, driving them out by using beer bottles as [mock] grenades.

Experiences of the second day were only those incidental to transportation supply, and pursuit of the fleeing enemy.

Experiences of the third day included: taking a patrol of three tanks from Avillers through Woel to the outskirts of Joinville, a distance of some five kilometers, leading the way for an infantry intelligence patrol, killing or putting to flight the crews of more than a dozen machine guns and a seventy-seven [millimeter German field gun]; bring up the rear of the battalion as it fell back; bringing in two crippled tanks, thus witnessing the violent bombardment of our evacuated position.

Experiences of the first day of the Meuse-Argonne attack of September 26th included seeing Captain [Harry H.] Semmes fall severely wounded while leading his company on foot through the almost impassable bog-infested, shell-torn, shell-swept region around Vaquois Hill and getting him and the other wounded evacuated; and getting the company through the region, taking Cheppy and Very.

Experiences of the second day of this attack included repeated attacks north of Very through a most violent artillery fire, direct, indirect and over the open sights; plunging from ravine to ravine, cover to cover, while the enemy fired over open sights and missed only by feet; killing or putting to flight a large number of machine gun crews; emptying a load of case shot into a Boche at ten meters; repeatedly establishing liaison with the infantry in order to find out what their next move was involving; being twice knocked down by explosions of shells; having brim of helmet smashed in by a fragment of another shell; waiting for a counter-attack until long after dark; and loading tanks with wounded and taking them through the shell-torn area to the first-aid station at Very.

Experiences of the third day included finding two tanks of the third platoon wrecked on the second day, and caring for the dead and wounded of their crews; assisting in the evacuation of wounded doughboys; taking the platoon by night to the support of "C" Company, between Charpentry and Baulny; platoon and truck loaded with gas, oil and rations; a truck with broken steering rod and magneto, involving hauling and back-towing and constant clearing of roads; and pulling of ammunition carts and ambulances out of ditches and shell holes.

Experiences of the fourth day included a daybreak attack with C Company in gas masks; skirting the eastern edge of the Bois de Montrebeau and then turning west and going into Exermont; pulling back to reestablish liaison with the infantry and to report that Exermont had been evacuated; plunging back through the heart of the woods to meet a counter-attack, which stopped on heights just south of Exermont, except for the drenching of the woods with gas and high explosive; gradually following the infantry back and then "standing to" in spite of concentrated artillery fire; and taking a position for the night in a ravine north of Charpentry.

Experiences of the fifth, sixth, seventh and eighth days were confined to patrol duty and to reconnaissance work and keeping up morale of men under steady and violent artillery fire and gas attacks, and preparing for the next big attack.

Experiences of the ninth day included the going over with the 1st Division; the dash through the enemy barrage; the cleaning up of numerous machine guns; the scaling of the heights northwest of Exermont; the crossing over into the sector of the 28th Division to put out a machine gun nest, which was putting down an enfilading fire on the 16th Infantry; being wounded in the scalp by machine gun fire and by splash;[6] having telescopic sight shot out and shield frozen by machine gun fire; having driver wounded by having anti-tank bullet pass through side of tank and two 37mm cartridge cases, causing the powder to blast out in face, and setting fire to four maps; fighting our blazing paper with our hands before it could explode our ammunition; starting the tank, which the driver had stalled, while the tank was stopping several anti-tank bullets, putting the gunner to flight; wrecking a 55mm [mountain gun], which had opened fire and driving a platoon of the enemy back over acres with a 37mm barrage; could not get to the crest to follow on account of an impassible stream; encountering over the open sight [direct] fire from 77's; trying to take remainder of platoon (and their acquired tanks) back into Exermont, an attempt given up on account of intense artillery fire, including many gas projectiles; vainly trying to reestablish liaison with company and battalion and finally leaving platoon in charge of platoon sergeant, with instructions to continue the attempt all night, and leaving it in order to get first aid and look up company and battalion personally; "passing out" on road to Baulny from loss of blood and effects of gas, being picked up by a truck and carried to Cheppy; escaping from mobile hospital and locating liaison officer of Tank Corps with First Division, and spending the night making reports by phone, especially as to location of tanks.[7]

Experience of the ninth day was being evacuated. Experiences since included seven weeks in hospital, acceptance of commission as first lieutenant, assignment to Company A, 329th Brigade; and routine service as company commander.

First Lieutenant Loyall F. Sewall, Company C, 344th Tank Battalion

I was relieved from being liaison officer with the 4th French group on the afternoon of October 3rd and reported to Major [Sereno E.] Brett at 1st Brigade, who ordered me to report to Captain [C. H. Ranulf] Compton at Varennes. I reported about 7:30 p.m. and was ordered to take five tanks to Charpentry to go over the next morning; H-hour was not given me and I was unfamiliar with the terrain. I made up five crews and found five tanks. I did not know the names of any of the men, but knew that they had never worked together before.

The roads were blocked with traffic and tank motors working badly, so I did not reach the heights northeast of Charpentry till about 11:00 p.m. The Germans were shelling Charpentry heavy with gas and HE [high-explosive shells] and had blown up an ammunition dump in that town which was still exploding beside the road. It was necessary to put on our masks and I waited for about two hours for a chance to get through the town.

About one o'clock (October 4th) as I did not know when H-hour was and as the Germans had let up a little, I ordered the tanks on. There was still a lot of gas in the valley and it was pitch dark, so I made very slow progress.

As I was crossing the bridge at Charpentry an HE shell exploded and blew off my mask and left a small piece in my leg and closed my right eye. When I came to I could not find the tanks, but found the driver of the tank I was leading. He had been blown out of his tank. I told him to find it and report to me on the hill south of Charpentry where I got together my tanks and reported to Captain [Courtney H.] Barnard.

We had an hour-and-a-half rest when we refilled our tank and started for Chaudron Farm under the command of Captain [Math L.] English. My tanks were in reserve, but on account of heavy machine gun fire and a 77 firing direct from Montrebeau Woods, and as the infantry kept calling for more tanks, I ordered them forward.

Captain English and his runner, Private Santana, both acted with exceptional bravery going from tank to tank under heavy fire, pointing out machine guns and giving advice. About nine o'clock he ordered me to report back for medical aid, but I was able to keep on for another hour, when I had to report back to the dressing station at Chaudron Farm, where I was evacuated.

Second Lieutenant Harlow A. Wood, Company C, 344th Tank Battalion

On September 26th my platoon attacked with the 35th Division infantry just to the left of Vauquois Hill. During the day we attacked as far as Cheppy where reorganization became necessary. The 27th September was spent in salvaging and reorganization. On the evening of this day we proceeded to Very. Here we waited orders until 10:00 p.m. of the 28th, when we proceeded to Charpentry and reported to [Lieutenant] Colonel [Henry W.] Parker commanding infantry there. During the night of the 28th we were ordered to attack from Montrebeau Woods to Exermont.

On Sunday the 29th, my platoon followed by 250 infantry attacked from Montrebeau Woods to Exermont, capturing that town and permitting the infantry to occupy the slope beyond that town. On the afternoon of that day the Germans came back and we were forced to withdraw as the infantry were all disorganized.

Captain [Math L.] English deserves special attention on this date for going back through the barrage and compelling the retreating infantry to take up a line and hold. He also found that our own artillery was firing on our men and sent a runner back to stop them. He stayed and kept our tanks there until the line was finally established.

Two men with a disabled tank were left in Exermont and we had no report for several days until their action was brought to our attention by a colonel of infantry (name not known) who said that they saved his life and that of 250 men by operating the 37mm gun from the disabled tank. They kept the Germans back, preventing them from surrounding and either killing or capturing this group of men. The colonel described it as the nerviest stunt he had ever seen. These men were Private [Harley R.] Nichols (now sergeant) and Corporal Gurrier, who were the crew of one of my reserve tanks.[8] After this attack we went back to Charpentry and stayed there until October 4th when we attacked with the 1st Division.

On October 4th my platoon attacked in front of the 18th Infantry of the 1st Division. We proceeded around Montrebeau Woods and towards Exermont. Before reaching there, I received some splinters in my right eye preventing me from going farther.

[Second] Lieutenant [Arthur] Snyder (then sergeant) whose tank had been put out by a 77 took my tank and continued on. He proceeded on until his tank was very badly damaged, his third driver for that day wounded and he himself wounded in several places on the head. He then carried his driver back until aid could be obtained. Snyder was assisted back later being in a very weak condition. His action on this occasion, as on others, deserves the highest commendation.

After the attack of October 4th, the remainder of my platoon returned to Charpentry where we stayed until October 9th, when we moved back to Varennes. I remained there until October 13th, when I was sent back here bringing only one man with me, the rest remaining in the composite company there.

Second Lieutenant Arthur Snyder, Company C, 344th Tank Battalion

September 26th, my company attacked to the left of Vauquois Hill. I was in charge of Captain [Math L.] English's runners, my company commander. About an hour after the attack started, a runner came to me with a message from [Second] Lieutenant [John J.] Dunn of the second platoon, ordering me to report to his tank, by the captain's consent. This I did, taking charge of Lieutenant Dunn's tank, while he led his platoon afoot. We encountered minefields, but we met no other strong resistance until we arrived south of Varennes, at about 2:00 p.m. Here, there was a great deal of "mopping up" to be done. Lieutenant Dunn took two tanks to attack machine gun nests on one slope of a hill. He put me in charge of another two, which attacked nests on the other slope of the same hill. We were successful in our attack, but we lost two tanks. With two tanks left, Lieutenant Dunn attacked the machine guns in the valleys south of the said town.

Here, his work as a leader was magnificent. His men were filled with confidence by his courage and successful leadership. He cleaned the above valley of machine gun fire and then we proceeded to Varennes, passing the village on the right and spending the night on the south slope of the hill, which is north of the town.

Here, Lieutenant Dunn and [Second] Lieutenant [Darwin T.] Phillips (345th Battalion) formed a full platoon, using tanks from both battalions. I was in charge of one of these tanks and had Private [Alfred] Truitt of Company C, 344th Battalion, as a driver. We attacked on September 27th at about 8:00 a.m. on the ridge just south of Charpentry. My tank got in a bad shell hole and was unable to get out. My platoon came out of action without me. This attack also proved successful and again Lieutenant Dunn did most excellent work, most worthy of mention. My driver, Private Truitt, showed great courage and devotion to duty under the trying experience of being in a crippled tank, which was in thick machine gun and shell fire. We manned our tank until our 37mm gun was put out of action. Then we crawled back to our infantry and advanced back to our tank with the infantry that evening at five o'clock.

On September 29th, I was in a platoon under [Second] Lieutenant [Edwin A.] McCluer of the 344th Battalion, which attacked around Montrebeau Woods. We were successful in silencing several machine gun nests far back in the woods, but the attack was not thought successful because of the infantry of the

35th Division failing to advance with us. My driver here was Private [Robert] Penick of Company C, 344th Battalion. He proved a most excellent driver and mechanic and was most cool and soldierly under fire and at all times.

On October 4th, I was in Lieutenant H. A. Wood's platoon of Company C, 344th Battalion. We attacked just south of Exermont with only two tanks, the others being lost upon the way to the point of departure. Lieutenant Wood was wounded about the eyes with splinters shortly after his tank went into action. Just as his tank went to the rear, a 77mm shell broke the tread of my tank. My driver and I crawled back to Lieutenant Wood's tank safely. Here, I went back into action in his tank, with his driver, Private [Horatio R.] Rogers, also of Company C. We were not into action long before Private Rogers got a similar wound to Lieutenant Wood's. The blood was ruining his vision, so I went to the rear for a new driver. I found a Private Hadley of Company A, 344th Battalion. He proved most courageous and a great devotion to duty, when he was wounded in the neck by splinters and our tank was "stalled" behind the German lines later in the day. An antitank gun bullet pierced our radiator and caused our engine to "stall" eventually. The 18th Infantry attacked between Exermont and Fleville and we were then able to get out of our tank and go to the rear with our wounds.

Both Captain English and Lieutenant Wood, I have personally known as excellent leaders of men, doing all in their power for the welfare of their men. Also, both being brave, skilled officers, it is with pride that I will always remember being one of their sergeants and a member of the 1st Tank Brigade.

Second Lieutenant George B. Heilner, Reconnaissance Officer, 344th Tank Battalion

The writer arrived in France from England December 27th, 1917, at La Havre. He was then 1st Sergeant of Battery 3, Training Battalion, 8th Field Artillery [FA]. The battery was commanded by Captain Dean Hudnutt and the battalion by Lieutenant Colonel F. B. (Spike) Hennessey.

After spending two days freezing at the rest camp, the battalion entrained in side-door Pullmans and at the end of two days and two nights rough riding, arrived at La Courtine (La Creuse). Although in the artillery, the battery had no horses or guns, so the work at La Courtine consisted in hikes and infantry drill.

While at La Courtine, the Training Battalion 8th FA was changed to the Field Artillery Replacement Regiment, 42nd Division, and on January 18th, 1918, moved to Montrichard (Loire et Cher).

At Montrichard the writer was promoted to the grade of battalion sergeant major. The routine was the same as at La Courtine. Here, the writer volunteered for services with the Tank Corps, and accordingly left February 17, 1918, with a detachment of enlisted men under the command of Lieutenant Colonel Hennessey and [First] Lieutenant William G. Robinson for Langres (Haute Marne). Arrived at Langres-Marne station February 18, 1918, at 1:30 p.m. and marched to St. Geosmes by Captain George S. Patton [Jr.]. This was the first lot of enlisted men to join the Tank Corps. On February 23, 1918, the Tank Corps moved from St. Geosmes to Bourg. The work at Bourg consisted at first in infantry drill, signaling and tank drill on foot.

Shortly after arriving at Bourg the writer was placed on special duty and detailed to instruct in map reading and sketching. Other classes at that time were Hotchkiss machine gun; 37mm [cannon] and signaling. These four classes were the first courses given in the Tank Corps.

About March 1, 1918, the writer was recommended for a commission by Major Patton and on April 5, 1918, was commissioned second lieutenant of infantry.

In April, the first consignment, about 20 in number, of tanks arrived at the tank center and the work of the Tank School began in earnest. The courses consisted in tank driving, gas engines, signaling, machine gun, 37mm [cannon], pistol, hand grenades, scouts and patrols and reconnaissance. The writer had charge of the latter and during his spare time managed to qualify in the other courses.

About May 12, 1918, the writer was re-commissioned second lieutenant, Tank Corps.

Work went on as described until June 8th, when an order was received creating two battalions (light tanks), the 326th and the 327th. The 326th Battalion was commanded by Major [Joseph W.] Viner. The writer was placed on the battalion staff as Battalion Reconnaissance Officer. The 327th Battalion was commanded by Captain [Sereno E.] Brett. The post of the Battalion RO, however, did not interfere with the reconnaissance class, which continued as before.

Work continued with little variety until August 1st, when the writer was granted leave to visit Treuville. This was a relief after being buried in Bourg for almost six months.

On August 26th, 1918, disguised as artillery officers, the writer left Bourg with Lieutenant Colonel Patton and [First] Lieutenant Harry W. Bolan, reconnaissance officer of the 327th Battalion, in Colonel Patton's car at 7:30 p.m. for the front. Arrived at Ligny-en-Barrois. Left Ligny the next morning, arriving at Beniote Vaux about noon. Here, the headquarters 1st Brigade, Tank Corps, was established. Here, the writer, together with [First] Lieutenant Maurice H. Knowles and Lieutenant Bolan, made a reconnaissance in the region at Handimont and Fresnes-en-Woevre. The working conditions here were ideal as the

Germans were very quiet and one could work with comparative safety. However, the reconnaissance went for naught except for the experience gained. Although the terrain was most excellent for tanks, the 1st Brigade was ordered to the Toul sector.

The move was made on September 7th, brigade headquarters being established at Ecrouves. However, the writer and Lieutenant Bolan were not destined to enjoy the luxuries of Ecrouves, but were sent to Manre. Here, they lived in what was once a good house. A reconnaissance was made from Bouconville east to the Bois de Hazelle. This sector, too, was fairly quiet, but not so quiet as the former. The Germans delighted in shelling the towns and roads, but did not bother individuals.

On September 8th the writer was informed that his battalion would arrive that night in a woods near Ancerville, that they would detrain, and to be there to lead them to a position of readiness. After waiting all night in the rain, the tanks failed to arrive. They were found the next day at Bourcq—one train. The tanks of the battalion were loaded on two trains. These were detrained in the yard in the daytime and that night were sent to the position of readiness, a run of 25 kilometers (to a woods two kilometers south of Bouconville). During the progress of detraining, the second train arrived at Bourcq, but it was decided not to detrain there. They were to go to the original detraining point. However, to tell the French railroad officials to go to a certain place is easy enough, but to get there is an entirely different matter. So, after riding around the vicinity of Bourcq for some five hours, they put the train on a spur three kilometers from Bourcq, uncoupled the engine and went off with it. Consequently, there was nothing left to do but detrain there. This made a run of nearly 20 kilometers for the remaining tanks. It took the rest of the night to detrain as the route was through woods all the way; the run from the detraining point to the position of readiness was made in the daytime. All the tanks were in the position of readiness the night of September 10th.

The writer was informed the night of the tenth to reconnoiter a route and pick out a parallel departure, in the vicinity of Xivray-Marvoisin. This was done the morning and afternoon of the 11th. The parallel of departure being about one kilometer south of Xivray-Marvoisin, the route was taped and instructions given to the engineers assigned to the tanks to post a man every hundred meters along the route. This was done as a precaution because the writer had no time to go over the route a second time or to go over it at night. This route made a run of about three kilometers and was across country from the position of readiness to the parallel of departure. The night was all that could be asked for for moving tanks and one that caused the writer more worry than any other time in his life. It was raining and so dark that one could not see his hand before his face.

The cause for worry was due to the fact that the writer was responsible that the tanks got to the position of departure. Due to the darkness, the tape could not be found and it was impossible to see any landmarks. Men were sent out in all directions to look for the tape, but without result. The interval of 100 meters for the engineers was too great and at first none could be located. The tanks reached their parallel of departure by posting men every ten paces along the route. The tanks though were not held up, but the men were sent out one after the other to post themselves, thus forming an endless chain. The trip lasted three hours, from 9:00 p.m. to midnight. H-hour was set for five o'clock the morning of the 12th. The artillery preparation was four hours.

The writer returned from the parallel of departure to the position of readiness in order to guide the supply tanks (leaving at H plus five), to the rallying point, which was less than one kilometer south of Nonsard. Owing to mud and breakdowns he arrived at the rallying point with only four tanks at 6:00 p.m. At 8:00 p.m. Major Brett ordered him to go to Menil-la-Tour as best he could (meaning on foot) get enough gas and oil for the battalion, have it loaded on trucks, and have them at the rallying point by 4:00 a.m. By hard walking and no rest he arrived Beaumont at midnight and found a captain there with two trucks loaded with gas, oil and ammunition. It was impossible though to get these trucks to the battalion before three o'clock the next afternoon, owing to traffic conditions and then only by getting the colonel in charge of traffic to give these trucks the right of way over all other traffic.

The 327th Battalion went from Nonsard to a point about two kilometers west of Woel and except for a slight skirmish a patrol of five tanks had in the vicinity of Woel with a 77, there was no further fighting in the St. Mihiel sector.

In order to give the reader some idea of sleeping conditions of a reconnaissance officer at the front the following record of the St. Mihiel sector is given:

Sept. 8th	No sleep. Reconnaissance all day. Up all night watching for tanks.
Sept. 9th	No sleep. Spent day hunting and detraining tanks.
Sept. 10th	Eight hours sleep. Spent day leading tanks to position of readiness.
Sept. 11th	No sleep. Made reconnaissance all day. Leading tanks to parallel of departure.
Sept. 12th	Two hours sleep. Leading supply tanks to rallying point.
Sept. 13th	No sleep. Trying to get trucks to Nonsard. Tanks moving to Vigneulles.
Sept. 14th	No sleep. Spent day getting to Woel and on patrol.

Sept. 15th	Two hours sleep in the morning from 6:00 to 8:00. Spent day making route reconnaissance from Bois de Thiaucourt to Bois de Haselle.
Sept. 16th	Six hours sleep.
Sept. 17th	No sleep—traveling.

Thus it will be seen that the writer managed to get eight hours sleep in 10 days, with one stretch of 60 hours without sleeping. It is also just about as hard for a reconnaissance officer to get food and one should feel very lucky to get a couple of cups of coffee and some bread or hard tack per day.

The writer left the Bois de Haselle the 16th for Recicourt, arriving there the morning of the 18th. This place was brigade headquarters of the 1st Brigade in the Argonne sector. A reconnaissance was immediately made here. The tanks arrived the night of the 20th, were detrained at Clermont and were run in a woods one kilometer north of the town before daylight; the total time in this case for detraining and running to the position of readiness being about seven hours. This included the entire battalion (two trains).

This sector was not as comfortable and healthy to work in as the other two. The Germans were shelling everything and everybody at any time and one had to be careful.

On the night of September 23rd the writer was ordered to take two truck-loads of gas and oil to the Cotes de Forimont (one kilometer back of the front line); the gas and oil being for the tanks to fill up on before going into battle. This night the Germans happened to be particularly active and while we were unloading they laid down a "Searching Barrage," around the same place and everyone spent a most uncomfortable 15 minutes, however, the men did not quit their job, but kept right on unloading, although they were right in the middle of the barrage. All escaped without a scratch and the gas and oil was safely stored in the woods.

The date was the 25th of September; just ten days after pulling out of St. Mihiel sector. The writer had one more close shave in the Argonne and one more long night walk.

On the morning of the 26th Major Brett, [First] Lieutenant [Theodore J.] Sledge, [First] Lieutenant [Harry G.] Borland, and the writer, with about ten enlisted men (runners), started out at nine o'clock to follow up the tanks, supposedly two or more kilometers ahead. They found the tracks and started to follow up the tanks, everything going alright until they reached a point about two kilometers northeast of Boureuilles, when suddenly they found themselves in a barrage coming from snipers and machine guns. The machine guns and snipers were firing from the front and sides. There were some French tanks on the left and some infantrymen on the left front, but there seemed to be nothing but Germans in front and to the right. They all picked a large shell hole, then sat there until things agreed to be a little more quiet, then they started to move. No sooner had they gotten out of the shell hole then everything came down again and one shell passed within five feet in front of them and landed less than 15 feet away. This meant another stop in another shell hole. As there seemed to be no let up and the infantry was coming back instead of going forward, they decided it would be better to move back to a safer place. Their next attempt was successful and all got safely behind a hill after a quarter of an hour ducking shell, machine gun and sniper bullets.

The last long night hike the writer had was on the night of September 28th, and it lasted from 7:30 p.m. to 7:30 a.m. [Brigadier] General [Samuel D.] Rockenbach wanted a list of casualties by ten o'clock the morning of the 29th, so the writer with [Second] Lieutenant [Frederick B.] Bond was sent out to find each unit and get a report from the commanding officer. The route west from Les Cotes de Forimont to Varennes, thence to Charpentry, Baulny, Montblainville, Varennes and back to Les Cotes de Forimont—a total distance of over 25 kilometers, and no transportation.

On the 6th of October the writer was taken sick with influenza and spent the time from then until November 19th at base hospitals. Since his return to the 302nd Center, he has been lecturing to the new units on the work of reconnaissance at the front.

327th/345th Tank Battalion

First Lieutenant William C. Louisell, Headquarters, 345th Tank Battalion

On the 23rd of September, I was put in command of three trucks with instructions to follow the tanks as closely as possible over a road that a Holt tractor would have found impossible. We finally found some tanks stuck in a trench and used these tanks to drag our trucks through the mud for about four kilometers. We were still "cussing" the reconnaissance officer who picked this road, which looked very nice on the map. Our orders were to meet the tanks at Apremont on the 26th of September, but found it impossible as the Boche did not leave Apremont until three days later, so [First] Lieutenant [Roswell] King and myself took a sight-seeing trip to the town of Varennes. On arriving there we found that the tanks were just coming in and the Boche just leaving. No doughboys had arrived as yet. After the Boche had withdrawn from Varennes, a very heavy artillery bombardment was dropped on the town, so Lieutenant King and I decided to move, which we did in a hurry. From our position in Varennes we were able to observe the work of the tanks on the east of the river Aire, followed by the infantry, which was at that time very badly "shot up," but it was a beautiful sight to be able to witness the tanks working with the infantry. The next two days were spent in getting supplies. By this time, over one-half of the officers of the brigade had been wounded and I volunteered to take a platoon, which was readily given me.

On the night of the 30th of September 1918, with five tanks, I proceeded to Montblainville, upon arrival reporting to [First] Lieutenant [Thomas C.] Brown. After a stay of about 30 minutes in Montblainville we reported to [Brigadier] General [Dennis E.] Nolan in Apremont. Upon arriving at Apremont, we inquired from one whom we thought to be an enlisted man, except that he looked a little bit worse than an ordinary enlisted man, where we could find General Nolan. He replied that he was General Nolan. We then reported we had tanks to be used in the attack, which we thought was to be made that morning. General Nolan ordered us to hold the position we were in and await orders. We thought we had better camouflage our tanks and he agreed with us. We were not used that day.

That night I slept in a tank after a three-hour conference with General Nolan and other officers of the 55th Brigade, 28th Division. I have never been able to decide whether it was the shell fire that made me shiver or the cold. At 5:00 a.m., next morning, General Nolan informed us that we would attack. Without any reconnaissance or information as to where the Boche line could be found, we started out. We were not in action but about 20 minutes and during that time we had four tanks destroyed by direct artillery fire at short range, eight men wounded and three men killed. We were relieved that night and returned to Montblainville. We were quartered in some Boche commanders' PC. We were very comfortable, but had no cover from shell fire. We were outranked from our PC by some artillery brigade commander and moved into a Boche dugout, where we were well entertained by rats, cooties, crabs and all other animals that were well cultivated by "Fritz."

On the 14th of October we again reported to General Nolan. Our action amounted to nothing. We were sent out on a patrol to ascertain whether or not it was possible to cross a bridge which led to Chatel Cherey. We were relieved that night and reported to Montblainville and from there withdrew all of our tanks to Varennes, there expecting to be relieved. Upon arriving at Varennes, we found that a provisional company was being formed. I was lucky enough to be given a platoon in this provisional company. This company moved to Exermont and there operated with the 42nd Division, which was unable to advance due to the heavy resistance met.

On November 1st was wounded south of Landres-St. Georges. After going through all the hospitals in France, more or less, arrived in Paris, much to my disgust. After being discharged from the hospital, I reported back to Bourg and was assigned to Company C, 328th Battalion (1st Brigade).

First Lieutenant Theodore J. Sledge, Headquarters, 345th Tank Battalion

The writer left God's country on the 14th day of August, 1917, on HMS *Andania*, had a very pleasant voyage to Halifax, and there participated in many boat drills, and many for boat No. 3, for he was unlucky and drew the same number boat as that of the general commanding the 1st Brigade, Coast Artillery.

He and two other fellow officers were assigned as permanent guards, to awaken the general in the event of being attacked by the Kaiser's Tin Fish. However, no such good luck for the Kaiser, and on September 1st landed safely in Liverpool, England. Thence to Camp Borden, where he soon dined and dined on water, sheep and goat, until he left for Southampton, where he went on board another of his majesty's ships and disembarked at Le Harve. Thence to Rest Camp No. 1, where everything was sunshine and laughter—NIX—finally landing in Camp de Mailly to begin training for our initial combat with the Hun.

For three months he studied electricity, direct and alternating current, French, Belgian and German type of telephones, the French system of liaison and on December 24th, received his certificate of proficiency. On December 28, 1917, orders were issued that he construct a telephone line from the gun emplacements at Houssimont to the target butts about 10 kilometers east. This was accomplished after several days of work in the snow, among droves of wild boars and deer.

On January 12, 1918, orders were received that he report to Captain G. S. Patton Jr. at Langres, France, for duty with the Tank Corps. He did, having great hopes of going into something exciting. On arriving he immediately began looking for tanks and Tank Corps headquarters, expecting at least to see signs in large glowing letters—HEADQUARTERS TANK CORPS—but no, he was conducted to a small room in a typical French mansion, with a small sign, "Tank Corps" hanging outside. On the inside was a chair, table and an empty paper basket, but behind this table sat the Tank Corps Captain George S. Patton Jr., who in a very few words thoroughly convinced the writer that the Tank Corps was really in existence and in time it would rain death, hell and destruction on the Boche. He started in learning the nomenclature of a Mack truck at the motor park in Langres, later at Bourg, the same schedule, with a few additions, such as driving nails, building roads and last but not least, shining the new "Sam Brown" [belt].

The night of March 21st, 1918, a cold, dark, rainy one, our first tanks arrived.

It was a great sight, the Tank Corps was at least on the map and all were sure then of our colors, Red (Artillery), Yellow (Cavalry), Blue (Infantry). Major Patton at the helm drove the leading tank to its berth in the "Mud Park."

Then began the days of toil in rain and mud, learning to drive the little "devels" over wagon ruts without letting them bump or racing the engine and keeping the doors closed. The days passed and no sign of excitement until one bright day in September, orders came to go into camp. Everything was secret, however, but all hands knew that the front was our destination. In pup-tents for three days, and these were three days of hell for the writer. Major [Sereno E.] Brett, (the Old Bad Major), Captain [Harry H.] Semmes, [Newell P.] Weed and [Math L.] English were at the front, and he being battalion adjutant was ordered by Major [Joseph W.] Viner to take command and prepare to get out. Things moved along smoothly and on Sunday morning, September 5th, Major Brett and the writer left for the Toul sector, making it in record time, having no mishaps, but hellish close; such as killing chickens that were getting their breakfast in the road; bumping into horses that were around an acute corner and could not possibly get out of the way of an automobile going at about 40 per; and making the corners on two wheels (Yes—the Old Bad Major was at the wheel). Being a soldier and visions of a scrap, soon he had to be brave, but was damn uncomfortable.

Toul was reached, a hurried lunch (the last for 48 hours), and he went with the Old Bad Major trying to find army and corps headquarters. We did not that day. Returning that night the Old Bad Major still at the wheel had his first accident, fell in a ditch and there remained until morning. At last army and corps headquarters were located and many marathon trips made—no sleep and little eats.

The fight was only a few hours off and he was evading the Old Bad Major for fear that he would be put on a special detail and not share in the glory of going over the top with the first American tank unit. It came. No tank for the battalion adjutant nor the battalion major. The Old Bad Major yanked a gunner out of the leading tank and sallied forth to battle, leaving the writer in mud, knee deep and one of the darkest nights he ever experienced. But fortunately, [First] Lieutenant [Harry E.] Gibbs came along and heard the writer's sobs and sighs, took pity and promised him a berth in the corps reserve that would leave at H-plus five-and-one-half hours. He left, but did not progress far on account of engine trouble. Tank was abandoned and he left half of his rations with the driver who had forgotten his.

He secured a pistol from a wounded hospital corpsman, later traded it to a doughboy for a rifle and belt; a brave man going forward with the infantry. In the meantime, he had collected about ten tankers and was progressing very nicely up in the front line until he heard a voice saying, "What in the hell are you doing here, get in a tank and that damn quick." He did and went forward into Nonsard with the Old Bad Major on the right, blasting snipers out of the church steeple, and Captain Newell P. Weed on the left. The first day over the tanks were assembled near Nonsard to gas and oil, and to eat if such was possible. Nothing doing until 7:00 p.m. when a sled loaded arrived with corn willy and hard tack; not enough, but they made out. Then to sleep, where, how, when—no blankets, no tanks, "The Major's Orders" to be delivered. At last when all others had finally crawled in or under a tank, he started looking for the Old Bad Major thinking perchance he would take pity on him and give him an invitation to share his blanket. But no, the Old Bad Major was nicely concealed in a tank, not a blanket to his name and he was left out in the cold again. At this moment Sergeant Major Dillon came along and offered to share his lone shelter-half with the writer, which he gladly accepted, and with this shelter-half for the bottom and the bottom of the tank for the top they crawled in to spend the rest of the night in asking each other "Are you cold?"

The next day was a day of travel, and the next finally stopping about two kilometers beyond St. Maurice, where he was sent by automobile to direct gas and oil to Lieutenant Gibbs and his disabled tanks. Not being a reconnaissance officer and without a map, got lost and went in some village where the Germans were just leaving one end. When he found where he was, he damn quickly left the other end and returned to St. Maurice where he got on the right road and directed the gas and oil to its proper place. He then returned to his proper place with the Old Bad Major and remained there the rest of the day. That afternoon at about 5:00 p.m. Boche avions [airplanes] came over and paid a visit shooting off a few star shells, which gave the artillery our location, and then the artillery opened up and the Old Bad Major and his armored cavalry moved out. That night was spent in riding, finally landing in the Bois de la Hazelle. There he remained for a couple of days and then went to the Argonne sector.

Things were more likely in this sector, and from all appearances the long looked for excitement would soon be had. It came. On the night of the 25th of September the Old Bad Major and his staff left the vicinity of Clermont and proceeded towards the front line. At about 9:00 p.m. they reached corps headquarters and billeted there for the night. The writer slept on the floor with the rats. Early the next morning the Old Bad Major and his flock started forward to see if they could see if any of the "little devils" had failed to jump off at the proper time. On they marched until about 9:30 a.m. when something happened. During their march the fog had been very thick and they had gotten the general direction, but did not know the exact location. All at once the fog lifted and hell broke loose, there were big ones; there were small ones; they were in the air; they were on the ground; they were everywhere, as well as with the Old Bad Major and his flock. It reminded one of an old hen and her small chicks when danger was near. They had followed the Old Bad Major into this, therefore they looked to him to get them out of this. He did, and after playing hide-and-seek in shell holes and trenches, finally reached a place of safety behind a hill, and there he spent another night with the Old Bad Major and two blankets in a German dugout on a wire bed. The next morning, after breakfast, each man cooking his own, which consisted of hard tack and a slice of bacon, they returned to Cotes de Forimont where the Old Bad Major was placed in command of the brigade owing to the fact that the colonel had been severely wounded the day before.

The writer spent the next few days in going to and from the front establishing a line of communication and getting information re-casualties. It was while sleeping in a French first aid station with rats and cooties the awful malady "flu" landed on him and he was evacuated to the brigade PC. Later, he took up the duties of liaison officer and then the real battles began, the battle of the Red Cross hospital at Rarécourt, Evacuation Hospitals #9 and #10; Battle of Verdun and the Battle of Bar-le-Duc. After these battles ware successfully fought and won, he reported to the Old Bad Major at Varennes and was sent back to Bourg to help get his old battalion in shape to return to the front. Thus ended the story.

Second Lieutenant William A. Dietz, Company A, 345th Tank Battalion

In November, 1917, Corporal Dietz was recommended for commission as a second lieutenant, but because of his tender years (he was not yet 21) the recommendation was not approved. (At that time the age limit for commissions was still in effect.) That was one of the few times he wished he had been born a few years earlier.

A second chance for a commission came in December, when he received an appointment to take the United States Military Academy entrance examinations. He was granted three months to brush up on his studies, for which purpose he went to Langres, the center of army schools, to attend classes to be given for men who were to take the examination. After about a month of this, he decided that should he go back to the States before the war ended, he would not in later years feel satisfied that he had done his full share of the work at hand. Therefore, he applied to GHQ to be relieved from the appointment. His request was granted and he left Langres in February to rejoin his old organization.

He found his battery in position in front of Mont Sec. It was occupying old, but excellent French gun-pits and dugouts, about 100 yards in back of what had once been the town of Apremont. The next two months were a pleasant vacation. That does not mean that nothing ever happened, for there were some highly interesting and exciting occurrences; but, in comparison with his later experiences, he knows that this was mere child's play. Corporal Dietz upon his return to his old battery, had immediately been assigned as gunner on the first piece of the battery, which, while he had been instructing on the other side of the country, had fired the first salvo fired by an American battery into the enemy lines. He had the pleasure of laying the first piece for several thousand more rounds destined for the same territory.

On April 1st an order transferring Corporal Dietz to the Tank Corps was received by him. He had requested this transfer because the tank service appealed to him as presenting opportunity for interesting, useful and exciting work. Then, too, it cannot be denied that he thought, since it was a new branch of the service, there would be excellent opportunity for advancement. He has found everything he had expected.

Upon his arrival at Bourg, where the Tank Corps was located, he was immediately impressed by the unusually high caliber of the entire enlisted personnel of the organization. Every man had come because he wanted to fight, fight hard, and fight immediately. They got their opportunity to fight, and fight as hard as men can fight, but the opportunity was far from immediate in presenting itself.

There were many months of training and fatigue. The training courses were gone over and over until they became monotonous. The fatigue details were more than plentiful. As the months went by, bringing no apparent prospects of the fighting for which they had all joined the Tank Corps, with the monotony of reiterated training courses, and over-much fatigue, the spirit of the corps gradually declined until it was barely discernible. Such expressions as, "Join the Tank Corps and get home safe," became current.

Finally, during the last week in August, came the definite news that the Tank Corps was to get to the fight. Once more the spirit of the men rose to its old pitch. Everyone was happy. The longed-for scrap was coming.

Corporal Dietz was by this time a sergeant in Company A of the then 327th Battalion, which is now known as the 345th Battalion.

On September 6th, the tanks were loaded aboard flat cars and they pulled out, destination unknown. However, no one cared where he was bound, just so that it was somewhere on the front. They finally reached their destination, which proved to be in the St. Mihiel sector. All hands spent the next two or three days, and nights too, toiling as hard as they could to get the tanks into the best possible condition to go over the top.

At 10:00 p.m. September 11th, they moved out in a blinding rainstorm for the jumping-off point, which Sergeant Dietz's company reached about 1:30 a.m. of September 12th. The last half-hour of the run was made to the music of preparatory barrage. Sergeant Dietz thought he had heard barrages in his artillery experience, but he hadn't. All others were as mere 4th of July celebrations as compared to this. One had to yell in order to make one's voice audible two feet away. It was terrific and it was wonderful.

The period of waiting till H-hour, five o'clock, should come, was a period of as great strain as any of them had gone through. There was not a yellow streak in the entire organization, but for most of the men, it was to be the first fight and the nervous tension was terrific. Five o'clock came at last and the fight started. All the world knows how it progressed. As a fight it was a picnic, but there was such work for the Tank Corps as conditions were very poor for tank work. However, all hands were well trained and willing, and the Tank Corps came out of the drive with flying colors.

They next moved up to the Argonne for the drive, which took place there. They were more confident of themselves now, for they had been through their first fight and had come out on top. Everything went along as smoothly as the most exacting soul could desire, and before long, the H-hour of the Argonne drive, 5:00 a.m. September 26th, arrived. The tanks went over, and at the outset, met as stiff a fight as their crews had ever dreamed of.

Sergeant Dietz's company was to have been in reserve the first day, according to orders, but the gods willed otherwise. They moved along through a fog, so dense that one could not see 10 feet ahead. Occasionally a few stray machine gun bullets whistled by, but there was apparently work for the reserve company to do. At about nine o'clock they suddenly emerged from the fog. About one half kilometer ahead of them was Varennes, a veritable beehive of machine gun nests and anti-tank guns. The company entered the town in column. The first two tanks fell out before long and Sergeant Dietz was ordered by his platoon leader to go ahead. He did so, but none of the other tanks followed, so he was soon alone. Arriving at the end of the street, he was undecided which way to turn. A group of 200 or 250 Boche, about 500 yards away, at the foot of a hill to the left, decided him. Starting toward them he opened fire with his machine gun. He emptied four belts into them and they seemed to fall like leaves. Then, after they had all fallen or disappeared, machine guns suddenly opened on the tank from all sides. He endeavored to cope with them with his machine gun, but met with poor success. After about 20 minutes, he was wounded, the engine was stopped, his driver had left, and the tank was burning merrily. Preferring death by machine gun bullets to being burned to death, he climbed out of his tank with a rapidity which still amazes him and broke all sprinting records traveling down a street that was strewn with the fallen walls of the houses that lined its sides. Much to his gratification and surprise, he was not hit again.

Getting out of Varennes was difficult business owing to the number of machine gunners and snipers still extant, nevertheless, he finally accomplished this feat, and after hiking several kilometers, reached a first aid station from where he was evacuated. Traveling from hospital to hospital until he had at last arrived at Bordeaux, after a month, by nagging the doctor every time he appeared, he finally received permission to return to the Tank Corps, even though his wounds were not entirely healed.

On his return to Bourg, he found that he was no longer a sergeant, but had been commissioned a second lieutenant.

Second Lieutenant Lester W. Atwood, Company A, 345th Tank Battalion

His first impression of France was more or less dismal. Landing at Le Havre in December was somewhat of a cold proposition. The hills were covered with snow and the atmosphere was very chilly. The first couple of days were spent at Rest Camp #1 and the cold made it anything but a rest camp. From there he traveled via box car, built to accommodate either Hommes [Men] 40 or Chevaux [Horses] 8, to La Courtine in La Creuse. Here it was not quite as cold and a little more comfortable time was enjoyed. He was in the famous "Spike Hennessey" outfit, with whom he had been at Fort Meyer in Virginia, and from whom he learned by experience the rudiments of being a soldier.

Corporal Atwood, for he was a corporal then, remained at La Courtine for the first three weeks in January 1918, and from there left for Montrichard, Loir-et-Cher. The climate was much milder here, so much so that some of the men in the battery even ventured to go in swimming in the river one day. It was at this place that Corporal Atwood had his opportunity to become a member of the Tank Corps. Thinking that by joining this organization he might see action quicker, he and several other companions transferred from "Spike's" outfit. After two companies of tankers were organized at Montrichard they left for Langres early in February. First, however, he was promoted to the grade of sergeant.

The two companies were met at the station by Colonel [George S.] Patton [Jr.,] who conducted B Company to the town of St. Geosmes, while [Second] Lieutenant [William H.] Williams conducted A Company to the same place, where both companies were billeted.

He remained at St. Geosmes for a week, and on February 22nd both companies moved to Bourg. The coffee of that first meal at Bourg tasted strongly of kerosene oil, since one of the cooks had put the kerosene can in the GI [Government Issue] can used for coffee.

At Bourg he drilled with his company out on the athletic field in the mud. Those first dismounted tank drills were rather discouraging, but brightened with the arrival of the first few tanks, which were viewed from a distance with more or less awe.

Things went pretty well for a time. Sergeant Atwood was made Sergeant First Class on April 16, 1918. In June, when the two original companies were split and became nuclei for the first two battalions, Sergeant Atwood became "Top Kicker" for A Company, 345th Battalion, and moved with his company to Brennes.[9] A parabola of the morale of the company, if such a thing could be depicted, would show somewhat of a declining line during those summer months. Much fatigue was the order of the day and this became more or less tiresome. However, spirits rose with prospects in September of going to the front, and remained high all the time up there.

Being First Sergeant, he did not rate a tank of his own so he went over that morning at the beginning of the St. Mihiel drive, September 12th, as a runner for the company commander's tank. The sight of all the rockets, star shells, sparklers, etc., was very pretty on that morning, but he had a few other things to think about than bright lights. After crossing our front-line trenches and getting towards the woods on the other side of the hill, machine gun bullets, both from a nest and from Boche planes, became so thick around that first tank that it was necessary to duck into an inviting shell hole near the tank for a few minutes. After crossing the Boche trenches, an occasional shell, coming in the direction of the tanks, helped to make things interesting.

Finally, the towns of Essey and Pannes were reached and the happiness of the liberated people was good to see. One French woman told him that there had been 15 Germans living in an upper room in her home and they had threatened her with a revolver at her head if she refused to comply with their wishes. Pannes was as far as he reached the first day; the night was spent in a barn with others of Company A.

The next morning a start was made at 4:00 a.m. for Boney, but later the tanks were brought back to Pannes and reformed into their proper companies and platoons. At 1:00 p.m. on Friday, the remaining tanks of the 345th Battalion took column formation and went from Pannes as far as St. Benoît. Here, it was found that the infantry had reached their objective, so the tanks returned toward Boney where they were camouflaged just in time to escape the vigilance of many German planes, which immediately came out.

One night was spent in this position near St. Benoît and on Saturday night the tanks were moved further back toward Pannes and camouflaged. The next night, Sunday, was spent in moving back to the lying in point in the woods near Bermicourt.

He remained here for three or four days and then a start was made to Clermont-en-Argonne. He slept on a flat car underneath a tarpaulin until Clermont was reached. Here, the company stayed on the safe side of a hill and from its comfortable quarters watched Clermont shelled daily.

Argonne first day. It will be remembered that the Argonne fight began on Thursday, September 26th. Here also Sergeant Atwood was tankless, so became a runner as in the former drive.

His company moved into position about 11:00 p.m. September 25th. There was little sleep to be enjoyed that night due to the artillery preparations going on. At 5:00 a.m. the tanks proceeded from their concealed position across our trenches and on towards Varennes.

Everything went fine for a time. There was little enemy artillery fire in the earlier part of the morning, possibly due to the presence of a heavy fog. Going along with the company commander's tank, there was not much to fear at first. Soon, however, a machine gun opened up and the safest policy then was to duck behind a bush and let it fire at the tanks which went on. By the time it was safe to proceed, the tanks were ahead in the fog and had changed their course going to Varennes. Sergeant Atwood followed in the direction he thought they were and ran into a German trench, which had just been captured by our first line of infantry. Here, the Boche machine guns, snipers and artillery played such a game that it would have been suicide to get up on a parapet since the fog had now cleared up. He stayed here with the infantry for a while, and hearing that the tanks were in the town of Varennes over to the right, resolved to go there, one way or another. Going along the trench in the direction of the town, he ran across one of the tank drivers of his company, namely Corporal Joline. Inquiring why this driver was here, Sergeant Atwood was informed that the driver's tank commander, Sergeant Wiley, had been shot through the jaw and had been taken to the rear. Finding the tank was quite near, Sergeant Atwood saw his opportunity to get a tank, which he had wanted all along. Taking his tank, he joined three others which were coming from Varennes going in the direction of the Argonne Forest. The woods were skirted and nothing was seen of the enemy, although an occasional machine gun was opened up. These four tanks went on to a hill directly west of Varennes where two German 77's were found, just recently abandoned. They were the guns which had been firing on the tanks and trenches from which he had just come. Here, a stop was made, tanks were gassed, oiled and watered and then the four tanks in charge of Sergeant Atwood proceeded towards Apremont as that was to be the first day's objective.

By this time it had become dusk and was soon dark. Proceeding possibly for a mile, he ran into a captain of some company of the 28th Division, who desired him to take his four tanks and go in search of some machine guns, which were bothering his infantry. As it was too dark then for the use of the tanks and as the ground was unfamiliar, it was decided to camouflage the tanks for the night and report back to Varennes for orders from some tank officer. With Sergeant Jones and Sergeant [Samuel F.] Reece he walked back to Varennes, but no one was found in Varennes, so after burying Sergeant Raymond C. Chisolm, who so bravely died making the supreme sacrifice, they returned to their tanks and went to sleep. At about 2:30 a.m. Sergeant Atwood was awakened by a lieutenant of the infantry who requested that he come to see the colonel of a certain regiment, in his PC, which was not far away. The colonel said that he wanted the tanks to be used in an attack that morning at 5:30 a.m. Although Sergeant Atwood had no orders from any officers in the Tank Corps to make such an attack, still he knew that the object of the tanks at the front was to help the infantry, so he resolved to take the chance.

Second day. Tanks were in the position designated by the colonel at 5:00 a.m. A barrage of cast iron one-pounders from two 37mm guns was all of the artillery preparation that they had. The attack was to start at 5:30 a.m. At this time it was too dark for tanks to see anything so the colonel put off the attack until 5:45 a.m. At 5:45 it was still dark and raining, so it was put off until 6:00 a.m., at which time it was just about light enough to see 50 meters ahead.

The four tanks took line formation with intervals of about 100 meters and proceeded at the rate of about 50 meters a minute. First one tank fell out, then the other two followed suit and Sergeant Atwood, with his driver, was left alone ahead of our own infantry and being fired upon with hidden machine guns, snipers, hand grenades and anti-tank guns. He had the satisfaction of routing out several Boche and chasing them way over to the woods. On the way back to his original position his tank refused to function properly and the driver could get little power from it. Not knowing what was the matter, and not wanting to be caught in an embarrassing position in German territory, they got back behind a hill in our own territory as soon as possible, where it was found that an anti-tank bullet had gone through the back of the tank and into the radiator, thus causing the water to run out and the engine to get red hot! It was also learned that the causes of the other tanks falling out were: that Corporal [James M.] Whitney had not been able to see anything through his sight, so had returned; that the fan belt of Sergeant Jones' tank had broken; and finally that Sergeant Reece, in the last tank, had been killed. They now had three available tanks, as the fan belt had been repaired. Sergeant Atwood took the tank previously occupied by Sergeant Reece, and with the other two tanks they skirted the woods over at the left where more Germans were routed out of their lairs. Later in the day Montblainville was reached and a warm reception was given from Boche 77's, none of which hit any of the tanks, fortunately.

The tanks were then put in charge of [First] Lieutenant [Thomas C.] Brown who arrived on the scene. The writer here would like to express his appreciation of the work done by Lieutenant Brown, who, with unceasing efforts, directed the affairs of his company during this drive, and who was so indifferent to heavy shell and machine gun fire in the face of the enemy. The tanks were sent back by him to Varennes for the night for gas, oil and water, and returned the next morning at five o'clock.

For the next two weeks Sergeant Atwood remained at or near Montblainville with his company. He was able in a few instances to participate in some of the tank patrols which were carried out in the vicinity of Apremont. It was near Apremont that Sergeant [Earling F.] Dutt, who was to be commissioned, Corporal [James M.] Whitney, privates [James M.] Casey and [Frederick J.] Wagner, were killed in action and although they, together with sergeants Chisholm and Reece will not be seen any more, still their memory shall live for the writer as long as he lives, and their example will be an inspiration for him in any future crisis of his life.

On October 5th he was sworn in at Montblainville in a dugout as a second lieutenant. Several days later the tank companies which had been operating in the Argonne were assembled at Varennes and as many tanks as possible were brought back, repaired, and made ready for the next drive.

With the exception of one Provisional Company under Captain [Courtney H.] Barnard, which stayed at Varennes, the rest of the men and officers returned to the Tank Center. Lieutenant Atwood, with about nine other officers, remained with the provisional company, which immediately moved to Exermont on Sunday, October 13, 1918, where Captain Barnard established his PC.

The next morning it was the first section's turn to make the attack so Lieutenant Atwood with [First] Lieutenant [Allan H.] Geddes and [Second] Lieutenant [Churchill C.] Peters started about 4:30 a.m. with 15 tanks for the jumping-off place. By the time that place was reached there were nine available tanks left. They passed from Exermont through Fleville and had just gone beyond Sommerance, when the first Boche were encountered. On this morning "Jerry" seemed to have an especial grudge against the slits in the tanks for he played on the slits with his machine guns in such a manner that the inside of the tank looked more like a Fourth of July celebration than anything else. It was a great source of satisfaction for him, however, to know that he got a few Boche that morning before he had to withdraw. Lieutenant Atwood received two splashes in the left forearm and hand and his driver, Corporal May, was shot in the mouth, so that it was necessary to turn back.

The other tanks which had been in the fight too, also turned back and after going just beyond Sommerance, which was under quite heavy shell fire, it was learned that almost everyone had been wounded, one way or another. Lieutenant Geddes thought he had a lost his eye. Corporal Williams, it is believed, did lose his eye. Sergeant Jones received a splinter in his eye, and others were incapacitated in various ways. Let it be said here that both Sergeant Jones and Sergeant Young, who were with Lieutenant Atwood that morning, did fine work all through the drive, and that while the writer did not personally see any act of especial bravery on their part, still he had it from authentic reports that both did commendable action in the hot fighting near Apremont.

The tanks, under orders, were withdrawn to Exermont and Lieutenant Atwood went to the first aid station and there his experience at the front ended and his hospital career began, for he went to no less than eight hospitals before he returned to the center for duty.

The foregoing account concludes the more important events which happened in Lieutenant Atwood's sojourn in France.

Captain Ernest A. Higgins, Company C, 345th Tank Battalion

The writer reported for duty with the Tank Corps January 17, 1918. At this time the Tank Corps consisted of 22 officers and no enlisted men. The equipment was one Packard truck in part repair. Immediately after reporting, he attended the automatic weapon school at Fort de Peigney for an 11-day course, reporting back at Touraine Barracks and commenced training with the means at hand. About the middle of February, the first troops arrived and Company A was formed at St. Geosmes. The detachment remained there for one week and then moved to Bourg.

The writer was assigned as machine gun instructor for the Tank Corps and began training at the Tank Center. In March, the first tanks arrived and tank training commenced. The corps was increased in size; Company B had been organized in February and on April 3rd, 93 men had arrived, out of which Company C was organized and the writer placed in command. Intensive training in machine gun, 37mm [cannon], tank driving and maneuvering continued throughout the summer. Notwithstanding the hard training, the spirit shown by the officers and enlisted men was splendid; all looking forward to the day of leaving for the front. The entire organization was keyed to the very highest pitch. On September 2nd, the 326th and 327th Battalions were ordered to go into camp preliminary to entrainment for the front. On September 5th, the writer received orders to join the 327th Battalion and was attached to Company C. On September 6th, he superintended the overhauling and testing of all machine guns and 37mm guns in the tanks preparatory to departure. Owing to some confusion, after having entrained on September 9th, and an uneventful trip to the point selected for detrainment, the actual detrainment did not take place until the night of the 11th. After a night march, through roads jammed with artillery and ankle deep mud, we arrived at Bois de la Hazelle, at H-hour plus 30 minutes or 5:30 a.m. September 12th. Due to the lack of gasoline all the tanks could not go forward at this time and the commanding officer of Company C, Captain Courtney H. Barnard, was ordered forward with eight tanks; the remainder remaining at this point in reserve. Nineteen of the original 20 tanks had arrived at this point.

Battle of St. Mihiel

The writer viewed the battle of St. Mihiel from the heights of Bois de la Hazelle. At 11:00 a.m. he went forward one kilometer with two tanks and pulled two tanks out that had been ditched. At 12:30 p.m. with the battalion commander, 327th Battalion, he went forward as far as the village of Bony, but met no resistance, everything having been cleared out before. On the following day, Friday the 13th, he reported to Pannes for gasoline and provisions. That afternoon he went forward as far as St. Benoît, and upon arrival was ordered to withdraw and camouflage his tanks in the woods near St. Benoît station.

On the evening of the 15th, all the tanks under the command of Major [Sereno E.] Brett started back to Bois de la Hazelle, a distance of 12 kilometers, arriving there after about 14 hours' march. The writer accompanied this column and remained at this point until Thursday the 19th, at which time he received orders to take 15 tanks and report to Bermicourt for orders. He had under his command 60 men and four officers. On arriving there, he found 18 five-ton Pierce Arrow trucks awaiting to load tank materiel. His orders were to load tanks. The trucks belonged to the French and between loading tanks and arguing with the Frenchmen, all were kept busy. It was necessary to remove the hoods and tails of the tanks and use a crowbar as a shoe horn to get the tanks loaded. About 9:30 p.m., after having loaded 11 tanks with considerable difficulty, the night being exceedingly dark and the rain coming down in torrents, orders were received to unload and release the trucks. This was completed at 11:30 p.m., everybody tired and wet and not in the best of humor. However, matters brightened a great deal when [First] Lieutenant Harry [E.] Gibbs announced that our "step-father" was awaiting with a hot meal. The "step-father" being none other than a German rolling kitchen captured at Pannes. It will remain a mystery to the writer where the men found billets that night, for search as he might, he could find none. At daybreak, another meeting was held, with "step-father" presiding. Lieutenant Gibbs, in charge of the ration and gasoline trucks and the rolling kitchen, never failed to make good in the subsequent six days, in keeping the men in splendid spirits.

Playing One-Night Stands to the Hun

At about 1:00 p.m. September 20th, narrow gauge flat cars being available, the loading of the tanks upon them was begun. At 3:30 p.m. 14 of the tanks were loaded, but no suitable car being at hand to load the fifteenth, and the track of this tank being broken in an attempt to load it sidewise, it was left with two days' rations for the crew and ordered to report to the 327th [345th] Battalion, which was entraining near her. The train left Bermicourt at 4:00 p.m., traveling by narrow gauge from Bermicourt to Tremblecourt, Rosieres and Bois de Nolon, the only incident of the trip worth mentioning was the derailment of one car, which was remedied in 30 minutes. We arrived at Bois de Nolon at 1:00 a.m., September 21st, and were most happy to meet "step-father" again. We remained in this wood until about 2:00 p.m., and then proceeded, in two sections, via Belleville, Bezaumont, Loisy and the Foret de Facq, arriving at the latter place at 8:00 p.m. on the same night. Unloaded immediately and camouflaged the tanks, and the following day made reconnaissance of the three routes to be followed that night to run into the German lines at the following named places: Lesmenils, Morville-sur-Seille, Port-sur-Seille. At 7:00 p.m. on the 22nd, three separate platoons, one commanded by [Second] Lieutenant [John W.] Rey, one by [Second] Lieutenant [Harry D.] Heitz and one by [First] Lieutenant [Robert C.] Llewellyn, proceeded to run into the German lines and executed a good American bluff.

In the course of this reconnaissance, Lieutenant Rey had run into quite a bit of trouble at the north end of Bois de Facq; however, there were no casualties. The writer remained at the train and as the tanks arrived about midnight, loaded them. All tanks had returned and were loaded before 1:00 a.m., September 23rd. We immediately left for Sivry. Shortly after leaving the Bois de Facq, Fritz turned his earnest attention upon that region with his artillery.

We arrived at Sivry about 4:00 a.m. the 23rd, finished unloading about 5:30 a.m. and set out to find a way to the Bois de la Fourasse. From there we went to make a run to Nomeny, Letricourt, Ajoncourt and Chenicourt. A peculiar situation developed here. Owing to the fact that at Sivry we had unloaded at the bottom of a saucer and could not get over the rim without being observed by the Hun, we remained at the bottom and made our unloading point our departure position for that night's operations. In view of the distance to be covered, the run to Nomeny was canceled and our attention divided to the other named places.

The same platoon commanders made the run successfully that night, all tanks returning and being loaded before 1:00 a.m. on September 24th. Our never failing supply officer, Lieutenant Gibbs, was on hand again with a hot meal. The return to Belleville was made the same morning and during the forenoon we loaded the tanks directly from the narrow gauge to the standard gauge cars with orders to report to Recicourt, Verdun sector. (The writer has since learned from a reliable source that the feint operations of these 14 tanks drew two divisions of German troops to that sector. If such was the case both officers and men feel fully rewarded for the hard work and hardship then endured on this trip.) This trip, which should have taken six or seven hours, took 48 hours. We were held up at Revigny for 12 hours, but this time we realized that we would be late for the fight which would start on the 26th. We arrived at Dombasle at 3:00 a.m. on the morning of the 26th with the preliminary bombardment in full swing.

Operation in the Argonne

Because the track was out it was impossible to get to Recicourt, so we unloaded at Dombasle. In unloading, two track pins, which had become worn with the excessive running of the tanks during the preceding days, broke. The writer started out to get in touch with the battalion, leaving the tanks with the platoon commanders to make such repairs as could be done with the limited means at hand. Some material was secured from the French tanks which helped immensely. Orders were received from the 1st Brigade headquarters to make a night march to the Cotes de Forimont. We got as far as Neuville, on the night of the 26th, at which place the last of the 14 tanks which started from Bermicourt limped in, about 2:00 a.m., on the 27th. Some had fan belts mended in three places and some of the men used their shoe laces to mend them. It is worth mentioning that from the 19th, when we first loaded at Bermicourt, the men worked almost continuously; the time not used in moving or maneuvering being devoted to the care of the tanks and such repairs as could be made. Not a single grumble was heard. In this connection, Captain Nash, of the engineers at Belleville, told the writer it was the most remarkable body of men he had ever seen.

The 27th of September was devoted to the repair of tanks. On the evening of this day a march from Neuville to Varennes was commenced. On account of the mine craters in the road, there was an acute congestion of traffic and it was impossible to get all of the tanks through. The writer received orders about 10:00 p.m. to report to the commander of the 91st Division, east of Very, with five tanks. At daybreak on the morning of the 28th, he succeeded in getting five tanks through to Varennes. After having been filled with gasoline, oiled and overhauled, and with two days' rations provided, the tanks started from Very, arriving there at 4:00 a.m. They were reported to Major General William H. Johnston, commander of the 91st Division, and assigned by him to the left of the 182nd Brigade as combat liaison between that brigade and the 35th Division.

At 6:45 p.m., without any preliminary bombardment, we went over the top.

We met very little resistance until about two kilometers out. The policy of the Hun gunners was to let the tanks pass rather than fire upon them. The writer was commanding a platoon. No reserve crews were available and only three runners to the entire platoon. After going forward two-and-a-half kilometers some bad ground was encountered slow and wet and filled with large shell holes and old trenches. Two tanks were ditched, the writer's going into a large shell hole, the other going sidewise into a ditch. Machine gun nests were known to be in the vicinity, but, to use the words of our colonel, "We had to get there." There was nothing to be done but get out and pull the tanks out of the holes. The writer and his driver dismounted and upon doing so received a warm reception from Fritz in the shape of machine gun fire from three different directions. One tank attacked the machine gun nest, which contained several machine guns, and the tank which was towing the others out covered the work of the writer and his driver with its fire. At this time, one of our Hun friends sent up a Very pistol signal, which in two minutes brought down a standing barrage. (The Hun did not live to see the result of his work for he was immediately killed by Sergeant Knotts of Company C, 326th [344th] Battalion.) The tanks were fortunately in a hollow and not subject to direct fire.

The writer had had many busy moments, but the next five minutes of that time will stand out as the busiest moments of his life. Both tanks were unditched and the four started for Fritz's stronghold, receiving an extremely warm welcome. The writer had four machine guns turned on his tank at almost 15 yards range, with the result that his driver was totally blinded and himself, wounded in his right arm and right eye. The coolness displayed by Corporal McGinnis, Company C, 327th [345th] Battalion, with both eyes out was remarkable. He continued to operate his tank under the direction of the writer until they could change places as there were no reserve crews and nothing could be done by withdrawing; much to Fritz's joy, if the tattoo of bullets beating on the tank was his way of expressing it. After driving back a kilometer, being unable to see clearly owing to wounds received, the tank plunged into a large shell hole from which it was impossible to extract it. The remainder of the trip to a dressing station was made on foot, the writer leading his driver, who presented a ghastly appearance, his entire face and chest being a mass of blood.

During this trip, between dodging hidden snipers and shells, we were kept quite busy. Upon arriving at the dressing station, in addition to having the wounds treated, we received hot coffee, which was welcome indeed, for it was the first that we had had in about 26 hours. That evening we were both sent to a field hospital and from there to a base hospital. This ended the part played by the writer in the battles in which the tanks participated as he was not again returned to the front.

First Lieutenant Harry E. Gibbs, Company C, 345th Tank Battalion

The air service can boast of their fighting squadrons and the infantry of their shock troops, but the stunt pulled by a small group of tanks on a little junket trip, between the two offensives at St. Mihiel and De Foret de Argonne (Argonne Forest), deserves some recognition. It did from the Germans, as shown by their intelligence report, will quote it later. It had none of the thrills of fighting, but for the thrills from cold, rain, mud, all work and no sleep, it had no equal. The "Traveling Circus" of the tanks was a nickname given to the trip by the men and I can say here, never was there a finer bunch of enlisted men brought together in a company. Not a growl from the start to the finish and all of them knew they had no fight to look forward to. And these men had been thru St. Mihiel, the Argonne and between, but when men are kept busy they always have better morale.

General [John J.] Pershing [commander of the AEF] wanted to make the Germans believe that we would attack directly after reducing the St. Mihiel salient, in the region of Pont-à-Mousson, the logical place in order to capture Metz, this feint to be made while the First Army was preparing for the fight at the Argonne that was made two weeks later. The job was given to the tanks.

Our orders were received at the Bois de la Hazelle on the afternoon of September 17th, the position where we had withdrawn after the St. Mihiel push. This place was knee-deep with mud and water and still raining. Captain Ernest A. Higgins was put in command with lieutenants Robert C. Llewellyn, Harry D. Heitz, John W. Rey and myself, 56 men and 15 tanks. We had an hour to assemble and be ready to start to our loading place at Bermicourt. We were ready and stood ready until 24 hours later when our orders came and we left for Bermicourt at 4:30 the afternoon of the 18th of September. Our tanks were the casts-offs of those not wanted by the battalion, so we had mechanical trouble before our column moved a hundred yards; towed several and all reported by 6:00 p.m. The distance being four kilometers raining hard, dark as pitch and no lights could be used.

This company had no repair unit. We did have a few extra track pins, fan belts and one track plate; no medical men and we were totally independent—get supplies where we could and just go. We did have a life-saver in an old German rolling kitchen that the tanks captured in Le Thillot. Without it we would have lived on cold meat, but with this old "step-father" as it was called, we were continually on the move and it did duty for 24 hours of the day.

For discouragement at the start we had it. We were to load our tanks on 5½-ton Pierce Arrow trucks, furnished by the French. They were there, 18, 15 for tanks and the other for personnel and supplies. We began to load at 7:00 p.m.

All tails of the tanks had to be taken off and also the domes. This was real work as every tail was loaded with bidons and camouflaged nets. Cribbing had to be built and also found first, and to have a French camion [transport truck] driver back up each time to our loading platform on a road heavy with traffic was a new experience, and cusses were as heavy and thick as the rain and mud.[10] By 11:00 we had 13 tanks loaded when the French sergeants stopped us and then the corps ordered us to unload as the use of the trucks had been changed in the meantime to carry artillery ammunition. And so our process was reversed, but not quite as easy as telling about it. We then hid the tanks in the ruins and camouflaged and waited for daylight. We were to load and go by narrow-gauge railroad. Our sections came by noon and we finished by 3:30 of the 19th. We were regularly blocked by traffic on the road and one tank broke a fan belt, track, and the other track off. We left with 14 in all, our destination Foret de Brule, some kilometers behind Pont-à-Mousson.

This trip was about 20 kilometers direct. The night was clear and cold. Boche planes were bombing the back areas; some were comfortably close. Our sections had to be split several times to get up grades and two cards "jumped the track."[11] This meant the loading and unloading process of tanks. Our supplies and rolling kitchen went by road direct to the woods on three trucks. We landed the following morning at the Foret de Brule and the men tried to sleep in the open flats, but it was too cold. There we "laid-in" until the afternoon of the 20th, when we left for the Bois du Facq directly in rear of the front lines. Unloaded by the next morning and no sleep again, but plenty of rain. These woods rivaled the trenches for rats and men had to have guards to sleep with ease. The night of the 21st, the company split into three platoons and ran up to the front lines over different and widely separated routes, and made as many tracks and as much noise as possible. They did it with fan belts off, tracks off, mufflers and engines red-hot, and all the time Jerry shelled the roads. One place he gassed. This maneuver was carried out with a hurried reconnaissance before dark that night, over new roads, and through French guards. Reloaded that night and started for Sivry; arrived the morning of the 23d, under the worst weather conditions possible—men riding all night on the little flat cars and no protection and with no instructions how to determine where we would maneuver that night. It was impossible to get near the front lines in the daytime on account of a ridge we would have to cross. All the tanks were cripples, so we could only get two platoons, but they covered a wide front. The shelling was especially heavy as Jerry was on the lookout. Trouble all the time mechanically. We loaded that night on the narrow-gauge for Belleville and reloaded on the broad-gauge the following noon bound for the Argonne with no plans for the fight or what we would do. Had a flatcar for each tank, one for gas and two "8 Cheveaux or 40 Hommes" (8 Horses or 40

Men) cars for the men and officers. Our trip was thru Toul and everywhere the tanks were given a welcome, and was a real treat for the men. Pulled into Revigny on the 25th and then the slow ride to Dombasle, where the freight trains were end to end. We arrived at 3:30 on the morning of the attack on the 26th, and were in it by the 29th.

The whole expedition was remarkable in the fact that all the tanks left Dombasle and arrived in Varennes, although between the two attacks, they covered at least 20 kilometers a night with no repairs, except those done by the men. Captain [Ernest A.] Higgins and Lieutenant Llewellyn were untiring workers and to this work all credit can go. It was being placed in a woods in an unusual situation and new territory and depending on your own resources to carry it through. Loaded and unloaded our tanks on narrow-gauge and broad-gauge, in rain, mud, dark and one time with same 400's, [400mm] railroad artillery, right alongside, barking every night for ten days, and yet the men worked without a word.

The result: that the Germans moved several divisions to prepare for an attack because 100 American tanks were moving into that sector. The "circus" didn't gain ground, but it did cover it with speed just to fool the Hun.

First Lieutenant Harvey L. Harris, Company C, 345th Tank Battalion

Every time I look out my window here I see a ridge which is the old valley wall of the now insignificant Aire River. It is about 400 meters from Varennes and by looking more determinedly, I can see the very place our tanks laid under its protection. We were there for two nights, i.e., the nights of September 27th and 28th. On the morning of the 29th, with the 35th Division having awfully hard going south and southwest of Charpentry, we were ordered up to assist.

I'd been up most of the night before and felt pretty rotten. At 4:00 a.m. we started to get ready. Our mess sergeant had been up since 1:00 a.m. Water for coffee had to be carried from a foot bridge here at Varennes, etc. At 5:00 a.m. we had coffee in the rain and dark. I felt better, but was too busy looking after the tanks of my platoon to do much damning of the Boche for making us get into the war. Just before leaving, a lieutenant stuck a bottle of something at me—"Boche cognac." Bien [All right], and I felt "trays beanser."[12]

About 200 meters from juncture of national highway, I could see that the Boche were shelling the junction with GI cans [artillery]. A captain, whom I knew was on the staff of 35th Division stopped me and said, "Thank God, we can't advance on account of machine guns." It wouldn't have made any difference to him if opposition was 420's [420mm howitzers]. He'd have wanted our little tanks to clean them up anyway. It's surprising what they ask us to do.

Doughboys to generals have sent us against places a battleship couldn't capture, but that's all outside the story. "There are snipers along the road. You'd better get in your tank," he cautioned. I walked a little further and saw a couple of doughboys go down—then decided to get aboard. It isn't an easy matter for me to get into the tank through those two small rear doors even when in training—let alone with haversack, pistol, belt, etc. I was hung up for a while, but got in and lumbered down the road. There didn't seem to be anything going on so I climbed out and sat just back of the turret, my feet hanging inside and my body almost entirely protected in front by the turret. I passed the general and his staff sitting in a gully at the side of the road. I'll never forget the appreciative "You're the man we're waiting for" expression as I rode by. This look did more to thrill me than words could possibly have done.

And still nothing stirring! As we approached this juncture though, things warmed up. The Boche weren't more than 500 meters away with their 77's and 88's, and they knew the importance of shelling roads!

I was jarred several times from concussions of exploding shells. Then I noticed my CO [commanding officer] at side of road (I spoke above of general and staff in gully—three feet deep—at edge of road). When one speaks of a general's PC (headquarters) he often imagines the "old man" is in a bomb proof shelter, orderlies running around, telephones ringing and the fight miles up ahead. Not so in this war! I haven't seen a brigade yet but what the general was up in front and his PC wherever he happened to be, along the road or in a shell hole.

He motioned for me to pull tanks over behind a hedge, which I did, and camouflaged them as best I could. But they'd been heard rumbling along. It would be luck if they weren't hit. But they weren't, although whizz-bangs [77mm field artillery], the kind you don't hear until they hit, came all around them all afternoon until the batteries that were firing had to withdraw. With artillery hidden and firing at your tanks, the only thing to do is hide yourself and them.

After the tanks were camouflaged, I went with my captain, several other lieutenants and the men to a gully nearby, this gully ran out into the Aire valley and after we'd settled down to an all-afternoon wait, I decided to see what I could by going to the edge of this gully and looking across the Aire valley about 1,500 meters. There, I was safe from every shell, and looking out across the river saw advancing tanks in line, infantry following at several hundred meters—just as pretty as the shows we'd put on at Bourg for the staff school.

At the far edge of the flats was the east edge of the Argonne. Everything seemed to be going well until a shell exploded amidst the infantry, then another in front of the advancing tanks, then another to the right. The doughboys immediately flopped down and the tanks continued, not knowing it. Then I saw a puff of smoke where the forest sort of jutted out towards me and a shell exploded within 10 feet of a tank. Several turned for a depression near the river, the others went for the woods, not knowing where the shots were coming from. And there I sat unable to do a thing, probably the only one who knew where those guns were, the flash had told me. With the aid of glasses I could actually see the Boche gun crews working, loading, and if my voice would have carried, I could have yelled the instant the #1 (man who fires the piece) had his hand on the grip and was going to fire. But that was out of the question. I thought of firing over at it with a 37mm from a tank—but probably wouldn't get within hundreds of yards. The range was, I should say, 2,000 meters; too much for a 37mm.

What to do? It was getting late. In half an hour it would be dusk. The doughboys, I could faintly make out, were digging in. The tanks were in the woods and might come any moment directly in front of the battery (for by this time I had been able to make out at least three guns) and be blown to pieces. Something had to be done damned quick.

I looked around and a captain and two enlisted men were approaching my point of vantage, which was darned good for an observation point. The men carried wire and field phones. As the captain came nearer I saw his crossed cannons [insignia on his collar] and before I could say a word he said, "I am going to set up our forward PC here, my battery is just back there a way. See anything to shoot at?"

"Well, I'll be damned," was all I could say, and pointed across the valley. What had sent him there at that minute? Three minutes later I probably would have gone back to the place I'd left the captain and he might not have seen the battery as it was fast getting dark.

Then I "came out of it" in a fraction of a second and told him the whole story. Meanwhile he'd ordered a phone rigged up from the battery. While waiting for this connection he set up his telescope and figured out his data, etc. "Hurry, hurry, hurry! In 10 minutes we won't be able to see a thing 100 yards away," I thought to myself.

"Hello. Yes, this is Captain (I don't remember his name). Is Lt.______ there? Take this data, work fast. Range 2200, (deflection something else)—HE sweeping." Four reports and they whistled over us. Four flashes, I estimated a couple of hundred yards short of target. "2600" and he kicked up the range 400. They were lost in the woods. "They ought to be worried now," he said. (The deflection was okay) "2400, three rounds on second piece close 5"—and 12 of 'em went over us, and eight at least landed right at that corner of woods. "That's got em." I saw two guns get direct hits. The crews must be finished too. And it got dark so that we could hardly see the valley directly below us.

"You've done something today, captain," I said. "Wasn't that fine," he answered.

I went back to the tanks and found that a runner had been looking for me for an hour. Most of the tanks had already gone back behind the hill toward Varennes. What a different night I spent to the preceding two. It was still cold, wet and raining—but I was warm within.

"Tomorrow I'll show him that observation tower near Apremont. Some more good fun," I thought as I sat on the running board of our Mack truck (the inside and underneath was crowded with enlisted men) and went to sleep as best I could.

Second Lieutenant Harry M. Mayne, Company C, 345th Tank Battalion

About September 1st, 1918, his outfit was ordered to entrain, and move to a position in the Saint Mihiel sector near Bermicourt. His battalion moved from the detraining point to the "laying in" point under cover of night. In this position in the woods, while waiting for "D" day, the time was spent repairing the tanks and getting them into battle condition. On or about the 11th of September, the battalion was ordered to the "jumping-off" point. They laid in overnight in a terrific rain storm. After an all-night barrage, they "jumped off" at about 5:00 a.m. The tanks moved forward toward a point in the German lines which had been previously designated. Owing to the fact that the barrage of the previous night had been so terrific, the tanks encountered great difficulty in crossing the trenches, but through the work of the engineer platoon assigned to the battalion, the trenches were filled in and made passable for the tanks. At this point the enemy artillery found our range and started to drop shells around us. Lieutenant Mayne's tank was put out of action and he continued forward in one of the other tanks in his platoon. After crossing the trenches, the tanks moved forward behind the infantry and came to a point where hostile machine guns were holding up the infantry. As soon as the tanks came into sight the enemy left their posts running, in this way showing their great fear of the tanks. The remaining tanks moved forward to Essey, and from there to Varennes, where the tanks ran out of gasoline and were compelled to wait a few hours for supplies. After the gasoline and ammunition had been replenished they moved forward and continued on with the infantry to the main objective, Saint Benoit.

After having attained the objective, the tanks were moved back to a position in the woods, about two kilometers behind the lines, and were prepared to assist the infantry in case of a counter attack by the Germans. After laying in for two days they were ordered back to the former "laying in" point and were there cleaned and repaired. A few days later the battalion again entrained and moved to a position in the woods near Clermont, in the Verdun sector.

In our new position a complete reconnaissance of the terrain was made by the battalion reconnaissance officers. On the night of September 25th, Company A moved to its new "laying in" position a short distance behind the front lines, and at 5:00 a.m. "jumped off" behind the infantry. Under a heavy fog they advanced in column, after having crossed the trenches. It was impossible to see in any direction, but the tanks were led by [Second] Lieutenant [Guy R.] Chamberlin, and through his knowledge of the territory and his fine maneuvering they managed to reach the town of Varennes, where Lieutenant Chamberlin was killed by machine gun fire, after having completed his duty. The town was full of machine gun nests and anti-tank rifles. Captain [Carl H.] McMillan called Lieutenant Mayne to his tank and told him to take his platoon forward and clean up the machine gun nests. The infantry was too far behind the tanks, and did not follow them into the town. At this time the enemy artillery got the range on the tanks and a great many of them were put out by this fire. Lieutenant Mayne's tank having been put out of action, he rallied the remaining tanks (six in number) and sent them forward, while he, himself, moved back to find the infantry to show them the way through the town. That night the reserve tanks arrived and Lieutenant Mayne rallied all of the tanks into action and reported with them to [First] Lieutenant [Thomas C.] Brown.

Lieutenant Brown and Lieutenant Mayne took the remaining tanks forward the following morning and were ordered by the infantry commander to move to the edge of the Argonne Woods and clean up the machine gun nests. The morning was spent moving up and down along the edge of the woods, cleaning out all the visible machine gun nests. After having completed this task, they moved forward to Montblainville. The following morning the tanks moved forward to Apremont. It was a very difficult task for the tanks, as they were compelled to attack this town several times, as the infantry was unable to follow them. Finally, the town was taken, and the tanks were rallied at Montblainville for the refill of gasoline and ammunition.

Second Lieutenant Harold H. Neff, Company B, 330th Tank Battalion

[Harold Neff's battle experiences were during his service as a noncommissioned officer in the 345th Tank Battalion on September 12, 1918. He received a second lieutenant's commission on October 2, 1918, and a subsequent transfer to the 330th Tank Battalion (see University of Virginia Alumni News, November 25, 1918, 54).]

The first day of the attack my company was supposed to be in reserve. After the attack had been well started, we got along, over trenches, down into a small valley. The incessant pop-pop of machine guns was heard not far away. The column stopped, as the leading elements were having great difficulty with a wide and deep trench. Suddenly, in the quietness, crash went a shell right over them. We decided that it was best to scatter helter-skelter until crossing could be negotiated. Machine gun bullets started singing quite a bit. Under the calm supervision of Colonel [George S.] Patton [Jr.] after several tanks had unsuccessfully attempted to cross and were ditched in the mire, first platoon in my company succeeded in passing, and were sent up the hill to get those machine gun nests. Before long, my tank, on account of various difficulties met by the others, was all alone. We kept on, not being certain where the Germans were, or whether any were really there, and popped a few shots into all the favorable cover. Suddenly, the front of the tank seemed ablaze with heat and smoke. I could not exactly understand what was on. I inquired of the gunner if he was firing. "No," he said. Then I guessed. We advanced, but on account of the lay of the ground could not exactly see what was before us. Suddenly, right in front of us, bobbed up, just like little Jack used to leap from the jumping-box, a whole bunch of Germans and went running all hunched over, like little lambs, up the way. It was comical to see them run.

We kept on going, toward a village that lay high on a hill, fair and beautiful with its distorted and crumbling walls. Nothing could be seen on either side. We arrived on a high precipice, and could find no course to descend it into the small valley, from which the village clambered up the hill. At last, after patrolling hither and thither, we attempted what seemed to offer a fair method of descent, and much to our disgust, owing to crumbling of the banks of a ditch that was overgrown with grass and partially concealed, we suddenly turned topsy-turvy, and lay there in the hollow. Then, while we were still pondering what we should do with our overturned steed, up on the precipice behind us came the rest of the tanks and let loose on the village with all their guns, right over our heads. And Fritz started back with a battery he had over there in the woods. The gunner decided to climb up after help, but when he stuck his head over, he saw all the guns of the tanks pointed towards him and he decided it would be perhaps the better part of wisdom to stay right where he was. The next day we finally succeeded in getting ourselves extracted.

301st Tank Battalion

Captain Franklin V. Tenkonchy, Headquarters, 305th Tank Brigade

Now that the World War is over, those that participated in that great struggle, that changed the political and economic conditions of all the countries in Europe, can now gather their senses and minds together and look back and tell us of their experiences, which I am sure will be very interesting to you all, as you sit by your fireside, and casually take up the deeds of some of our brave and courageous boys who went over and done their bit.

The experiences and memories of Captain F. V. Tenkonchy, TC, Tactical Officer of 305th Brigade, Tank Corps, USA are filled with the self-abnegation of a body of red blooded Americans ready and willing to do their share of real honest to goodness fighting and thereby assist in ridding the world of German Kultur, as defined to the universe by that eminent authority, the spokesman of Prussian barbarism, the Kaiser, who later developed to be the last ruler of the Hohenzollern family to reign over the arch criminal nation of the world, namely Germany.

At last the day, which had been so fervently yearned for, arrived and with it came orders for Captain F. V. Tenkonchy, Engineer, RC [Reserve Corps] who was stationed at Camp Lee, Petersburg, Va., on duty with the 305th Engineers to proceed overseas, and report to the commanding officer at England for duty. The captain received these orders with utter amazement and dumbfoundedness. He had to read the orders two or three times to be absolutely sure, that there was no mistake. This habit of being sure of his orders came in two ways, the first, the underlying principle of military training, that of being very sure that he understood the order; second, that after ten months of drilling and teaching men squads east and west in the United States, and when everything seemed to be the darkest as to his possibilities of coming over into either the Flanders mud, Land of Picardy or to sunny France, the orders struck him like a thunder-bolt out of a clear sky. The captain, who was now the happiest officer in the army, went about his work of preparing for his trip, and overseas duty, like the small boy feels on the first day of school vacation.

The captain embarked on the SS *New York* which was known then as SS 650 on February 8, 1918, and after a trip lasting eight days, which was devoid of all exciting events, that is there were no submarines encountered, arrived in Liverpool, England, on February 16, 1918. On the following day he arrived in London, and there he experienced his first air raid. This was the captain's first experience under enemy shell fire. He being of an inquisitive nature and not knowing the dangers ventured out during the raid in order that he might better see the performance. His eagerness to see the show resulted in a manner that taught our captain that it is not profitable to body, to exhibit his fool brave traits. During the raid the captain suffered a superficial wound, caused by a ricochet, which he camouflaged from his commanding officer, because he violated an order, in venturing out while the raid was in progress. After a two-day stay in London the captain was ordered to the British Tank Center, Wool, England, to attend a machine gun school.

At Wool, England, the British Tank Center, we find the captain applying himself zealously to his new duties. We find him eager, keen, [and] ambitious.

He is making good at the assignment laid down to him, because he sees a trip across the channel, at an early date that will take him into the heart of the fighting zone. The opportunity for which he so long yearned is now about to be realized and perseverance rewarded. Little does he know, that his ambition is to be thwarted. We find the captain passing the course with a very high grade, and upon the completion of his instruction, he is assigned to be chief instructor on the Hotchkiss machine gun, much to his disappointment; but he like a true soldier obeys the orders of his supervisors, and again puts his whole heart and soul in the work of imparting his knowledge to what is to be the first and only American battalion of heavy tanks to get into action, and help to destroy the menace that threatens the liberty of the whole world. At last the [301st] Battalion thoroughly trained, receives its mobilization orders. The captain still hoped that his efforts, or rather his desires would be recognized, and he would be ordered to depart with the battalion; but no, he was again to face disappointment. The battalion left and our captain was left behind to help train the 302nd and 303rd Battalions that came over from the States.

We now find the captain a broken-down individual; but yet, still doing his best by his government. The truth of that old saying "every dark cloud has a silver lining," is to be exemplified in the captain's case. Again like a thunder-bolt out of a clear sky, the captain receives orders appointing him adjutant of the 2nd American Tank Brigade, and also orders to join the 301st American Tank Battalion attached to the 4th British Tank Brigade immediately.

Pursuant to the orders received, the captain started out to comply with the instructions which had an unknown destination. At Amiens, from which the Boche have been driven just about two weeks previous, the captain met Major [Ralph I.] Sasse waiting for him there with a car, which was to take him to the advanced brigade headquarters at Manancourt. This trip took the captain through country which had been fought over two or three times. The wreck, ruin and devastation along this 40 mile trip was beyond all human conception. The devastation was not the kind that you would expect from the ordinary results of shell fire. It was destruction of the vandals who, as they went, swept wreck and ruin on all sides. Everything went, regardless of the fact whether the objects destroyed offered any strategic value to the allies or could offer any protection.

The captain having arrived at Manancourt at about 9:00 p.m. was treated to a rather severe bombardment of HE shells. Upon the captain's arrival he found the battalion ready to attack the following morning, on the Le Catelet—Bony—Gouy sector, this sector contained the strongest points of the famous Hindenburg Line. Our often disappointed captain was now in high spirits at the prospect of getting into action in about six hours after his arrival in the sector; but again, he did not know that another disappointment was in store for him. Just about one hour before the battalion jumped off, he received orders to stay back in advanced brigade headquarters and look after details of an administrative end of the office and the office routine duties. After these duties were completed and the headquarters put in proper shape and arrangements made of conditions after battle, we find the captain dodging German shells, machine gun bullets and mustard gas on the battlefield, doing all classes of work with one aim in view, that of doing all that he can to help the cause which he thinks and believes is right and just.

The captain had gotten up to the battle line about one half hour after the infantry of the 27th Division jumped off. The sight of those "doughboys" going over the top together with our own barrage, which was producing the most terrific screeching and heartrending noises overhead, was a sight, that never can in anybody's life who had been there, be forgotten. Their march, which was also in the face of a counter barrage laid down by the Boche, was as steady as though they were marching down Pennsylvania Avenue in Washington. Such veterans as the Australians remarked that never in their four years, had they witnessed such a spectacle. Not content with this sight the captain worked his way up forward, as far as he could which was not very far. On his way up he had to wear his gas mask all the time. Visibility was almost impossible, due to a combination of mist, fog, and smoke making the march very difficult, as well as dangerous; but the captain kept on; how he escaped with his life without even being wounded, is and will be a mystery.

Along about ten or eleven o'clock the fog and smoke lifted sufficiently to see down the valley, and to his eyes was disclosed the destruction of a large number of tanks. Looking at the destruction, and then let your mind wander back to the conditions under which the boys fought, the admiration of the courage displayed by his pals in attacking such a formidable strong point was immeasurable. The captain now worked his way backward to headquarters and to visit the dressing station en route to get data for official reports.

After the battle, when the roll had been called, it was discovered that several of his friends, officers with whom he made the trip over the Atlantic, had gone west [died]. In spite of losing some of his best friends, he worked on assisting in different ways, the survivors. Captain [Kit R.] Varney [Company A, 301st Tank Battalion], bunkie of our captain, while leading his tanks over, made the greatest sacrifice that falls to lot of the soldier, by paying with his life; that right, and not might, shall be supreme. This momentarily put a damper on everyone's effort because Captain Varney was a jovial fellow loved and honored by his fellow officers and men. His demise, regretted by all, caused everybody to work harder for the next show, that his death might be avenged.

Reorganization having been effected in the battalion, preparations were made for another attack. All preliminary work being completed, the battalion jumped off at day break of October 8, 1918. This attack was a complete success from every point of view. The tanks did wonderful work in cleaning out all obstacles. The results of this attack had a wonderful effect on the part of those that went in. They felt happy, that they were able to revenge the loss of their pals, and put the Boche on the run, and as it later developed, the Boche never stopped running until his legs gave out, and then he shouted "Kamerad."

With everybody in a happy frame of mind over the outcome of the show, work was started again to prepare to administer some more Yankee medicine to the Boche. Reorganization being effected, the battalion and advanced brigade headquarters moved up to Serain. They went into this town about two hours after the Boche had left it. Conditions in this town were ideal, as compared to the other towns or places where our captain had to put up for the nights. In this town for the first time in a month, he had his meals cooked on a real kitchen stove, served on real chinaware and on a real table. He slept on a real feather bed and under a real roof. To live in such luxury again, after spending over a month living in dugouts several feet underground was the change that our captain encountered. This change had a rather peculiar effect on the captain. He was going about, in sort of a daze due to the wonderful reversal of living conditions.

Preparations being completed for a battle which was to take place on October 15, 1918, was cancelled, due to a lot of conflicting information concerning the river Selle, as to whether or not tanks could or could not make a crossing. This condition made it imperative that a reconnaissance of the river be made to establish definitely if tanks could cross. The captain together with the Battalion Reconnaissance Officer started out that night, each armed with two automatic pistols and six Mills bombs, to make the reconnaissance. This trip during the dead of the night, into the mysterious piece of ground, known as "No Man's Land" was full of both amusing and serious incidents. The captain together with the Battalion Reconnaissance Officer cautiously crept over the river bank, their eyes glued on inky black atmosphere, looking for the movement of the enemy sentries and with their hands clutching their trusty 45's [Colt .45-caliber semiautomatic pistols] ready to lay the enemy sentry cold, should he make himself visible. Cautiously creeping along in this manner, they crossed the river, the water which was only about 12 inches deep, on into the heart of what was supposed to Boche country. They noticed an object moving, not exactly towards them, but what they thought standing like a sentry on an advanced post. At this time their excitement was running high. They decided to fire, but on second thought they both decided not to, but to creep up as close as possible to the object before firing in order not to attract attention. They figured that possibly they might capture the sentry, or rather what they thought was the sentry, and bring him back to our lines. They began to see visions of decorations and medals by the score, but only to be disappointed.

As they began to draw up to the object, what they thought was a sentry turned out to be a small blackberry bush. Bang, went all their dreams of decorations and their spirits dropped about 100 percent; but they accomplished this purpose, and obtained information that made the battle of October 17th, 1918, a complete success.

The above are the memories and experiences of one red-blooded American who, at the country's call, dropped his civil training and volunteered his service to the cause that would make the world safe for democracy and forever crush the thoughts of a nation which practiced the policy of might not right shall be supreme.

Major Roger B. Harrison, Commander, 301st Tank Battalion

Major Roger B. Harrison, "301st Tank Battalion in the Offensive Towards Maubeuge, September 29–October 23, 1918, " Personal Experience, The Infantry School, Fourth Section, Committee "H," Advanced Course 1930–1931, Fort Benning Georgia.

Introduction

By the time the United States entered the World War, tanks had demonstrated their worth as an offensive weapon and it was essential that steps be taken to provide our army with this invaluable aid to the infantryman.[13]

Recruiting for the Tank Corps was begun in February 1918, and under the name 65th Engineers, the organization that was to become the 301st Battalion, US Tank Corps, was assembled at Camp Meade, Maryland, late that month. Early in April, 1918, the battalion was sent to Wareham, England, for a period of training in the British Tank School and here it remained until August 24, 1918, when it was sent out to France to be attached to a British tank brigade for a tour of service at the front.

The original plan contemplated that the battalion would be equipped by the British and would remain with them until the weather became unfavorable for the use of tanks, at which time it was to be returned to the American army and equipped with the new Mark VIII tank which was then being built. The end of the war came before the latter part of this arrangement was carried out and the battalion saw all of its active service attached to and—to all intents and purposes—a part of the British Tank Corps.

Due to a shortage of tanks, the British were unable to furnish a complete armament for the battalion and the high water mark was reached with 47 Mark V and Mark V Star tanks just prior to our first engagement.

The battalion spent the first two weeks of its stay in France in various moves; drawing tanks and other equipment; and in convincing General [Hugh J.] Elles, Commander in Chief of the British Tank Corps, that it was ready for any task he might assign it. The day finally came when the battalion was attached to the Fourth British Tank Brigade and was informed that its first assignment would be to lead the 27th American Division of the II American Corps in its assault on the Hindenburg Line on September 29, 1918.

Action on September 29, 1918

General Plan

The Australian Corps with the II American Corps attached, was to resume the offensive in a general northeastern direction from their present front line. The II American Corps was to attack with both divisions in line, the 30th on the right and the 27th on the left. After breaking the Hindenburg Line, these divisions were to push on and capture Nauroy and Gouy. (The 1st objective). When this objective was taken, the 3d and 5th Australian Divisions were to pass through the 27th and 30th Divisions respectively and capture the second objective.

The III British Corps, on the left, was to advance with the 27th American Division as far as the canal.

After the 27th Division had been passed by the 3d Australian Division, it was to exploit to the left with one regiment (105th Infantry) to assist the III British Corps in crossing the canal.

The entire area was to be heavily bombarded and gassed, more than a thousand guns being concentrated on a 6,000-yard front. The attack was to be led by a rolling barrage consisting of high explosive (40%), shrapnel (40%) and smoke shells (10%), which was to continue to the second objective.

The 301st Battalion was allotted to the 27th American Division with orders to allot one platoon (five tanks) to each battalion of the assault regiments and two platoons (10 tanks) to the regiment detailed for the flank offensive. The remaining tanks of the battalion, seven in number, were to be placed in Fourth Tank Brigade Reserve.

In compliance with these instructions, the companies of the battalion were assigned as follows:

A Company—15 Tanks—to 108th Infantry on the right
B Company—10 Tanks—to 105th Infantry for flank exploitation
C Company—15 Tanks—to 107th Infantry on the left.

Preparations

At a conference on the morning of September 19th, the Commanding General, 4th Tank Brigade [Brigadier General Edward B. Hankey] informed the battalion and company commanders of the 301st Battalion of the general plan of the attack and, on September 25th, the battalion commander had a conference with the commanding general, 27th Division [Major General John F. O'Ryan] at which nothing was accomplished. The division commander had a very poor opinion of tanks and did not care to have them lead his troops due to the moral effect their getting blown up would have on his infantry. On the following afternoon—September 26th—there was a conference at Headquarters, 27th Division, during which the various details of the coming engagement were explained and tank company and platoon commanders were sent to get in touch with the infantry regimental and battalion commanders with whom they were to work.

No time was available for any training with the infantry, so that both the tanks and the infantry went into action with only theoretical knowledge of what to expect of each other and without that fundamental feeling of respect and confidence in each other's ability, so necessary for perfect team work.

Air Force

The 8th Squadron, Royal Air Force, was assigned to the Tank Corps for all air missions except photography and arrangements were made with this organization for noise planes to cover the last stages of the approach march and for contact planes during the operation.

Due to the noise made by the tank engine, it was necessary to find some means of preventing the approach of the tanks becoming known and thus informing the enemy that an attack was about to be launched. Experience had shown the British that this could best be done by low-flying planes as the noise of their motors was quite similar to that of the tanks and the presence of low-flying planes dropping bombs and using their machine guns on the ground troops was no novelty at this stage of the war.

Reconnaissance

Due to lack of time and transportation it was not possible for all of the individual tank commanders to be brought up to observation posts where they could see a part or all of the territory behind the enemy lines. The battalion and company reconnaissance officers, however, made a very thorough and complete reconnaissance of the forward area and each tank commander was given three maps to take into action with him. These maps showed his route and objective; all known and probable obstacles such as sunken roads and wide trenches; the location of land marks to help him keep oriented and an abbreviated barrage table for his particular area. In addition to these maps, each tank commander carried oblique air photographs of the area he was to cover.

Routes to the front line were to be taped by the company reconnaissance officers, and this was done by C Company, but the entire detail of A Company was either killed or wounded by a shell while laying the tape and this route was not completed, the tanks being led to the "jump-off line" by members of the reconnaissance staff.

Approach Marches

When the battalion was detailed for this operation it was approximately 25 miles in rear of the front line and 15 miles were covered by train. This was the only rail movement made by the battalion with its tanks during the war and was accomplished without difficulty. The entire movement was made under cover of darkness and unloading was accompanied by a very noisy, but otherwise ineffective air raid.

For secrecy, all movements were made under cover of darkness and, on the night of September 27–28, the tanks were moved to the vicinity of Villers Faucon, a distance of 10,000 yards. All tanks completed the move on schedule and were camouflaged before daylight. The tanks were given final overhaul at this place and were completely filled with gas, oil and grease and, in addition, carried one half fill to be used just before reaching the start line.

The approach march from Villers Faucon to the start line covered 8,500 yards and was a very different affair from that of the preceding night. The latter part of the route was constantly shelled with high explosive and gas. No tanks were put out of action by the enemy, but the wearing of gas masks made it extremely difficult for the drivers to handle their tanks in the dark.

Of the 40 tanks that started the march, one broke a track and five developed mechanical trouble, leaving 34 that actually crossed the start line at H-hour.

Conditions

(a) Weather.—On the morning of D-day, a slight mist hung in all the valleys in the area of operations; however, this cleared by 7:00 a.m. and the remainder of the day was fair.

From H-hour on D-day until about 8:00 a.m. a slight breeze carried all smoke toward the enemy. From then until 10:30 the wind was either stationary or toward our troops and the entire battlefield was covered with a dense smoke from our own barrage. Tanks were unable to see their infantry and cooperation was practically impossible.

(b) Ground.—Ground conditions were good and offered no serious difficulties for tanks. The Hindenburg Line was expected to be a serious obstacle, but it was crossed without difficulty by the few tanks that succeeded in reaching it.

A number of tanks were ditched in trenches and sunken roads but, in every case, this occurred due to the inability of the driver to see and could have been avoided with proper vision.

Operations

Before the attack could take place it was considered essential that the high ground along the general line Quennemont Farm—Guillemont Farm—The Knoll be captured and the entire battle was planned on the premise that this line would be in our hands prior to D-day. The infantry start line was placed along this general line with the artillery start line 200 yards in front of it.

The III British Corps made numerous efforts to capture this line and reached their objective several times, but were unable to hold out in face of the determined counterattack that followed each of their efforts.

When the 37th Division took over this part of the line the desired ground was still in the hands of the enemy and the 106th Infantry assisted by 12 tanks from the 4th British Tank Battalion, was ordered to capture it. On September 27th this regiment made a very determined attack and, while small parties reached their objective, their efforts fared little better than those of the British before them and the front line remained practically as before.

Due to the fact that numerous small groups of Americans were known to be holding out in the contested area and also that many American wounded were in the area and could not be reached, it was decided that the barrage would not be brought back to go over that area again on September 29th, but that it would come down as originally planned. The infantry was instructed to leave their present positions in time to work their way forward and be on the designated start line by H-hour. This message reached the assault regiments of the 27th Division on the afternoon of September 28th and they immediately started to work their way forward to the designated line, but met with so much resistance that the brigade and regimental commanders held a conference and decided to wait until H-hour the following morning before continuing. This decision placed them from 500 to 1,000 yards in the rear of what was to have been their protective barrage, and, during the entire engagement on the following day, they were completely out of touch with it.

When the 107th Infantry attempted to leave their trenches on the morning of September 29th they were met by heavy enemy fire from the positions which were to have been in their possession prior to the start of the battle and they and the Australians, who were to pass through them on the first objective, spent the entire day in a vain effort to establish themselves on what was to have been their line of departure for the initial assault on the enemy's position.

Tanks

On the morning of September 28th the battalion commander was informed that, due to the obscure situation on the front of the 27th Division, orders had been issued for the assault troops to leave their present position one hour before H-hour and work their way up to the designated line of departure. As some resistance was expected, the tanks were to cross the present front line at H minus one hour and assist the infantry in reaching the start line. This message was delivered by the commanding general, Fourth Tank Brigade, in person and he was asked by the battalion commander what action should be taken by the tanks in case the message failed to reach the infantry or that the infantry did not start as directed. The reply was to go ahead regardless of the infantry and arrive at the start line in time to cross at the first lift of the barrage and that the infantry would either be on the start line and ready to go with the battalion or would catch up with it before it had advanced very far. These instructions were promptly communicated to the company commanders and, by noon on September 28th, all tank commanders were thoroughly familiar with the new situation.

The tanks crossed the infantry line at the designated hour, but were informed that the infantry would not move out until H-hour and, pursuant to the instructions of the tank brigade commander, they moved on forward to the line of departure which they crossed at H-hour—5:50 a.m. This put the tanks assigned to the 107th Infantry approximately 1,000 yards in front of the troops they were to aid and here they fought an independent action completely out of touch with the infantry they were to support and in violation of one of the basic principles of the employment of tanks—tanks must always keep in close contact with the infantry they are supporting.

"A" Company, on the right, had better success and succeeded in establishing contact with the 108th Infantry, to which it was able to render some assistance.

Early in the morning it became apparent that the attack was not progressing according to schedule and that the 105th Infantry would not be able to make the flank exploitation for which it had been detailed. It soon became necessary to use this regiment to reinforce the 107th Infantry which was being subjected to heavy counterattacks. This change cancelled the assignment of the 10 tanks from "B" Company and the company commander immediately put them into action to assist in clearing up the situation on the left flank. Only two of these tanks reached the Hindenburg Line, the others becoming casualties shortly after entering the battle.

The reports of the tank commanders were unanimous in stressing the difficulty of vision on this occasion. The dense smoke made it impossible to orient themselves; the drivers could not see where they were going and thus many tanks were ditched in trenches and sunken roads that ordinarily would have been avoided; gunners could not use their guns effectively because no targets could be seen.

Anti-Tank Defenses

The nature of the terrain in this general sector made it extremely difficult to use tanks on any but the front of the II American Corps, the St. Quentin Canal presenting an impassable obstacle. On the II American Corps front the canal went underground through a tunnel and the Germans were well prepared for the advance of tanks over this area.

In order of their effectiveness we met the following:

(a) Field and Anti-Tank Guns.—Firing with direct laying over open sights [firing along the line of sight] at tank targets. These guns exacted a heavy toll from the battalion which, no doubt, would have been greater had not smoke blanketed the entire field.

(b) Anti-Tank Rifles.—Numbers of these were found on the battlefield and they had no difficulty in penetrating the tanks. However, the German soldiers did not like to fire them due to their heavy recoil. A few casualties were caused by these rifles, but no tanks were put out of action by them.

(c) Armor-Piercing Bullets.—These were used in great numbers and all tanks were pierced in numerous places. Most of the energy of the bullet was expended in getting through the armor and very little damage was done to the personnel and none to the machinery inside of the tanks.

Casualties

Casualties in this operation were very heavy both in personnel and in tanks. The battalion lost three officers and 17 enlisted men killed; 15 officers and 70 enlisted men wounded; seven enlisted men missing; a total of 112 or approximately one-third of the men engaged.

Of the 40 tanks scheduled for the operation, six failed to get in it. Of the

34 that crossed the start line 16 received direct hits from artillery or anti-tank guns and were destroyed; two were blown up crossing a British mine field that had been put down some months before and of which no information had been given to the battalion; nine were ditched in various trenches and sunken roads; five reached the Hindenburg Line.

Results

Both from the tank and the infantry point of view the attack in the 27th Division sector was a failure. On the right, the British and the 30th American Division had reached their first objective and the Hindenburg Line was broken. On the right of the 27th Division's zone of attack the line had been carried forward by the success of the 30th Division. It then bent sharply backward to the left where it rested on what was to have been the line of departure that morning.

The infantry at least had made some advance, but the tanks had accomplished nothing to compensate for the loss of their machines and personnel.

Comments and Criticisms

In considering the action on the front of the 27th Division, it must be borne in mind that this was a small, though important part of the attack along the whole front which extended well down into the French sector.

The principle of simplicity was violated in that two start lines were used for the infantry and what was supposed to be a minor operation was to be carried out before the main attack. The minor operation—the advance to the designated line of departure by the infantry—proved to be a major operation and the delay in accomplishing it disrupted the entire plan in this sector.

The principle of cooperation was violated in the orders that placed the tanks out of contact with the infantry they were to support and in the orders that caused the infantry to be so far behind their protective barrage that they derived absolutely no protection from it.

The plight of the 107th Infantry on the left appears to be due either to a lack of information or to faulty information of the true status of affairs in its immediate front at higher headquarters. Although the 106th Infantry had failed to consolidate the line of departure desired for this operation, the Australian corps commander assumed that the 107th Infantry would have no difficulty in advancing 1,000 yards in an hour before the main attack and would arrive at the start line in fit condition to take part in the main assault. Under the conditions as they actually existed, nothing but faulty information could have caused this erroneous estimate of the situation.

This same assumption caused the tanks to be sent into action on the left flank completely out of touch with the infantry whose cooperation was essential to their success.

It appears that, in order to save the time necessary to clear up the situation in their front and thus delay the general offensive and disrupt the time schedule of the higher command, the troops in this particular sector were sent into action under the most unfavorable circumstances.

The result of this action emphasized the necessity for the joint training of infantry and tanks. Had the 107th Infantry received the benefit of this training they would have realized that they were losing invaluable aid when they allowed their tanks to pass through their lines at H minus one hour.

In view of the situation as it developed, there is ample room for doubt that the tanks could have placed them on the designated line at H-hour, but there can be no argument against the statement that great assistance could have been rendered the infantry in overcoming the storm of machine gun fire that swept over them when they attempted to go forward. All 15 tanks assigned to this regiment crossed its front line and passed on.

The survivors of this battle were thoroughly in accord with the statement that had been constantly made to them while in the British Tank School—"Tanks without infantry support can hold nothing."

The period immediately following the battle was spent in salvaging tanks and equipment from the battlefield. All tanks had had very hard service and it was necessary for them to be overhauled before they could be used in action again.

On the day after the battle, General Hankey, commanding the Fourth British Tank Brigade, appeared at battalion headquarters. He was greatly perturbed at our heavy losses and began to apologize for starting us out with such a difficult assignment as he was afraid of the effect our defeat would have on our morale. The battalion commander assured him that the morale of the battalion was unimpaired and that all the battalion asked was a chance to get their own back. As later events proved, this statement was repeated verbatim to General Elles, Tank Corps commander in the field, and our opportunity was given us on October 8th.

Operations on October 8, 1918

General Plan

The Fourth British Army was to resume the offensive with the IX British Corps on the right, the II American Corps in the center and the XIII British Corps on the left.

Two objectives were given for this attack, the second being called the line of exploitation.

The 301st Battalion was allotted to the II American Corps and was to accompany the infantry as far as the first objective. Here Whippets [medium tanks] were to take over the tank assignment and carry on to the line of exploitation.

The attack was to he launched under cover of a barrage, which was to cover the advance as far as the first objective, after which, special arrangements had been made for artillery support to the line of exploitation.

The II American Corps was to attack with the 30th Division in line and the 27th Division in reserve.

The 59th Brigade of the 30th Division was to lead the attack with the 118th Infantry on the right and the 117th Infantry on the left.

The 118th Infantry was to attack with two battalions in line and one battalion in reserve.

The 117th Infantry had one battalion in line; one battalion in reserve; and one battalion in brigade reserve.

One battalion from the 60th Brigade was moved to the vicinity of Joncourt and made subject to the call of the 59th Brigade for flank protection or use in repelling counterattacks.

Tanks

Due to the heavy losses in tanks on September 29th, the battalion had only 23 tanks fit for use in this operation. No replacements were available and, to get something approximating normal combat strength in the platoons, the battalion was reorganized into two companies.

13 Tanks were allotted to the 118th Infantry on the right.

10 Tanks were allotted to the 117th Infantry on the left.

Preparations

The usual conferences were held and the tank platoon commanders arranged a set of signals by which the infantry could indicate to the tanks what was holding them up and the general location of the resistance.

Reconnaissance

Reconnaissance differed from the preceding engagement only in the important fact that all tank commanders were able to get forward to observation posts where they could see the country over which they were to operate back of the enemy's lines. This proved of great value in keeping them oriented during the attack.

Approach Marches

On the night of October 5–6 the tanks moved up to the vicinity of Bellicourt, a distance of 9,000 yards. This march was accomplished without incident.

On the night of October 7–8 the tanks made another march of 9,000 yards and crossed the "jump-off line" at H-hour, which was 5:10 a.m. The night was pitch dark and numerous sunken roads and wide trenches had to be crossed. During the last half hour, the battalion was bombed by air planes and heavily shelled, but no casualties resulted. An enemy search light looking for our low-flying "noise" planes was a great aid in keeping direction as it was located in the approximate center of our objective and was in operation most of the night.

Of the 23 tanks that started, 20 jumped off at H-hour, the other three going out on account of mechanical trouble.

Communications

One wireless [radio-equipped] tank operated with the battalion on this and also our previous engagement. This was an old tank unfit for further fighting. It carried an officer observer and a wireless crew of two men. The set itself could not be used inside the tank, making it necessary to halt the tank and put up the set before messages could be sent.

The tank was given a fixed route and a time schedule, copies of which were given to all tank officers in order that they might know where to send runners. Due to the excellent weather conditions, the observer was able to send back much information of great value both to the tank and the infantry headquarters.

Tanks carried pigeons on this occasion, but they proved of no value. One pigeon message was sent which arrived at battalion headquarters about midnight, long after the officers who sent it had reported in person and informed the battalion commander of the contents of the message.

Due to the fine visibility, the contact planes were able to keep up a steady stream of messages throughout the engagement and the battalion commander had accurate information of the location and condition of his tanks at all times.

Conditions

(a) Ground.—The area covered was ideal for tanks, there being no wide trenches and few sunken roads.

(b) Weather.—A slight breeze blew all smoke toward the enemy and atmospheric conditions were favorable throughout the engagement.

Operations

The attack was entirely successful. The first objective was reached on scheduled time and by 2:15 p.m. the line of exploitation was in the hands of the attacking infantry.

All tank commanders report that they had excellent targets and much ammunition was expended.

Tanks worked in close cooperation with the infantry and the number of crushed machine guns and dead gunners testified to the aid they had furnished. One light railway bank was heavily held with machine guns, all of which were promptly handled by the tanks.

The principal organized resistance came from Brancourt-le-Grand and here again, the tanks carried the infantry through the village.

Casualties

Casualties to personnel were very light in this engagement. Two enlisted men were killed while three officers and 13 enlisted men were wounded; a total of 18. Of the 20 tanks that started, 11 reached their objective and rallied, four received direct hits from artillery or anti-tank guns and were destroyed, [and] five developed mechanical trouble and went out of action at various stages of the attack.

Comments and Criticisms

This action was a decided contrast with that of September 29th. The infantry and the tanks started from the same line of departure at the same hour, working under the same orders. Close contact between the tanks and the accompanying infantry was maintained at all times.

The 30th Division had worked with British tanks on September 29th and showed the benefits gained by their experience on this occasion.

While the infantry could probably have made the same advance without the aid of the tanks, there is no doubt but that they would have taken much more time to make the advance and would have suffered many more casualties.

In conversation with officers of the 30th Division after this engagement, the battalion commander was informed that the tanks had so simplified the advance for the infantry that many of them reached their objective without firing a shot.

The opinion of the commander of the 301st Tank Corps is shown in the following note which was received shortly after the battle:

Adv. Hq. Tank Corps
9th Oct.

> My dear Harrison
> A note to congratulate you and your fellows on the splendid results you got today.
> I am more glad than I can say that you have had the opportunity of getting your own back on the filthy Hun.
> Yours sincerely
> [Lieutenant General] Hugh Elles

On completion of this engagement, work was started getting the tanks ready for the next assignment, which came on October 17th.

Operations on October 17, 1918

General Plan

The offensive was to be resumed by the entire fourth British Army with the IX British Corps on the right, the II American Corps on the left.

The II American Corps placed both divisions in the line for this attack, the 30th on the right and the 27th on the left.

The attack had four objectives. It was not expected that the fourth objective would be reached that day, but it was given to provide a line of exploitation should the enemy resistance collapse. Tanks were to accompany the infantry as far as the third objective.

The artillery was to conduct a general bombardment from H minus 48 hours to H-hour and was then to fire the usual rolling barrage for the attack.

The 301st Battalion was again allotted to the II American Corps. The 30th Division, on the right, advanced with the 59th Brigade—117th and 118th Infantry in the assault followed by the 60th Brigade—119th and 120th Infantry—in support.

On the left, the 27th Division advanced with brigades abreast, each brigade being in column of regiments. The 53d Brigade was on the right with the 105th Infantry leading and the 54th Brigade was on the left with the 108th Infantry leading.

15 tanks were assigned to the 30th Division.

10 tanks were assigned to the 27th Division.

Preparations

The usual conferences at corps, division, brigade, regimental and battalion headquarters arranged the details of the operation.

Air Force

In addition to their regular "noise" and contact planes, arrangements were made with the 8th Squadron, Royal Air Force, for planes to watch for and bomb any anti-tank guns that could be located. Planes were to carry smoke bombs to assist in screening any tank that might be in difficulty.

The squadron was asked to make a low-flying reconnaissance of the Selle River for the purpose of determining possible tank crossings. This was promptly and efficiently accomplished.

Reconnaissance

All tank commanders were taken to observation posts where they could locate landmarks [in] back of the enemy's lines.

The battalion reconnaissance officer went out with an infantry patrol and succeeded in reaching the Selle River behind the enemy outpost line. He waded down the river and marked all possible tank crossings on his map.

On the afternoon of October 15, the tanks were moved to the vicinity of Busigny, a distance of 4,500 yards. They spent the next day under cover of the railroad bank at this place and moved out about midnight, October 16–17, for the "jump-off line." This march covered 5,500 yards and the heavy work the tanks had been doing took its toll as five of them went out with mechanical trouble and did not get in the battle.

Communications

Communications were exceedingly poor in this battle. Due to the heavy fog, planes could not fly, the observer with the wireless tank could see nothing and runners promptly became lost.

Conditions

(a) Ground.—Due to the excellent work on the part of the battalion reconnaissance officer and the 8th Squadron, Royal Air Force, the Selle River proved to be a very slight obstacle to the tanks. Two tanks were ditched in crossing the river.

One of these attempted to cross outside of the designated crossing limits and the other got mired in marshy ground approaching the river.

(b) Weather.—The weather was decidedly unfavorable for the use of tanks and was largely responsible for the poor showing made by the tanks on this occasion. From H-hour until noon—5:10 a.m. until 12:00 p.m.—a heavy fog enveloped the field and it was impossible for the drivers to see where they were going and the gunners could not recognize targets to fire on. Compasses were used to keep the general direction and tanks cruised through the fog in a vain effort to keep in touch with the infantry. By noon, when the fog lifted, the tanks had used up their gasoline and were forced to leave the field just at the time when they could have been of real service to the infantry.

Operations

Due to the facts that the known crossings of the Selle River were in the 30th Division sector and that the river was only about 500 yards in front of the 27th Division, that division was notified that their tanks would not join them until they were across the river. The tanks were to cross in the 30th Division's sector and then work to the left and catch up with the 27th Division. These tanks crossed the river as planned, but became lost in the fog and never gained contact with the division.

In the 30th Division's sector the line was further from the river and the tanks did good work in helping the infantry that far forward but, after crossing the river, they too became lost in the fog and were of little assistance to the infantry.

Casualties

Casualties were slight in this operation. One officer and one enlisted man were killed, while eight enlisted men were wounded. One tank received a direct hit from artillery and was destroyed; one tank caught fire and burned out; two tanks were ditched; [and] eight tanks developed mechanical trouble.

Results

Only two tanks reached their first objective. This was due entirely to the fog as only one tank was put out of action by the enemy.

In spite of the adverse weather conditions the infantry made progress and, by evening, had established themselves on their first objective.

Comments and Criticisms

Everything possible had been done to assure the success of this operation and the unusually heavy fog which caused the tanks to fail could not be foreseen.

The tank crews did their best under the circumstances but it would have been much better for all concerned had the tanks been held out of the engagement until the fog lifted. They would have then been able to assist the infantry in their final efforts of the day and the infantry advance undoubtedly would have been greater.

The failure of this operation to accomplish greater results was not caused by the violation of any basic principles, but was due to the unusual weather conditions which prevailed and which could not be foreseen.

No replacements were available and, after this engagement, the battalion was reorganized into one company with only 12 tanks fit for action and, with these, we fought our last battle,

Operations on October 23, 1918

General Plan

This was a combined attack which was carried on by the First, Third and Fourth British Armies, the Fourth Army being assigned the task of forming a defensive flank facing east to protect the main operations which were to be carried out by the First and Third Armies.

There was to be no general preliminary bombardment by the artillery although specially selected roads were to be bombarded and counter battery work and harassing fire would continue.

The 301st Battalion was allotted to the IX British Corps, which in turn, allotted it to the 6th British Division.

The IX Corps was to attack with the 1st Division on the right and the 6th Division on the left. The movement of the 6th Division was to conform to that of the division on its left (25th British) and "it was to form an ever-lengthening defensive flank facing east, as that division gained ground."

As the moon was full and the nights very light, H-hour was set at 1:20 a.m. in order to take the enemy by surprise.

Only 12 tanks were fit for action and they were divided into three platoons of four tanks each. These were assigned as follows: 1st Platoon—four tanks—two missions—

(a) To left battalion of the lst Division; then

(b) To right battalion, 18th Brigade, 6th Division.
2d Platoon—four tanks—to 18th Infantry Brigade
3d Platoon—four tanks—to 71st Infantry Brigade.[14]

Operations

This was a very simple operation and was accomplished without the loss of a tank or a man. It is mentioned solely on account of the fact that it was the only night attack which the battalion took part.

The moon light was very bright at H-hour and the drivers and gunners had no difficulty in seeing their routes and targets. Later, clouds and mist came up and the enemy sent over a number of gas shells. The wearing of gas masks in the dark made it extremely difficult for the drivers and effectively silenced the gunners. However, the enemy put up a very little resistance and such opposition as was encountered was speedily overcome.

On this occasion, tanks proved that daylight was not essential to their operation and there is no doubt that they would have been used in other night operations had the war continued any great length of time.

Comments

(General)

The battalion spent its entire active career as a part of a British tank brigade. All tank actions in which it took part were planned by the British and very detailed instructions were received from tank brigade headquarters usually days before any information could be obtained from the infantry with whom the battalion was to work.

All tank actions were based on the doctrine that, to be effective, tanks must be used in mass by surprise. Mass was always employed and tanks were concentrated where it was desired to strike the hardest blow. Surprise, in many cases, was only relative. The prolonged bombardment prior to the assault on September 29th informed the enemy that an attack was imminent, but the intensity and duration of the bombardment was such as to give the enemy no indication of the hour of attack.

It was a foregone conclusion that tanks would be used in any assault on the Hindenburg Line and that the sector most favorable for their use was where the St. Quentin Canal went underground. That the enemy was aware of this is shown by his elaborate and effective preparations to handle such an attack in this sector.

The attack on the front of the 27th Division was doomed to failure from the start and the only question is—would there have been any greater success if the infantry had started forward when the tanks passed through them? This action on the part of the infantry would have brought on the battle in this sector one hour prior to the time it was scheduled to start, but it would have given the infantry the aid of the tanks in moving forward. It would have made little difference in the ultimate fate of the tanks for the German defenses were such that tanks were bound to suffer heavy casualties. The infantry launched their attack without any aid from the barrage and there is no question but that the tanks would have overcome many of the enemy machine gun nests before they themselves were put out of action.

The attack on October 8th is an excellent example of a well-planned, coordinated attack working according to schedule under favorable conditions. The plan was simple and the artillery, tanks and infantry worked with perfect cooperation against an enemy weakened by his previous defeats.

The operations on October 17th demonstrated that the best of plans and preparations do not always insure success. Everything that could be foreseen—even the possible collapse of the enemy's resistance—had been provided for, but the forces of nature smiled on the enemy and disrupted the attack.

For the tank crews, the only novel part of the operation on October 23d was the fact that they were in action against the enemy. All of their approach marches had been made under cover of darkness and many of them under worse conditions than they found themselves in when they crossed the "jump-off line." Night operations with tanks are possible, but will always be accompanied by a gamble on the weather. If the moon shines, the tanks will be able to function, otherwise, they will prove of little value until daylight.

First Lieutenant Thomas N. Miller, Company A, 301st Tank Battalion

A sense of justice and admiration for the gallant officers and men who fought in his section prompts First Lieutenant Thomas N. Miller, commanding 3rd Section, Co. A, 301st Heavy Battalion, to make this a narrative of their acts, rather than of his own.

The Hindenburg Line, between Bellicourt and Le Catelet, was the scene of their baptism; men hitherto untried proved their worth a thousand fold, on that cold, dreary dawn of September 29th, 1918. Five tanks (the full section) started the approach march; six officers and 51 men set out gaily for the great adventure, happy in thought that at last they were to be of use to the great world army pledged to thwart the ambition for world dominion so dearly cherished by the Hun.

In the column were second lieutenants John R. Webb, Joseph J. Gutkowski (contracted by his comrades to "Murphy"), Hugh S. Taylor, Clarence J. Hartt and Harold R. Dean. The Hun let loose a great many HE shells that he didn't need, and a prodigious amount of gas the tankers didn't like, consequently the approach march became anything but an enjoyable outing. The Hun gassed them and he shelled them, and he shelled them and gassed them, until there was no choice as to which was the worst. Dean's bus broke a track on a turn; the track twisted out of the flanged rollers, and the bus was finished for that action. One man remained behind to guard the tank, while the remainder of the crew went forward with machine guns and ammunition; they were distributed between the four remaining tanks of the section. That terrible night will long be remembered. Through dense concentrations of gas, with frequent explosions of HE shells close aboard, ahead, behind and on both sides, these men felt their way to an appointed filling-up point before deploying to go into action. For three-and-a-half hours gas masks were worn; a saint could have "cussed" Kultur that night.[15]

Their reconnaissance staff suffered severe casualties, and Dean, commander of the disabled tank, "carried-on" for the wounded officers, until he too fell seriously wounded. At last, after weary months of training and waiting, all four tanks got off on time, into action at last! The Hun got into action too; he threw his great ammunition factories at them! They wondered what Sherman would have said had he been a tank commander![16]

Everyone came back that day. Some came back in their tanks, some walked, and many came back on stretchers. The dressing stations got 31 of the 57 officers and men who went into action.

Murphy blew up in a minefield, and although himself wounded, assisted in getting his casualties to the rear. Before they sent him to the rear, he wrote an accurate message to his section commander giving his casualties and the map location of his burned-out tank. The message was written on the back of the only scrap of paper he saved from his tank—the picture of a wee wifey back home.

Hugh Taylor came back, calm and unperturbed as ever, driving his own tank and with but one of his crew on his feet—Corporal Roy A. Smith, six-pounder gunner—the smallest man in the section, of the biggest scrappers of 'em all. The tank had eight machine gun armor piercing holes in the side and an anti-tank rifle hole on the starboard. Lieutenant Taylor and the corporal fought the tank alone, after the remainder of the crew became casualties, and they withdrew only after the single six-pounder they carried went out of action. When Taylor got out of the driver's seat, his leg was stiff—a nice "cushy Blighty" if he wanted it. Instead, he pulled off the surgeon's tag consigning him to the hospital, limped out of the advance dressing station, and rejoined his section.[17]

John Webb was ditched, badly ditched, while running in thick smoke. Boche machine gunners close at hand called to him to surrender—their bodies were found later. Other machine gunners on their flank made life even more miserable, until they were picked off with a rifle. Lieutenant Webb took the lead and every man dug; dug with stones, screwdrivers, tin hats, fingernails, anything. The old bus came back from Jerry's lines, a wounded man in the driver's seat. Did they quit when there seemed nothing else to do? There just naturally ain't no quit to John Webb's "Pole Cats."

Clarence Hartt, he of the unmilitary and off-duty title of "Flossy," commanded what he fondly termed the "Bear Cats"; one of them got a bad dose of splinters in his eye, and sank to the floor, exclaiming, "My eye is gone." "Aw Hell, keep a scrapping," answered Corporal Connelly, "Yu' got another eye, ain't yu." That was the spirit of the Bear Cats! They would attack the Kingdom of Hades without a bucket of water, and come back too!

Since that memorable day, the section went into action on three other occasions, participating in every action in which the 301st Battalion was engaged. One tank was lost in a minefield and turned over to salvage; the other four ready for action up to the signing of the armistice, when two of them were turned back to the British. The remaining two are still on the job.

What did they do? They did their damnedest to force the Hindenburg Line at a particularly strongly fortified point, and hit it such a wallop that the next day it was forced. They assisted in the capture of Brancourt; crossed the La Selle River between McLain and St. Martin Rivière, and wound up their fighting career in conducting a moonlight excursion into enemy lines and turning over to the infantry La Haie Tenneile and Gimbroment, near the Bois de L'Eveque.

And what of the men? Originally 52 strong in the enlisted personnel, the section actually fought 103 men, including replacements and an entire crew from Company C that participated in an action with them—for actions, objectives reached in three of these four engagements, with not a single fatality.

Morale? Who likes to sleep night after night in the mud, between two tanks, with a leaky tarpaulin overhead? Who likes to wake up in such a bed of roses, wet and chilled to the marrow, to partake of a dainty breakfast of "Corn Willie" (they know him well) and hardtack, when "there ain't no coffee?" Who really enjoys those things, added to days and nights of hard, fatiguing, nerve-racking work? Nobody! They put up a mighty good bluff that they did enjoy it, those men; sometimes their section commander almost thought they did. Certainly they never let up on their work.

Second Lieutenant Hugh S. Taylor, Company A, 301st Tank Battalion

Nor was it long before the battalion moved out for its first action in a column almost a mile long. The first night was spent in trekking to the "laying up point."

Then followed the day of studying maps and aerial photographs, that all might learn the ridges to be avoided, landmarks and probably enemy strong points. The carefully gained and thorough information imparted by [First] Lieutenant [Thomas N.] Miller, the platoon commander, was responsible for his tanks being where and when they should have been, when the much-anticipated "Z" night arrived.[18] All that night the tanks trekked along passing through curtains and clouds of gas. That night, were it not for the odor of the gas, it would seem like a bank of harmless fog.

Dawn had just brought to light the general outlines of the surrounding hills when the tank reached the "jumping-off" point. Time synchronized well, for just then the barrage opened up. That was a sight to behold! All along and behind the German lines the sky lit up with masses of rockets and stars of all hues and descriptions.

The first machine gun bullets to hit the sides of the tank sounded more like rain than anything else, but when the armor piercing bullets came through the plates they did not seem as harmless as drops of rain. Then an anti-tank bullet made its appearance in a dashing manner and knocked out the driver. In all, nine members of the crew were wounded by piercing bullets. Fortunately the motor was not injured and "carried on" in its noisy manner.

Corporal Roy A. Smith, now the only one left on his feet to operate the guns, repaired the only big gun aboard while sitting on the floor. Tis well he did so, for several machine gun bullets passed uncomfortably close above his head, but he got his gun fixed and silenced several machine gun nests in quick order, and with a certain amount of satisfaction, too. Of the remaining two men, one was driving and the other gassed in the rear of the tank. Thus the tank "carried on."

Second Lieutenant Kenneth P. Watts, Company A, 301st Tank Battalion

During the operations relative to and including the four battles in which the battalion was engaged, Lieutenant Watts, was in the first battle, as Company "A" tank commander, in the second, Company "D" assistant reconnaissance officer and in the third and fourth, Company "A" reconnaissance officer.

The first battle took place on the morning of the 29th of September. The objectives were the Hindenburg Line and the canal tunnel between Vendhuile and Bellicourt, with the starting point about 1,000 yards east of Ronssoy. It was during this operation Lieutenant Watts realized that a "Tank trip" under war conditions leaves much to be desired. Lieutenant Watts was to have remained in reserve at the tank-drome,[19] but due to a mishap to one of the combatant tanks on the approach trek, he was instructed to follow the battalion about three hours after its departure. He did not know the route, so it was necessary to follow the marks left by the battalion. The night was very dark, making it difficult to find the way. He trekked until dawn and then camouflaged his tank. By the aid of a map, he discovered the battalion must be about two miles to the north, he having branched off and followed the truck marks of a British battalion. It was then necessary for him to report to his battalion commander for instructions and data relative to the battle, which was to take place the next morning and also to reconnoiter the intervening country for a suitable route to enable him to reach the battalion after dark, before its departure for the starting point. This was done and he joined the battalion and his respective company. The trek forward to the starting point was a hard one particularly while passing through Ronssoy, which was shelled and gassed. His company arrived about 30 minutes before "starting over." This just gave time to fill up and prepare for action.

As the spot was under heavy shell fire, 30 minutes seemed quite long enough. At a given time he advanced with three other tanks of his section and after covering about 1,000 yards, he lost sight of the other tanks and supposed they were either a little behind or "knocked out" as shells were coming hard and fast, bursting uncomfortably near and playing havoc with the infantry just to the rear of the tank. After advancing another 500 yards, a shell tore away part of the unditching gear and ricocheted off the track, another following almost immediately took away the signal arms. At this time his driver, who had been steering the tank along a communication trench, got too close causing the side to give way and allowing the tank to slide sideways with it. After trying a number of times to get the tank out, it became hopelessly ditched. He then ordered his crew to evacuate, taking machine guns with them to help the infantry, who were hard pressed at the time, or if necessary, to help defend the tank. Just then, a section commander ([First] Lieutenant [Herbert W.] Warden [Jr.]) appeared and after a short investigation continued on his way. No sooner had Lieutenant Warden departed when another shell burst just to the rear of the tank, seriously wounding one of the crew. The concussion knocked Lieutenant Watts off his feet, leaving him with but a hazy idea of what followed for some little time. Later the advance progressed favorably and he decided to seek the rallying point, leaving his ill-used tank to the tender mercy of the salvage company. It was then he discovered two of the other tanks in his section had been ruined and the third had mechanical trouble soon after "starting over." During this operation Lieutenant Watts had but three or four hours' sleep for three days and two nights. He was ably assisted throughout by his crew.

The second battle took place on the morning of October 8th. The objectives were Brancourt, Ponchaux and the intervening area. The lying-up place was just north of Bellicourt. It was Lieutenant Watts' duty to reconnoiter the ground between the lying-up place to a farm located about 1,500 yards northeast of Estrees, about 1,000 yards from the front line, for a suitable route for the approach trek. This work was carried out, the total distance amounting to about four miles. On the night of the approach trek he led the tanks to the farm without trouble and in time to allow the crews to rest before going into action. The night was exceptionally dark and in many instances it was necessary to send a runner ahead to locate landmarks, and on this account tape was used for the following operations.

The third battle took place on the morning of the 17th of October 1918. The objectives were Ribeauville and Mazinghein. The lying-up place was just north of Busigny. Lieutenant Watts was to reconnoiter the area from the lying-up place to the starting point for a suitable route, and to obtain all possible information regarding the enemy areas opposite his sector. This was done and the tape laid just after sunset, on the night preceding the battle. He was warned by enemy machine gun fire when to bring the tape to an end. It was during preparations for this battle, [First] Lieutenant [Theodore C.] Naedele, battalion RO, distinguished himself. Information was required as to whether the river Selle was an obstacle to tanks or not. It was in the hands of the enemy, and not visible from OP's [Observation Posts]. On the night of October 15, 1918, Lieutenant Naedele crawled through the enemy lines and made a personal reconnaissance of the river bed at much danger to himself. We obtained information which greatly helped towards the success of the operation.

The fourth battle took place in the early morning of the 23rd of October. The objective was L'Eveque Woods. Lieutenant Watts reconnoitered the ground between the lying-up places and the starting point on the night preceding the action, helped to lay the tape and later accompanied the tanks on the approach trek. This work, apart from a little shelling, entailed little danger. The approach trek was carried out quite successfully and the tanks went into action as scheduled.

Second Lieutenant Roland T. Adams, Company A, 301st Tank Battalion

On the 29th of September 1918, the 301st Battalion took part in its first show. The show was to take place in the Cambrai, St. Quentin sector, with Le Catelet and Gouy as objectives. Previous to zero hour the Hun was to be subjected to a bombardment of 48 hours duration.

As the outfit left the lying-up point in column of tanks, everything was in top-notch shape. As it neared the jumping off point, after passing along several batteries on its route, the battalion separated into platoons of five tanks each, as each platoon had a separate jumping-off place.

The second platoon of A Company, of which the writer was in command of the left tank, went to a point on the road between Ronssoy and Hargicourt. To get to this point, the platoon had to pass through a valley which was filled with mustard gas and smoke. On arriving at the refilling point the tank crews started to refill tanks and the mechanics to replenish the oil canisters and grease cups. The platoon at that point, owing to some unfortunate occurrence, was under fire of machine guns.

It was decided to start off without completing the fill. As there had been some casualties in the reconnaissance department, the platoon went down the same road and over the crest of a hill where it deployed to a line of some 100 yards between each tank, with the exception of the mopping-up tank, which followed the other four tanks at a distance of about 1,100 yards. There, the fireworks commenced. At that point the war began with a vengeance, as far as the second platoon was concerned.

Before the show, the tank commanders had been told to keep the infantry in sight. The writer, up to that time, had not seen any infantry, so after about 10 minutes of travel, he reversed and in a moment picked up the line of infantry, and then went forward again. The German barrage had been laid down by that time, and the tank went through it. It was as heavy a barrage as could be imagined.

The writer crossed one line of trenches and yards upon yards of wire, meanwhile using his two six-pounders with good effect. The machine gunners were very much on the job and did good execution.

In the rear trench of the Hindenburg out-post line, the tank was struck. In crossing a trench at a traverse, the side of the traverse gave way and the left track of the tank fell in. There was very much machine gun fire at this point.

A British tank came along, and he got his tail in the trench and didn't have enough motive power to pull out. At the other side, an American tank in command of [Second] Lieutenant Elliott P. Frost was ditched while in the act of running down a machine gun nest.

The writer got out of his tank and went to the British tank to speak to the tank commander. On returning to his own tank, he noticed a group of German prisoners being formed to be marched to the rear. He was on his way to get some infantrymen to get a German machine gun nest that was firing at the three tanks, same machine gun nest being concealed so well that it was impossible to find where it was, and passed in front of Lieutenant Frost's tank, which although stuck had its motor running. He looked in at the front flap and saw Lieutenant Frost in a dazed condition, called to him and he wouldn't answer, so the writer climbed on top of the tank and opened the top flaps of the after turret and saw that the crew were also in a dazed condition owing to the petrol fumes. The writer called for one of his men, Private [Virgil] Miller, and the two dragged out Lieutenant Frost and his crew, laid them out on the ground in the fresh air and administered aromatic spirits of ammonia to them. It was necessary to lay them behind a small hummock as the Hun was sniping with a 77mm field piece from the Hindenburg front line trench about 300 yards further on.

Later on in the afternoon, the British tank got out and hauled the writer's tank out. The writer's tank was immediately prepared for action and went on toward the Hindenburg Line. It was headed for a trench whose occupants had been bothering the tank crews all day. At a point about 100 yards from the trench, the tank received a hit by a 77mm HE shell that knocked four track plates out. The tank was evacuated and the crew ran for a trench.

Captain Carleton Reynell, Company B, 301st Tank Battalion

Lieutenant Reynell received his orders assigning him to the Tank Corps (Engineers) in January 1918. After landing in England he spent several months in the British schools and acting as mechanical instructor to the 301st Battalion, Tank Corps, USA. After completing a reconnaissance course in the British schools, he was assigned as battalion reconnaissance officer with the 301st Battalion and left England for Bermicourt, France, on August 31, 1918. On his arrival at British Tank Corps headquarters, he was attached to the 15th Battalion, British Tank Corps, and sent immediately to the front to join them at the town of Courcelles-le-Comte.

He had trained with the 15th British Battalion in England and was very pleased to be attached to the organization commanded by Lieutenant Colonel Ramsay Fairfax, a former naval officer and experienced soldier in tanks and other branches.

During his stay with this battalion three attacks were launched on the strongly fortified town of Vaulx-Vraucourt, about six kilometers northeast of Bapaume. In the first two of these attacks the tanks took the infantry to their objective beyond the town and the infantry were driven back by counter attacks. After the second attack a British general remarked to Lieutenant Reynell, "I wish we had American or Australian infantry here to hold this place. Our men are too played out."

During this time Lieutenant Reynell worked either with the battalion reconnaissance officer or second-in-command of the 15th Battalion, studying their methods and observing their tactics. After this he was ordered to return to his own battalion, which was relieving the 10th British Battalion in the 1st British Brigade.

On the night of September 27th the tanks moved up to Enfer Wood, a distance of about 800 yards and 8,000–9,000 yards from the front line. One tank bellied on a stump, but made the trip all right. This was a record in the British Tank Corps for number of tanks taking a long night march safely. They laid up in Enfer Wood all day. That afternoon at 4:00 p.m. (September 30th) orders came in to the effect that due to the failure of an attack the day before, our infantry had failed to bring their starting line up to the infantry starting line of the coming attack and would consequently be left 1,200–1,500 yards behind the barrage starting line. The plan given the tanks was roughly: the tanks to leave their line at zero minus one hour and fight their way up to the "infantry starting line" at zero and not to open fire until they arrived at that line for fear of wounding our own infantry. Orders to the same effect were sent to battalion headquarters.

It looked like a tough proposition for the tanks and infantry to start the battle before the artillery barrage started, but the boys had been straining at the leash so long that they were about ready to start almost anything that looked like a fight.

Lieutenant Reynell went with the wireless tank, which was manned by British Tommies, seasoned tank men. [First] Lieutenant [Sibley P.] McCluskey, battalion reconnaissance officer, insisted on going forward and seeing that the tape was laid correctly by the company reconnaissance officers, though arrangements had been made for the infantry detail commanded by tank company reconnaissance officers to do this. Lieutenant Reynell snatched an hour's sleep with Captain Kit R. Varney on a tarpaulin near a tank before starting up.

The approach-march up was fairly successful, one tank being laid out with a broken track. The Boche threw over a great many gas shells and about half the march was spent wearing a mask. Ronssoy was being shelled pretty heavily and A Company had to go through the town, but Captain Varney led them through without a casualty.

Word came up that Lieutenant McCluskey and [First] Lieutenant [Theodore C.] Naedele, reconnaissance officers, had been wounded and Sergeant Charles Butler, a draughtsman, killed laying tape and that Lieutenant McCluskey had important information to convey. A messenger was sent ahead to the dressing station to get it. The message was to the effect that tape had not been laid, but that Sergeant Grace and Corporal [Adam E. M.] Paff, draughtsmen, were going to lead the tanks of that section in.

When the B Company tanks arrived at regimental headquarters, 107th Infantry, it was found their orders differed from the other tank orders and they were going to jump off at zero, practically 1,200 yards behind the barrage and sometime after the other tanks went in. While the tanks were refilling at this point, enemy shelling was very active and once they dropped some gas shells just behind the tanks.

The tanks left the infantry front line just before the sun rose and were fighting as soon as they left the tape. Major [Ralph I.] Sasse and Lieutenant Reynell stopped the wireless tank at the end of the tape and wired in that the tanks had gone over. [Second] Lieutenant [Albert L.] Hilliard came back with his tank, almost crying, because he could not get the engine to run properly and had to go out.

Headquarters was established at Bihucourt, about four kilometers northwest of Bapaume. Work was started immediately on the reconnaissance of the Cambrai front and practically every day was spent in the front line by the reconnaissance officer using observation points in Ravrincourt Wood and in the trenches around Denicourt. The British had fought over the ground several times and very valuable data was collected from officers and men who had been on the former campaigns, and transferred to a record map of the whole sector until finally details of every stream, road, bridge, etc., behind the enemy lines were collected.

The battalions were ordered transferred to the Fourth Army (British) and a copy of this record map turned over to the 1st Brigade, British Tank Corps, for use in their attack on Cambrai. Lieutenant Reynell was transferred to the headquarters 2nd Brigade, USTC [US Tank Corps] at this time as reconnaissance officer and attached to the 301st Battalion for duty during present engagements.

The battalion was ordered to Manancourt and Lieutenant Reynell and Lieutenant McCluskey, the battalion reconnaissance officer, proceeded ahead to select a tank-drome. Manancourt was being shelled intermittently with HE shells and after the tank-drome had been selected and the battalion was moving in, shells were dropping over occasionally. One of them fell three yards from one of the trucks, but there were no casualties. The first night spent at Manancourt was a rather unpleasant one as shelling was almost continuous during the night and several bombing raids were made by the enemy. Sleep was impossible and as very little cover was available, it was quite miraculous that there were no casualties in the Tank Corps bivouacked near their tanks.

Reconnaissance of the enemy front was started immediately. The American sector took in the towns of Le Catelet, Gouy, Bony, Bellicourt, and several strongly fortified farms in that neighborhood. The Hindenburg Line was just opposite the allies' front and the tunnel of the St. Quentin Canal gave the enemy complete cover from artillery bombardments.

This was the only point in this sector of the front that tanks could be used to cross the canal and for this reason the Boche had fortified it as strongly as possible. The Hindenburg Line, St. Quentin Canal, tunnels with slag heaps along the top, and the Escaut [Scheldt] River all offered formidable obstacles to tanks and had been wonderfully fortified with acres of wire and a great amount of artillery.

The towns of Ronssoy and Hargicourt were on our immediate front and were constantly shelled with HE and gas. Observation of the enemy's territory was very poor and only by carefully picking one's way from one shell hole to another was it possible to get far enough forward to see the town of Le Catelet through field glasses.

Lieutenant Reynell attended the preliminary conference at headquarters 27th Division, USA, where preliminary details were talked over and another conference the following day where final details of the coming attack were settled. The wireless tank moved up toward the Hindenburg Line and set up again in a valley where they could see the tanks go over the hill beyond.

Our own barrage had started by now with the most terrific screeching overhead. In the grey dawn the infantry could be seen coming over the hill behind and it was a sight which could never be forgotten. They came on as steadily as though they had been on parade and the British soldiers said they had never seen troops go in so steadily.

The Boche laid a barrage down on the tanks almost immediately and it was a pretty sticky spot to stay in with 105's [105mm artillery] landing all over the place and machine gun bullets singing by. To add to the general discomfort, the wind blew smoke from our own barrage back over the tanks and some gas shells were mixed in the Boche barrage.

The crew of the wireless tank could do nothing but stand still with their gas masks on and dodge shells. Visibility was impossible beyond five yards. One shell burst near the side of the tank and everyone jumped against the tank. There were pieces of shell between them and the tank when they straightened up after a miraculous escape. One of the men paced 18 paces from the tank to the center of this crater. Several wounded men were dressed on their way back and one or two wounded in shell holes revived. A continual rattle of machine guns could be heard along the front of the Hindenburg Line. One man in the wireless tank was hit by a piece of shell and wounded in both legs. Major Sasse and Lieutenant Reynell crawled out ahead of the tank to find out if visibility was possible ahead. They finally lost sight of each other and had to find their way back to the tanks by yelling through the fog. The fog lifted for a moment and a troop of cavalry could be seen going in. I've heard since they did not come out.

Several tanks could be seen on the ridge in front and the wireless tank prepared to move forward, but the smoke fog settled down again. One of the captains said afterward that he tried three times to get to the wireless tank, but could not get near on account of the shell fire.

After about two hours the smoke lifted and the wireless tank turned to the right and swung down the valley followed by nine shells from a battery at Le Catelet, all about 50 yards short. Several tanks could be seen in flames. Some tank crews were coming in and the wireless tank set up behind a hedge and sent back another message. One of the British soldiers set up a fire and cooked a wonderful lunch with food picked up from dead soldiers on the field; the first meal for 10 hours.

The wireless tank came back through the rallying point, which was heavily shelled and through the town of Ronssoy, which was full of gas and shell fire and crowded with wounded, to St. Emilie. The Hindenburg Line had been taken.

Several of the officers and men had "gone west" [been killed] and it put a great damper on any jubilation which could be felt. Captain [Kit R.] Varney, loved by every officer and man in his battalion, had been killed leading his tanks in with a revolver in his hand. The following day when the casualty list came out, everyone felt blue, but there was so much work to be done that one had little time to think of anything else. Salvage work was started immediately and preparation for the next action begun.

The reconnaissance officer immediately started work in the forward area, preparing for a future attack and a few days after a conference was called at headquarters 30th Division to plan our attack on Brancourt. Details were arranged and the 301st Battalion moved to Bellicourt two nights before the attack. Lieutenant Reynell and [First] Lieutenant [Theodore C.] Naedele, battalion reconnaissance officer, slept in a cellar the night of the attack and went up with the infantry in the morning. The attack was a great success, the tanks doing great work, completely cleaning out a line of machine gun nests along a railroad bank; in one place putting a field [artillery] piece out of action. Some of them stayed out 'til all their ammunition was exhausted and when they returned to the rallying point everyone was jubilant at having revenged the loss of their friends killed in the former action.

After this action the tanks had hard work to keep up with the rapid advance of the infantry. Everyone worked almost night and day trekking up or replacing worn out parts.

The battalion moved into Cornin, a town taken over by the Americans two hours after the evacuation by the Germans. Living here was luxury after life in the shell-torn area from Perrone to Le Catelet. Work was begun on the reconnaissance of the enemy territory and an attack planned across the La Salle River. Three days before the attack Lieutenant Reynell was ordered to his present station at the 302nd Center to instruct and prepare the units of the brigade for the reconnaissance work.

Second Lieutenant Roy M. Lester, Company B, 301st Tank Battalion

After receiving about three months of tank training in England under as near actual fighting conditions as it was possible to produce without being in the front lines themselves, we were sent to the front with the 7th Brigade of British tanks for a little of the real stuff. We watched them capture Bapaume and then returned to Achiet-le-Grande to get our own tanks, which we received about August 28, 1918.

We were equipped with "Mark V" and Mark V Star tanks in all three types, viz., male, female, and morphodite.[20] After "trimming" them up in the best of condition and equipping them for action, we moved to Malancourt where we rested until the 26th of September.

On the evening of the 26th we received instructions to enter the fight the next morning. Our objectives were assigned and each tank commander was given a map with his route marked out. My tank was to cross the Canal du Nord, proceed through the village of Le Catelet and Bony and then to attack the German trenches to the north. As the point of departure which was assigned to us was still held by the Germans, all of our plans miscarried.

We operated with the 27th and 30th American divisions. There were also Australians operating in our sector.

Zero hour was designated as 5:05 a.m., of the 27th, and after trekking all night we moved forward at exactly 5:05 a.m., under a heavy barrage from our artillery. Of course I had given full instructions to each one of the 10 men in my tank crew before starting.

We encountered the first enemy machine gun about six o'clock and wiped it out easily. This was about one kilometer east of Ronssoy. We then continued forward under very severe fire from the Boche machine guns and artillery. Fortunately, we were able to continue on our course, but owing to heavy smoke shells, which our artillery were throwing over, we were forced to rely entirely on our compass. It was not accurate and this caused us to go about 3,000 meters to the right of our real course before we found out the mistake.

We passed without difficulty the German first line trenches and here their machine gunners proved themselves to be true fighters, for nearly every one fought to a finish. We crushed one machine gun, hidden in an old shell hole, completely.

We continued forward for about 900 meters to the German stronghold—the Bony trench—where we had the misfortune to be ditched. My driver, Sergeant (blank) tried his best to pull us out, but without success. Meanwhile my machine gunners were busy answering the enemy's fire, by which we were completely surrounded. One of them was hit twice in quick succession by anti-tank bullets. As his wounds were both in his knee, we were able to administer first aid easily and at once.

About this time, we began for the first time to notice the presence of gas, but we were unable to use our masks, with success, as the heat inside of our tank was terrific. One of my men was overcome by the heat and fainted, causing us considerable trouble and delay. We were forced to use our masks as best we could, which was to discard the face part and breathe through the mouth-piece.

After about 20 minutes, which seemed like an age to us, the smoke lifted and we found ourselves about 1,000 meters from the enemy's artillery. We then received two direct hits; the second one hitting us within five seconds after the first. The first shot, being a dud, merely passed through the top right side plate without exploding. The second one, however, pierced the side of our tank, striking the engine squarely, taking off both legs of the machine gunner on that side and wounding four of the other men. The force of the explosion knocked me off my seat and to the rear of the tank, but I received no wound.

The tank immediately caught on fire, but as we always left the doors unlocked, we managed to get our wounded outside without delay. On the outside we found ourselves under the direct fire of a machine gun. One of my crew was hit almost immediately by several shots in quick succession. The rest of us separated and found cover—shell holes—near the tank.

On account of the haste in which we were forced to leave the tank, we were unable to take our machine guns with us for protection and our infantry was nearly 4,000 meters in our rear. They were gradually coming forward, however.

About 11:30 a.m. "Jerry" started a barrage which lasted for two-and-a-half hours and caused his own machine gunners to take cover, where they stayed until the barrage lifted and then resumed their former positions and took occasional shots at the place where they supposed us to be. I managed to return their fire with my automatic, but without any apparent effect. The steady advance of our infantry attracted their attention more and more and about 5:50 p.m., we found ourselves relieved by a detachment of the 27th Division. We immediately retired to the rear.

During all the confusion and uproar I was only able to keep three of my men with me, the others being picked up and given first aid by the doughboys. Of a crew of 11, we had seven casualties.

After recuperating from the effects of the gas and a slight machine gun wound, for a few weeks in a rest camp, I was ordered to the front again and given a new crew and a new tank.

I entered action on October 23rd and my objective this time was the southeast section of the Mormal Forest, which was a distance of about 8,000 meters. We were working this time with the British 4th Army Corps and it was the first time that our tanks had gone into action at night. Our barrage started exactly at 1:30 a.m. With an accurate compass and under cover of a very good barrage, we reached our objectives about 4:30 a.m., being followed all the while at two or three points in our course.

We waited about two hours for the infantry to gather and dig in and then returned to our point of departure under severe enemy shell fire, but arrived there without mishap.

Without a doubt this night attack was one of the most successful during the war. We caught the Jerrys by surprise and caused them to retreat rapidly in confusion toward Belgium. It was this attack which eventually led up to the capture of Valenciennes and Mons a few days later. This was also the last show that the tanks were in.

Second Lieutenant David E. Heaphy, Company B, 301st Tank Battalion

Had you been an observer in the second major operation of the 301st American heavy tank battalion working in conjunction with the 30th US Division on a front between Beaurevoir and Joncourt, you would have started from a small French town called Bellicourt on the edge of the famous St. Quentin canal. Orders were received that the tanks were to leave at 6:00 p.m. for the jumping-off point, which should be reached a few minutes before zero hour the following morning. The trek was to be about 2,000 yards, skirting the village of Estrees, which seemed to have a special fascination for Jerry's HE's. The night was pitch dark and having made a personal reconnaissance, you knew full well that there was plenty of barbed wire and a few of the Beaurevoir outpost trenches to cross. Two companies were formed in line, the RO leading with the section commanders walking ahead of their respective platoons. In order that your sergeant will not go wrong or shake up the crew to any great extent, you walk about 10 yards ahead and enjoy the odors emitted from the exhaust of the bus [tank] ahead. Here, you find your white handkerchief very useful in signaling your driver. Bang! Suddenly a 9.2-inch battery opens up nearby and when you come down to earth, you start thinking the nicest things about your poor RO. You are all settled down and going fine, when you suddenly find yourself lying in the bottom of a trench, all mixed up in barbed wire. You suddenly remember the approach of your bus and make a mad scramble to get out of its path and clamber out of the trench.

After a time, which seems a month of Sundays, you reach the filling-up point. Oh, at last a chance to rest. Suddenly, a terrific barrage opens up to the north with a most elaborate display of fireworks. Is it a counter-attack or is it merely our own barrage laid down to cover our approach? While you are pondering over this question, the captain approaches and orders, "Get some sleep." You require no further urging, but pick out a nice dry spot and prepare to snooze. For about 10 minutes you really try to sleep, but that infernal barrage keeps reminding you that there is a war on.

Wee! Zow! They are dropping on a road about 300 yards away. You jump up and suddenly take a great deal of interest in the fireworks and joke with your men as at the meaning of these little green lights which Jerry is sending up. You try to pass it over by remarking that there must be some Irish left in Germany, though you know very well that they are tank SOS signals. Soon, the display stops as quickly as it started and orders come to your section commander to move the section up to the jumping-off point.

Here the real fun begins. You swing out of column and start across a sunken road only to find it filled with infantry ready to follow up. You are greeted on all sides by shouts of "At a boy" and "That's the stuff to give them." In a few minutes you pass them and leave with a few cheery remarks. You halt and know you have finally arrived at your jumping-off point. You give the order to load and to orient the tank. You are still some 800 yards from the front line, so you proceed to enjoy a little lunch. The word is given to start, so with a few parting remarks of "See you at the RP [Rallying Point]," you shove off. Everything is still quiet and you are in the front seat of the driver in order to watch the compass and time your speed, so as not to reach the barrage line too soon. Suddenly, out in front of you it opens up, a clearly detailed line of bursting shells and you wonder at the accuracy of modern artillery. Putt! Putt! Putt! Oh! A Jerry! Your left machine gunner opens up and you climb out of your seat and take your post in the turret. You see flashes, along the railroad just in front of you. So this is Jerry's strong point of which you were told by the RO; now for some good hunting.

You cross the railroad and your six-pounder opens up at close range with case shot, while all your machine guns are firing at top speed. Jerrys were soon running in all directions, affording excellent targets. Shells were dropping all around, indicating that Jerry is putting up a strong counter-attack. Suddenly, a bang and a flash, and you find yourself resting on the floor of the tank, unhurt except for a few splinters in your face. Good old armor plate! You take your post again. Somebody tugs on your coat. Your forward machine gunner has received a machine gun bullet in the arm. A first aid dressing and he returns to his post. You have scarcely regained your post when your muffler disappears and the same shell disarranges your petrol feed system, causing your motor to stop. After a hasty examination you find that the trouble cannot be remedied, so you decide to evacuate. As your driver is getting out of his seat, Jerry registers another hit on the tank, wounding him severely. All take shelter in a nearby shell hole, which covers any approach to the tank and await the arrival of the first wave.

The first to arrive were the aeroplanes flying very low and directing a harassing fire on the retreating Boche. Upon the arrival of the first wave, you offer your services, but as everything is progressing smoothly, they are not needed. Meanwhile you have received a slight wound, so after seeing that your men are properly cared for and reporting to your station commander, you are told to report to the CCS [Casualty Clearing Station] for clearance to the hospital. You follow instructions with visions of a good bath, white sheets, pretty nurses, n'everything.

Second Lieutenant Claude E. Gans, Company B, 301st Tank Battalion

The time is "zero hour"—the barrage has opened and is immediately behind you, the dull hum of a powerful motor is heard above all the noises of battle. Turning and looking about, you see a heavy tank crashing forward through the semi-darkness. Through the haze, you cannot keep from noticing that all its guns are prepared for action and the wonder of the thing almost amazes you, for you realize that it is no less than a "traveling fortress." You decide to take up at once a vantage point to witness the whole "show."

Keeping your glasses glued upon the tank, you watch its zig-zag course over ruins, across trenches, shell holes, ditches and small streams, through roads and hedges—you lose it for the moment as it plows into a smoke cloud or the dirt and debris through running unexpectedly in front of a Jerry machine gun position, spitting fire and smoke like a dragon of olden times. You see it lumbering along, halting briefly now and then, but—always going forward. The command is "Carry on!"

Who are those foolhardy men following closely behind "your" tank? Notice how carefree they are—why, they are even smoking and chatting as they plod along; guns slung over their shoulders and helmets tilted cockily on their heads. How can that be possible? Your answer is simply the tanks.

With your glasses you are able to notice the confusion behind the enemy lines—men running wildly around in every direction. The enemy is in a sad state of disorganization—you realize that they have discovered the tanks and you must give credit where credit is due.

Your glasses now wander about to pick up "your" tank—yes, there it is—still going forward, always forward. Following it closely, you notice it patrols up and down in front of your own infantry—it has reached its objective and the infantry is "digging in." A little later "your" tank makes an "about face" and gallops toward home in "fourth" much like the winning colt at a derby, and you set out at once for the rallying point.

The tank rolls up just as you arrive, and its commander is outside, map in hand, just making sure that he has brought his tank to the right spot. A sergeant and a corporal are busy—yes, they are helping the rest of the crew, or rather what is left of the crew, out of the tank, and you soon learn that there have been some casualties. You ask the tank commander for his story and finally draw the news out of him that the tank had received a direct hit, killing two men and wounding four others—yet the tank had "carried on," reached its objective and returned triumphantly.

You have one more desire—to go over the ground just covered by "your" tank—and you immediately start out. Here is the old front line—here are the tank tracks. Following these you come to the old enemy lines. Enemy dead are lying about in countless numbers—here is a machine gun nest, squashed by "your" tank. The innumerable dead astound you—then it comes to you like a flash; "tanks take no prisoners." Finally you reach the new line—a young infantry officer greets you with "Boy, Howdy! Things went like a movie this morning. Aren't the tanks great? Why, we cross five thousand yards and our losses are almost nil."

Now, you are fully convinced that the tanks are THE THING and you solemnly say, "I swear by the tanks."

Second Lieutenant Paul S. Haimbaugh, Company B, 301st Tank Battalion

It is in the cold of early morning, October 8, 1918, and the tanks of B Company of the 301st Battalion, US Tank Corps, uncouth and gigantic crawling monsters with their 35 tons weight, lay stretched in sinuous line along the tape waiting the zero hour. Silent they are, looming bulky in the darkness, soon to awaken and plow their way through the strongly held German lines. You stifle a yawn and shiver with cold and anticipation, and you impatiently pace up and down the line, snatching hasty glances at the luminous characters on your watch dial. It reads 4:30 a.m. and zero hour approaches. Time to go. You rouse your crew and crank up. The engine hums a deep throated cacophony as the line of tanks moves slowly forward. We must be at the "jumping-off" point when the barrage starts. A small mass in front dissolves into men who hastily scramble to their feet and move from our path. Looking about, you see dark forms stretched flat on the ground. It's the infantry, good old American infantry, fighting like yourself, with the British. Good luck to them today.

Then the heavens flame and the air vibrates with the opening crash of our barrage, which resolves itself into a steady booming roar. Right on the dot is the barrage. Five-twenty to the minute; we'll give Jerry enough today. Things aren't going well with him on this Cambrai–St. Quentin sector just now. Perhaps two snappy American divisions and our battalions are worrying them.

The doughboys spring to their feet and start forward. You urge your tank on until you are nosing the barrage, ahead the German distress signals flare in the sky. In a minute the enemy barrage will fall. Here it is. And it's disconcertingly close. You think maybe you better zig-zag a bit. Maybe you can dodge them. The doughboys trudge steadily on; here and there one sags into a heap (shell splinters). One shell nearly gets you as it bursts nearby with the rending crash peculiar to high explosive. Seems like it nearly lifted your tank into the air. Hello! A dozen pneumatic hammers start playing a tattoo on the sides and front of your tank, and splashes of hot metal enter the cracks and sting your face and hands. The infantry, 150 yards back, are prone on the ground; too hot for them. Well, it's up to you to locate the enemy machine guns and put them out. Observation from the peepholes reveals nothing. You pop your head through the trap door and take a quick look around. There they are. A hasty command to the six-pounder and machine gunners. Crash goes the port six-pounder and the tank is filled with fumes of cordite. A hit. A couple more in the same place and a machine gun nest. Come on infantry. As the tank passed you see the grey forms sprawled grotesquely around their guns. You're glad the "bus" is a mole, for those six-pounders certainly do the work.[21]

Up ahead is a railway embankment and a sunken road, a likely place for machine gun nests. Tat-tat-tat, they've already begun to strafe you. Slipping from your seat you shout commands to your gunners. Picking their targets, they pepper away with the machine guns and the two six-pounders thunder. The noise is terrific and the tank is filled with cordite and gasoline fumes. There is a sickening smell of hot oil about. You're pretty close now so you order case shot, and the six-pounders rake the embankment and road with iron case shot, with deadly effect. The place is a shambles—grey forms sprawled in the road—huddled in funk holes—lying in queer broken positions about their guns. Its war and you had to get them first. A half dozen Boche scramble to their feet with hands upraised and you let them pass back towards the rear. Come on infantry!

Your tank, snorting and panting, surmounts the embankment; your hair raises for on a ridge 500 yards ahead are two 77's, sacrifice guns, left behind to get you. Crash! a shell lands 50 yards to your left and short. Your starboard six-pounder lets go. Crash! another one which lands close is sending up a shower of dirt and stones against the side of your tank. Working like mad your gunner sends four shells after the two guns. Good work, for they are silenced. One member of the gun crew flees back.

Beads of perspiration stand on your forehead. Hot work this. The combination of powder and gasoline fume; the smell of hot oil and the exhaust begins to daze you. But you pull yourself together and rumble on. The infantry swings along behind, bombing dugouts and "mopping up," assisted by your running mate, a female tank armed with machine guns only.

It's but a mile to your objective now, but it's a mile of thrills. You get "shot up," put out a half dozen machine gun nests; clean up another sunken road with machine guns placed every ten feet along it. A one-pounder [37mm gun] in a hedge scares you with several well placed shots before it "goes west." Some German artillery observer way back spots you and chases you over the landscape, dropping now a shell in front and then in back of you. Here's your objective. You wait for the infantry to come up, and your crew enjoys a breath of air. After the infantry has dug in and consolidated its position, you turn towards the rallying point. Proudly, the tank lumbers homeward, conscious of its black and blistered sides bearing the honorable scars of machine gun fire. You loll on top, grateful for the fresh air, and a satisfied feeling rolls over you—hard work well done.

Captain Ralph de P. Clarke, Company C, 301st Tank Battalion

After months of training in the schools of the British Tank Corps in England—interesting and necessary, but exasperating to men eager to be at the front—the 301st Battalion, Tank Corps, finally went into the line early in September 1918. Company C relieved the 10th Tank Battalion (British) and took over their remaining tanks, the other companies drawing new tanks of the largest type from the base. For two weeks, while they itched to get into action, the tank crews, inordinately proud of having their own busses at last, adjusted and cleaned them to the last degree by day—and—at night listened to the guns and watched the attempts of ubiquitous Boche planes to come over bent on bombing. They could not yet be told that plans were being evolved for a tremendous smash at the only vulnerable point in the famous Hindenburg Line, a drive the success of which would mean much to the allies and in which they were to have the honor of leading.

Then came the night when 40 heavy tanks crawled out at dark on the beginning of a long trek to the "lying-up place." Dawn found them just nestling under their camouflage again while the tired crews literally threw themselves down for what rest they could get before the strenuous night and day to follow. Toward dusk, the tank and platoon commanders were assembled for final instructions and checking up of details—and that never omitted ceremony of synchronizing watches with the time obtained from headquarters.

Shortly before midnight the actual approach march began—the movement that involves bringing the tanks to the "jumping-off" line just at zero hour, without lights or noise. An approach march tires all concerned—but it tries the very souls of the officers. Over muddy fields and sunken roads, through barbed wire hedges, across abandoned trenches and shell holes—always without light and noise, and most of the time under the searching fire of the enemy artillery. The company commander groping for the way a hundred yards ahead has his nerves strained to the point of breaking for fear of losing the way and not arriving in time, or an accident or a chance hit putting part of his command out of commission. The platoon commanders constantly pass up and down their particular tanks to keep all going well. On foot in front of his tank, its commander guides after the preceding one, his only means of communication with his driver the frantic waving of a glowing cigarette.

The approach marches are much alike, some worse than others, but this first one will never be forgotten. Up ahead the reconnaissance officers were crawling out in front of the infantry lines, laying the tape that serves as a sure guide over the last and most important thousand yards or so. Halfway there an orderly brought word that [First] Lieutenant [Sibley P.] McCluskey, while so doing, was badly wounded and his sergeant assistant killed. A bit further on a bad "pocket" of gas and smoke seriously threatened further progress, but they were led through somehow—officers frequently removing their masks in order to see if possible, and in several cases going on their hands and knees, coughing and gagging, actually finding the way by feeling the tracks.

Company C met its RO, [Second] Lieutenant [Harry M.] Woods, at the beginning of the tape, and arrived at the other end without a casualty.

[First] Lieutenant [William M.] Rosborough, commanding a platoon, jumped into [Second] Lieutenant [Hannibal E.] Potter's tank with his two orderlies. This tank drove straight for its objective, until, while knocking out machine guns in the outposts of the Hindenburg Line, it received a direct hit [from a German 5.9-inch field gun], killing six of the crew and seriously wounding all the other occupants. Hastily evacuating under heavy fire from close by, the survivors took up position with their Hotchkiss guns in a nearby shell hole. In this scant shelter, Lieutenant Rosborough dressed as well as possible the wounds of the others. Then, although wounded and burned himself, he made the precarious trip back to our infantry to try to get help—while Sergeant Frank J. Williams Jr., his orderly, also badly wounded, insisted on staying with Lieutenant Potter, who was in a serious condition. Eventually help reached them and they were removed to hospital, but Lieutenant Rosborough was taken prisoner while crawling along. While being conducted to the rear through a trench, he pushed over one of his guards, hit the other in the eye, scrambled up over the side and got away. After hiding that night and the next day under his derelict tank, he succeeded in working his way back to a dressing station.

Many tanks that day went gallantly on until wrecked by a shell—not one faltered. [Second] Lieutenant [John D.] McKay, twice wounded at his post, was killed while trying to get out of his tank to be out of the way. His crew evacuated upon receiving a direct hit, several badly wounded; although they had stood to their guns as long as the tank would run. While in a nearby shell hole under heavy machine gun fire, Private William Burns three times crawled back to the tank to get things for the wounded, once more dressings, again for a coat, and finally for the dead officer's gas mask to replace Corporal [Samuel B] Hoffar's destroyed by the shot that wounded him.

[First] Lieutenant [Oscar] O'Kane's tank received a hit that wrecked it completely, fatally wounding him and one of his crew. Other tanks shared the same fate, but their crews fared better, although many were wounded—for the Boche had direct observation and concentrated his 77's on the tanks. But all were going straight and did splendid work against the machine guns to the last.

[Second] Lieutenant [Earle B.] Dunning's tank in some way missed being hit for a long time, while it went on across trench after trench, through machine guns and wire until far behind the German lines it was knocked out. Until after dark, the crew hid nearby, then started an almost hopeless attempt to get back. Seven were taken prisoners, but the lieutenant and Sergeant [Carl E.] Rosenhagen, after hours and hours of patient, agonizing crawling and wiggling and waiting, reached the British lines and by the next night reported to the battalion. They were sick from gas and exposure, exhausted, soaked, torn to ribbons by the wire,—but related their story and turned in their valuable information. Lieutenant Dunning was decorated with the Military Cross and Sergeant Rosenhagen with the Military Medal of the British.

After a few days reorganizing crews and repairing of tanks, the company was ready to go in again—not a whit daunted by their terrific initiation. They were veterans now, and no show would ever hold the interest the first did. The chance came on October 8th, when the remaining tanks of Companies A and C combined in one company, led an attack on the village of Brancourt. All went well, all tanks reaching their objectives and returning, wiping out machine gun nests and clearing the village. [Second] Lieutenant [Aubrey F.] Holmes had the bad luck to get a bullet square in the eye, but his last words to his driver as he lapsed into unconsciousness were to go right on.

[Second] Lieutenant [John W.] Dinsmore's tank succeeded in knocking out, by a well-placed shot from its six-pounder, a gun in the church steeple that had harassed the infantry for days. Then, after reaching their objective, it went voluntarily to the assistance of a British unit of the corps on our right, advancing alone and clearing a wood of Boche guns so that this unit could go on.

The Germans were retiring fast by this time, and it kept the officers and crews under a night-and-day strain keeping up the pace of open warfare. But they did it, and went in again October 17th in an attack on the river Selle. Part of the approach march for this show was a nightmare. For three hours, from one to four a.m., it was necessary to lie in position, engines stopped, nothing possible to do but sit tight while shells burst on all sides. All but a few necessary officers were kept inside the tanks in their gas masks while the platoon commanders wandered from tank to tank looking in and passing a few casual remarks to keep down the inevitable tendency to panic under inaction. But it was a relief to all when the time came to go on, with only two casualties and one tank disabled.

Just before zero hour, when approaching the starting line, [Second] Lieutenant [Richard A.] Parke's tank burst into flames in full view of the enemy, drawing the fire of a dozen machine guns; but this officer quickly had it turned into a nearby wood, shut down and abandoned before it could betray its mates or furnish a useful target for the artillery. In this action also, lieutenants Dunning of Company C and Frost of Company A, cooperated; after fighting to their limit in refilling Lieutenant Frost's tank with the remaining ammunition and petrol from Lieutenant Dunning's, making a temporary crew out of the volunteers from both, so that Frost could go back in and do all the damage he could.

Once more the remaining tanks of the battalion operating as one company participated in an attack on October 23rd. It was a night affair, Zero Hour at 1:20 a.m., but in spite of the dark, the tanks did splendid work. Again lieutenants Frost and Dunning distinguished themselves. With their allotted jobs done, and done well, they looked around, hungry for a scrap. In conjunction with an infantry officer met in Bazuel, a little private show was arranged when the two with their tanks led a couple of platoons to a new position of advantage half a mile further on.

After this show there was a 10-day period of reorganization and repairs—when everything was newly adjusted and additional tanks drawn. Then on to Le Quesnoy, recently liberated, from whence the battalion stood ready to go into action the following morning—when the Armistice was signed.

This brought to an end the longest consecutive period a heavy tank battalion has ever been in the line. Only those who have worked with tanks, in the dark and mud, can fully appreciate what this means. The days of heavy backbreaking repairing—the heart breaking treks, the strain of the night approach marches, and yet all performed with a cheerfulness and energy that won the battalion the respect and admiration of the experienced British Tank Corps. Like praise from an older brother—that was not easily won, but meant so much more when won.

Second Lieutenant Harry M. Woods, Reconnaissance Officer, Company C, 301st Tank Battalion

As Reconnaissance Officer of Company C, my part in the operations of the 301st Heavy Battalion, US Tank Corps, was largely one of office work on maps and aerial photos and field work, comparable to a preliminary look-over for a survey, for the purpose of selecting rear area routes, tank-dromes, lying-up points, etc. My active part, where all my "experiences" such as they were, occurred, consisted in the main of three parts: tape-laying, to guide tanks to their jumping-off place; load-up tanks before an attack; and getting reports.

For our first and hardest "show" on September 23, about 2,000 yards of tape was laid on the night of September 28–29, with the assistance of a detail from the 107th US Infantry. The first 1,500 yards was laid with only the discomfort incidental to darkness, rough ground and a few gas shells. The last 500 yards extended from a trench where the American troops were not sure whether they were outposts or not, directly toward the German lines. According to infantry headquarters, tape could have been laid nearly 1,000 yards further than we went, but it proved later that it was well we stopped when we did, for we had laid the tape almost into the German outposts then. But as we did not know it at the time, it did not "get our wind up" and the only untoward incident of the tape laying was Jerry's ill-timed notion to drop half a dozen HE shells on a track-and-trench crossing just as we were passing that point. Aside from scaring us badly, however, he did us no damage.

The tape laid, I went back and met the tanks and led them up to and onto it. The approach march was successful but, due to heavy gas in one valley and heavy shelling at one point on the tape line, where everybody except the company commander sought comparative safety inside a tank, [it was] unpleasant. The tanks were refilled with gasoline near infantry headquarters while the company commander and I argued with the infantry commander, whose operation orders differed from ours; a blunder which contributed to the heavy infantry casualties of the next day. We left the refilling point in time to "jump off" at zero hour and deployed the tanks at the end of the tape line; a disagreeable task, as the point was persistently shelled. It was when we started back with the tanks deployed that the infantry's misinformation as to their forward positions served us badly, for before we could get back to the "show," both sides opened up and caught the company and platoon commanders, their runners and myself in front of our actual line, between the German machine gun fire and our own. Fortunately, we all got back safely, mostly by means of two tanks that had to go out of action with mechanical trouble.

I left the tank, on which I rode, back at the first trench line and hastened to the dugout of the infantry commander, feeling sure that he would be anxious to learn of the tanks' start. I was so zealous to deliver the news, in fact, that I ran at top speed all the way. A heavy German barrage was falling at the time. I spent the forenoon at or near headquarters and after lunch spent the rest of the day meeting returning tanks and crews, getting their reports and directing them to a new rallying point, that originally selected proved untenable.

The tape laying for our second show was rendered difficult by reason of a long distance to go, a very dark night and difficulty in getting the tape from supply. But from the enemy we met with no molestation. The possession of the railway where our tape was to end was in doubt and we were rather anxious as we approached it, but it proved to be safely within our lines and we were "more scared than hurt." The tanks arrived at the beginning of the tape in time to get a good start along it and we left them to deploy by themselves after crossing the railroad to which the tape led. As for the "bolos," we had the privilege of watching from a beautiful OP the whole show, which was a complete and early success. Some of the tanks returned with their work all done before 8:00 a.m., and by noon all were rallied or reported.

The tape for our third show of October 17th was laid with very little difficulty. A misty night of poor visibility made it possible to work while there was still considerable light and the tape was all down and we were back at the laying-up point by 8:00 p.m. Again, we had been misled as to our front line positions, but machine gun fire at fairly short range warned us when it was time to stop. A and C Companies were acting as one for this action, which made three RO's available. As there was no need for more than one with the tanks, we matched coins to see who should go and as my lot fell to stay behind, I did not see the get-away. The next morning, a very heavy fog interfered seriously with the attack and precluded the obtaining of any reports until after noon. Not long after lunch, however, the tanks or crews began to get back to the rallying point and by nightfall all were reported.

The fourth show on October 23rd was a small, moonlight affair with only nine tanks participating and zero hour 1:20 a.m. Due to a last-minute change of plans, my part became the laying of 2,000 yards of tape practically where we had drawn our line on the map. Heavy shelling at two points ahead of us where we were going to lay tape "got our wind up," but it ceased before we got to the places and the scare was the only damage done us. The tanks got up to the beginning of the tape soon after we returned, and as there was nothing more for me to do except get them onto it, I went back and reported to battalion headquarters, where I spent the night and most of the next day; for with all the battalion RO's available to work with nine tanks, report-getting did not fall to my lot that day. So my part in active operations ceased when I left the tanks on their tape line the night before.

After that my work consisted in helping load up the tanks on rear-route treks in a vain endeavor to keep up with a war which was leaving us faster than we could follow, until November 11th and the armistice put an end to all our expectations of future action.

Second Lieutenant John A. Logan, Company C, 301st Tank Battalion

Arriving in France, about the middle of August, the 301st Battalion, USTC, proceeded immediately to Bermicourt, near the center stores of the British Tank Corps. The battalion had men "hand-picked" in the States, received five months tank training in England and physically and mentally were in the pink of condition.

One private expressed the wish of the entire battalion when he said, "Show me the way to the war that we have come so far to take part in." The British said we were fit, and anyone who knows the British methods will know that our training must have been thorough indeed. Tanks were issued to A and B Companies. C Company proceeded to Achiet-le-Grande to take over the tanks of the 10th British Battalion. This battalion had just aided the New Zealanders in the capture of Bapaume and many of the tanks were left on the field where they had "conked" out. It was up to C Company to get these tanks into shape for the initial battle, where we were to have our baptism of fire.

Before going to Achiet-le-Grande the writer had the privilege of taking part as an observer with the 11th British Tank Battalion, in the breaking of the famous Drocourt Queant-Switch line. The experience was well worthwhile. Two sergeants of the observing party were killed.

After leaving the British battalion, we joined our company at Achiet-le-Grande.

The particular tank assigned to the writer was in the battlefield where it had been left by the British. It was the famous old "Jellico" and all it needed was a new engine and several patches for holes in the armor plate.[22] The crew worked eagerly and soon the tank was in tip-top shape.

Our next move was to Manancourt. We had been under shell fire for a few days at Achiet-le-Grande, but here Fritz was sending them over at regular intervals, but we were becoming used to it. [Second] Lieutenant [John D.] McKay's tank and the "Jellico" or rather the "Arizona," for the crew had decided to give the big lumbering bus a regular American name, were side by aide. "Black Sammy" as he was affectionately known by his brother officers was a congressional medal man and had seen service with the marines all over the world. Little did we think that our first fight would be "Sammy's" last, and that his would be the supreme sacrifice.

Then came one morning that we all had been looking forward to. With orders to be prepared to leave at night, everyone knew his part. Cheering news came with the order that we were going over with the Yanks, the hard fighting bunch, the 27th ["Yankee"] Division. A Company was to go over with the 30th Division. We made an all-night march with our tanks, and believe me, a trip to hell is nothing compared to leading over trenches and wire in the black darkness. Arriving at the lying-out point, the tanks were camouflaged and everyone turned in for a few hours' sleep; some in the mud and some in the tanks. The writer remembered falling between a box of shells and the engine, and being too tired to get up, slept there.

Working feverishly at our engine, we were able to put it in shape for the approach march that night. After leading our tanks through much shell fire and gas we arrived at our jumping-off point. We afterwards told the reconnaissance officer jokingly that he was in league with the Germans, for the end of the tape at which we were to jump off had been laid actually within the German lines.

The barrage started and we were off. The crew of the "Arizona" were as cool as could be. The sight of the American doughboys, strolling along, for that is exactly how they looked, smoking cigarettes, was enough to put courage in the weakest. In about three seconds though, we couldn't tell where we were. It became very foggy and we rocked like a ship for Fritz had put down a barrage and shells were falling very close. We could see the other tanks mopping up the trenches to the left of us and four tanks to the right, which we thought were from our platoon. After fighting alongside of these four tanks for a while, we discovered them to be from A Company, so we turned to the left to join our own company. We were lucky to do so for in a few minutes those four tanks ran into a minefield and were blown up. We had just cleared up a trench of Jerries when our engine went dead. We thought that an armor-piercing bullet had fixed us, but after a few minutes cranking we managed to get a couple of cylinders coughing so that we were able to get the tank into the trench so as to repair the damage. Suddenly, I heard a yell and turned to see a mass of flames shooting from the engine. The whole tank seemed to be on fire. The driver and I tried to get out through the top, but the door stuck, so back through the flames we went. I tried to put the fire out with pyrene, but the fumes made me groggy almost instantly and but for the fact that Sergeant Hoberts dragged me out, I would have surely been badly burned. We were scarcely outside when a German aeroplane flying low dropped a couple of flares. Just then business began to pick up, for the shells began to fall all about us and then a German machine gunner spotted us. The gunner had managed to bring out a couple of machine guns and we mounted them.

There was fighting further down the trench and I saw an American doughboy bayonet a Boche as clean as you would like. We found 22 Boche machine guns in the trench and a couple of anti-tank rifles. The shelling was intense and I became separated from my crew with the exception of a sergeant. Everyone was lost in the fog and smoke. Later in the morning I found [Second] Lieutenant Richard A. Parke, whose tank had been put out of action. We stayed with some Australians that night and found our battalion next morning. Our losses had been very heavy, but they told us that the Hindenburg Line had been taken.

I drew a reserve tank with a new crew and a week or so later we went in again at Montbrehain. This fight was a picnic and we evened up for our losses in the first show.

On the Selle River we went over with the 30th Division. It was very foggy and we were lost for a while. My tank, the "O'Hell," was to mop up with three others. It sure was fun, for we had good ground to travel on. In Bohain we were obliged to shoot up the houses for the Boche machine gunners kept firing from them. Our crew suffered no losses and we picked up [Second] Lieutenant [Roscoe C.] Little's crew, whose tank had been stuck in the river.

Those boys from the South are a game lot and there is one officer that I would like to see again. While we were lost in the fog, I was outside my tank trying to get a map location. He came up while we were studying our map. He was covered with blood and bits of flesh. Two of his companions had been blown to pieces right beside him with a shell, but it never affected his nerve a bit.

We wound up the season at Le Quesnoy near the Belgian border, for the armistice put an end to the open season on Huns, and here we are at Saulty; still with the British, each one with but a single thought, "When do we go home?"

Second Lieutenant R. E. Hughes, 301st Tank Battalion

It was with the gallant 301st American heavy tank battalion, BEF [British Expeditionary Forces] that you could see starting for the night show or on the approach march at about 6:00 p.m., October 22, 1918. Your tank commander walking just ahead to direct their way, it becoming too dark for your driver to see his way. You would see him fall into holes and over wire and then would come his wild yell to the driver to stop. Yes; yelled as he never yelled before. To stop the "bus" from crushing him, the driver would apply all his force on the brakes. This is only one of the many close calls of death you have had to contend with. It has been experienced many times by all brother tank commanders.

Not stopping to brush off the dirt and mud you get in front of your tank again, command the driver to move on. You arrive at the filling-up point near midnight, there to refill all tanks again. Give to all the necessary instructions as to their duties. A bite to eat and a little drink, as it may be many days before another chance may be had to eat again. A last word of cheer and good luck to all other brother tankers and then comes the order, "turn her over." Everybody inside all doors and hatches secured and the guns loaded and in position ready to fire. The tanks move and the tape is followed; that tape which the brave reconnaissance officer has laid to within the enemy lines. At the end of the tape, the jumping-off place. The platoon commander bids you farewell saying, "Give them the American argument, boys." And that is what they got. The word was given to fire and you could hear the German machine gun bullets knocking at the door and once in a while an HE [shell] would explode nearby and move the tank to one side and then another push it back.

The driver had orders to keep 75 yards to the right and abreast of a brother tank. The peepholes being too small to have a clear vision, the shutter was opened and not until the guns were fired, could you see the other tank's position. Many hedges were encountered and passed through. The great question was, would the ground on the other side hold your tank. In going through an orchard, the other tank was missed or were we lost? The tank commander got outside and encountered a British patrol and from questioning them with the aid of his map, came back and started the tank on its proper course, but not before drivers were changed, because the first driver had succumbed to gas, which was plenty.

Tank commander sat alongside of the new driver and conducted the tank to its final objective and returned to the rallying point with all his men, arriving about 10:00 a.m.

Everyone, slightly gassed and very hungry, made for the kitchen to eat and then rest, knowing that the day's work of pushing back the Huns had been completed, and successfully.

Brigadier General Samuel D. Rockenbach, Commander, US Army Tank Corps, American Expeditionary Forces, France, 1918. (Library of Congress, Prints and Photographs Division, 101–199 Independence Avenue SE, Washington, DC, 20540, Call No. LC-B2-4814-7A)

Lieutenant Colonel George S. Patton Jr., Commander, 304th Tank Brigade, with a Renault light tank at Bourg, France, 1918. (https://www.army.mil/e2/-images/2007/04/22/3578/army.mil-2007-03-28-152527.jpg)

Major Sereno E. Brett, circa 1919, commander of the 344th Tank Battalion during combat operations in France in 1918. (https://en.wikipedia.org/wiki/Sereno_E._Brett#/media/File:Sereno_E._Brett.jpg)

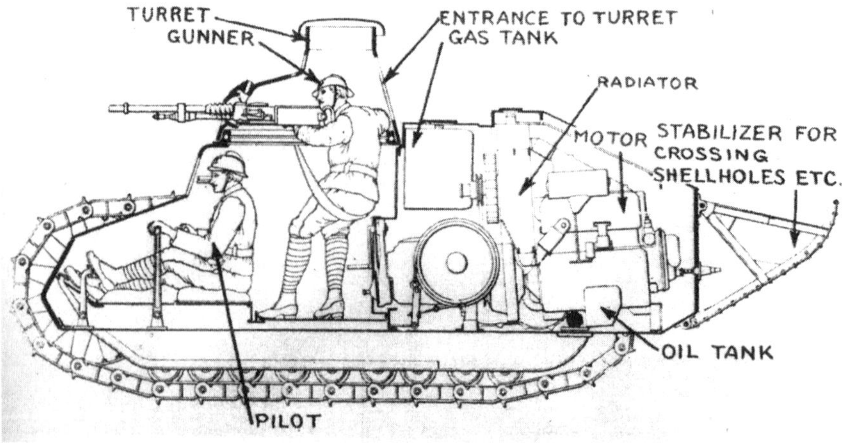

Schematic of Renault light tank armed with a .30-caliber Hotchkiss machine gun. (*New York Times Midweek Pictorial*, December 5, 1918, 1)

US Army Tank Corps Renault light tank with two-man crew. (*New York Times Midweek Pictorial*, October 17, 1918, 5)

Renault light tank, Company C, 345th Tank Battalion, in action in France, September 1918. (William E. Moore and James C. Russell, *Official Pictures of the World War* [Washington, DC: Pictorial Bureau, 1920], 197)

Renault light tanks loaded on rail cars, September 25, 1918, in anticipation of operations the following day in the Meuse-Argonne Offensive. (William E. Moore and James C. Russell, *Official Pictures of the World War* [Washington, DC: Pictorial Bureau, 1920], 232)

Renault light tanks of the 344th Tank Battalion near Boureuilles, France, September 26, 1918. The lead tank is armed with a .30-caliber Hotchkiss machine gun, followed by one armed with a 37mm gun. (William E. Moore and James C. Russell, *Official Pictures of the World War* [Washington, DC: Pictorial Bureau, 1920], 327)

Renault light tanks of the 344th Tank Battalion with gas cans (bidons) strapped to their tails, near Boureuilles, France, September 26, 1918. (William E. Moore and James C. Russell, *Official Pictures of the World War* [Washington, DC: Pictorial Bureau, 1920], 236)

A German Mauser 1918 T-Gewehr 13.2mm anti-tank rifle examined by a French soldier, September 1918. (*New York Times,* September 22, 1918, sec. 6, 2)

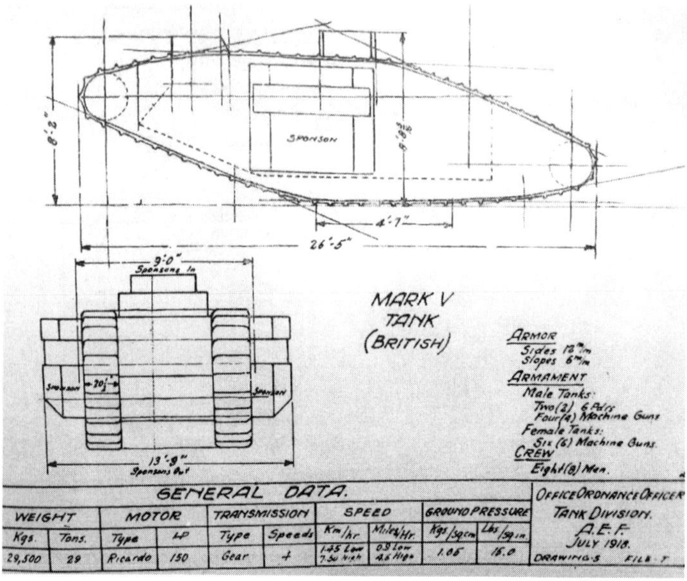

Mark V tank diagram, July 1918. (George S. Patton, Jr., Papers, Manuscript Division, Library of Congress, 101–199 Independence Avenue SE, Washington, DC, 20540, Box 55, Folder 3)

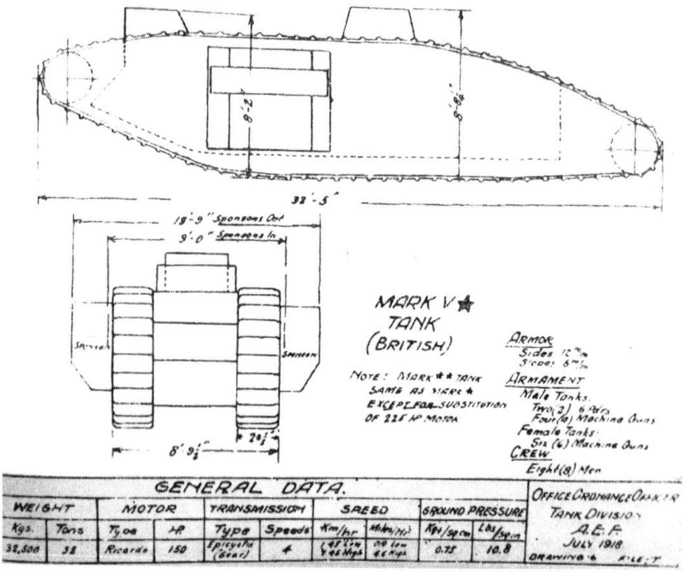

Mark V Star tank diagram, July 1918. (George S. Patton, Jr., Papers, Manuscript Division, Library of Congress, 101–199 Independence Avenue SE, Washington, DC, 20540, Box 55, Folder 3)

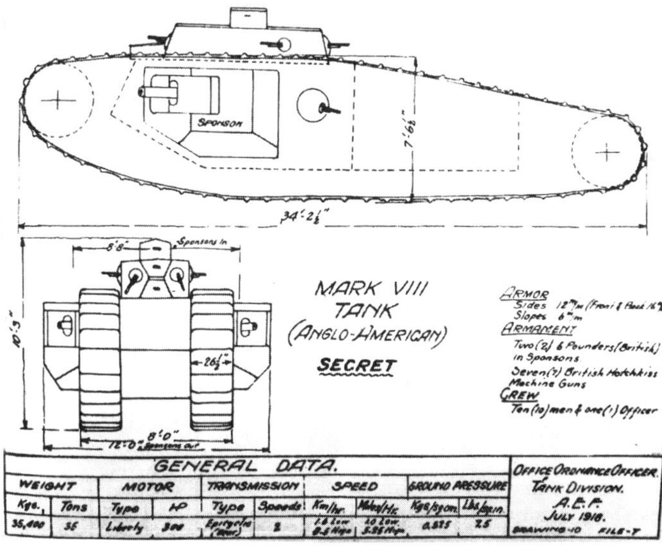

Mark VIII tank diagram, July 1918. (George S. Patton, Jr., Papers, Manuscript Division, Library of Congress, 101–199 Independence Avenue SE, Washington, DC, 20540, Box 55, Folder 3)

Sectional view of Anglo-American Mark VIII tank design, 1918. (George S. Patton, Jr., Papers, Manuscript Division, Library of Congress, 101–199 Independence Avenue SE, Washington, DC, 20540, Box 55, Folder 3)

A 301st Tank Battalion tank advancing through enemy barbed-wire entanglements. (*New York Times Midweek Pictorial*, January 2, 1919, 14)

A platoon of the 107th Infantry Regiment, 27th Infantry Division, lying behind a 301st Tank Battalion tank as it advances against the enemy. The tank at right is laying a smoke screen. (*New York Times Midweek Pictorial*, January 2, 1919, 14)

301st Tank Battalion Mark V tanks (*in the background*) with cribs advance for the attack against the Hindenburg Line near Bellicourt in late September 1918. The cribs, located on the front of the tanks, were hexagonal-shaped frameworks of timber braced with steel that could be dropped in a trench to provide better traction in trench crossings. (American Battle Monuments Commission, *American Armies and Battlefields in Europe* [Washington, DC: Government Printing Office, 1938], 376)

IV

Unofficial Personal Accounts

George S. Patton Jr., Personal Correspondence

George S. Patton Jr., letter to his wife, Beatrice, June 13, 1918 (George S. Patton Jr., Papers, Box 8, Folder 7, Manuscript Division, Library of Congress, Washington, D.C.; hereafter cited as Patton Papers)

Dear Beatrice:

One year ago today we reached Paris full of desire to kill Germans. We are still full of desire but so far as I am concerned there are just as many Germans as there were then. Sometimes I deeply regret that I did not take the infantry last November instead of the tanks. The regiment I had the chance to join has been at it now for five months. Of course I have done a lot but I keep dreading lest the war should finish before I can really do any fighting. That would destroy my military career or at least give it a great setback.

The only cheering prospect is that there are very many infantry battalion commanders and only a few tank commanders.

If the war lasts long enough it will work out greatly to my advantage but the unknown is always full of terrors and I wake up at night in a sweat fearing that the d___ show is over.

I am having too much routine for my health at least health of mind.

I trust that it is doing my character a lot of good for I keep at it in spite of constant difficulties and discouragements. But unless I get into a fight or two it is all wasted effort. . . .

George S. Patton Jr., letter to his wife, Beatrice, September 16, 1918 (Patton Papers, Box 8, Folder 18)

Darling Beat:

The news is out, so I can give you a brief account of the battle of St. Mihiel, etc. At 10 a.m. August 22 I got a telephone message to report to [Brig.] Gen. R [Rockenbach] with my reconnaissance officer ready for protracted field service. I did, at 3 p.m. We were at Army HQ and had been told the plans, which as you know, contemplated the attack by Three Corps. I was to command the tanks in the Five Corps. The rest of the tanks were to be supplied by the French. At 6 p.m. I reported to your old friend [Brig.] Gen. [Wilson B.] Burtt (Capt. in Mexico) who was chief of staff. Next day I went to French corps headquarters to get permission to visit the front. On going there I was told it was a marsh where tanks could not move. As I did not believe this, I went out with a French patrol that night to the Bosch wire and found the ground hard and dry, though in winter it is probably a marsh. We worked hard and got all ready to fight; also got our tanks, for on August 22 we had only 22. I had to patrol and make plans and then travel back to the center every other night, a four-hour ride, to arrange things there. We thought that "D" day would be September 7. On September 4, I got ordered to leave the Fifth Corps and report to the Forth Corps near Toul. Here I got a new job and had to start all over again, which was a bore; still it had to be done.

I walked down the Rupt de Mad by day to the bridge at Xivray, which is in No Man's Land and was not shot at. I had to do it to see whether we could cross the stream.

Then we started to detrain and that was awful for four nights. The French made every mistake they could, sending trains to the wrong place or not sending them at all. The last company of the 327 Battalion detrained at 3:15 a.m. and marched right into action.

We attacked at 5 a.m. on Thursday, September 12. At 1 a.m. 900 plus guns opened and shock till 5. It was dark with a heavy rain and wind. I was on a hill in front of the main line where I could watch both battalions and 30 French that I had also under me.

I could see them coming along and getting stuck in the trenches. It was a most irritating sight. At seven o'clock I moved forward 2 miles and at nine o'clock I decided I had to see something, so I took an officer and three runners and started forward.

There were very few dead in the trenches, as the Bosch had not fought hard, but you never saw such trenches—8 feet deep and 10 to 14 feet wide. At the first town we came to, St. Baussant, the Bosch were still shelling and it was not pleasant. At ___ [Maizerais] I found the French stuck in a place under shell fire. I talked to the major and went on. I had not gone 20 feet when a shell, 6 inches, struck the tank he was working on and killed 15 men. I went on toward Essey and got into the front line infantry who were laying down. As there was only shell fire, I walked on smoking with vigor; most of the shells went high. Here I met [Brig.] Gen. MacArthur (Douglas) commanding a brigade. He was walking about too, so we stood and talked, but neither was much interested in what the other said as we could not get our minds off the shells. I went up the hill to have a look and could see the Bosch running beyond Essey fast, then five tanks of my right battalion came up, so I told them to go through Essey. Some damned

Frenchman at the bridge told them to go back as there were too many shells in the town. The lieutenant in command obeyed. This made me mad, so I led them through on foot, but there was no danger as the Bosch [were] shelling the next town.

Some Germans came out of dugouts and surrendered to Gen. MacArthur.

I asked him if I could go on and attack the next town, Pannes. He said sure, so I started. All the tanks but one run out of gas. When we got to Pannes, some two miles, the infantry would not go in, so I told the sergeant commanding the tank to go in. He was nervous at being alone, so I said I would sit on the roof. This reassured him and we entered the town. [First] Lieut. [Maurice H.] Knowles and Sgt. Graham sat on the tail of the tank. I watched one side of the street and they the other. Pretty soon we saw a Bosch who threw up his hands. I told Knowles and Graham to go get him and I went on outside the town toward Beney. I saw the paint fly off the side of the tank and heard machine guns so I jumped off and got in a shell hole. It was small and the bullets knocked all of the front edge in on me. Here, I was nervous. The tank had not seen me get off and was going on. The infantry was about 200 meters back of me and did not advance. One runner on my right got hit. If I went back the infantry would think I was running. If I did not, they would not support the tank and it might get hurt. Besides, machine gun bullets are unpleasant to hear. Finally, I decided that I could get back obliquely, so I started as soon as the machine guns opened. I would lay down and beat the bullets each time. The captain of doughboys said he could not advance as the troops on his right were not up. I asked him to send a runner to the tank to recall it. He said it was "not his tank," so I went and I burned the breeze too, so did the bullets. I kept the tank between me and the bullets as much as possible and finally got it back. By this time four more tanks had come up, but there was no officer. I put Lieut. Knowles, who had caught 30 Bosch instead of one, in the tank and asked the infantry if they would follow. They said yes, so I started the tanks. In the meantime, some of our machine guns had pushed out in front and one tank thought they were Bosch and began to shoot at them. I had no time to get someone, so we went out again. The tanks went on to Beney, but the infantry swerved off to the right and I sent a lieutenant out to change direction of the tanks. Then, I followed the advance on foot, but there was not much shooting. The tanks had scared the Bosch away.

From here I walked along the line of battle to the left flank at Nonsard where the other battalion was. The captain who would not send a runner was killed at this time. I was very tired indeed and hungry as I had lost the sack with my rations and my flask of brandy. At Nonsard I found 25 tanks. They had taken the town and only lost four men and two officers, but they were out of gas. All my runners were gone, so I started back 7 miles to tell them to get some gas. That was the only bad part of the fight. I had had no sleep for two nights; nothing to eat since the night before except some crackers I got off a dead Bosch. I would have given a lot for a little brandy, but even my water was gone.

When I got to ____ it had been raining two hours and the mud was bad. Here I met an officer sightseeing and he gave me a lift. This was lucky as the car got stuck in a jam and went slower than the men on foot and an airplane dropped a bomb on the road and killed two soldiers who had been walking just back of me.

I got a motorcycle and got the gas and reported to the court.

The 13th we did nothing. I will tell you of the 14th later.

This is a very egotistical account of the affair full of "I" but it will interest you.

I at least proved to my satisfaction that I have nerve. I was the only man on the front line except Gen. MacArthur who never ducked a shell. I wanted to, but it is foolish, as it does no good if they are going to hit you, they will.

I had in this section 144 tanks and 33 French tanks; quite a command. We lost two tanks with direct hits and eight men and three officers only, one killed and one lost an eye.

All the losses were small, absurdly so. The great feat the tanks performed was getting through at all. The conditions could not have been worse. Only 40% did it the first day, but we had 80% up by morning. The men were fine. Nearly all the officers led the tanks on foot.

Gen. R. gave me hell for going up, but it had to be done, at least I will not sit in a dugout and have my men out in the fighting.

I am feeling fine and just at present have little to do. . . . Personally, I never fired a shot except to kill two poor horses with broken legs.

George S. Patton Jr., letter to his wife, Beatrice, September 19, 1918 (Patton Papers, Box 8, Folder 16)

Darling Beat:

. . . We are getting ready for another show and I am sitting in the only remaining house of the village. They have not shelled us yet, but doubtless will shortly, as Americans don't seem to be able to conceal themselves very well. I just got back from a reconnaissance where I was dressed like a Frenchman. I hope I did not get any bugs, but one cannot be too particular. I fancy our next show will be less easy than the first that is if the Bosch fight and I think they will. The ground, however, is better for us, being less of a swamp than the St. Mihiel salient proved to be. Still, as it has been raining all the time, it may get muddy here also. I just got through writing a report on the last action and recommended certain officers for gallantry. I hope they get something.

We start to unload tonight in a swamp, but it will be hard for the Bosch to see us.

To complete the account of the battle of St. Mihiel on the 13th. We did nothing except get one battalion up on the line. On the night of the 13th the left battalion started to move up and look for the division it was supposed to be with. We could not find it. I joined the battalion at 7 a.m. and we decided to go onto a road which ran along our front, or supposed front, and on one end of which was the other battalion. We had nearly reached this end, having seen no troops, when an officer told us that two kilometers down the road were the Bosch at Woel. We thought of attacking, but having no infantry, we decided not to, and hid the tanks in some bushes and sent an officer south to look for our division and one forward to hunt the Bosch. In the meantime, we ate canned corned beef and coffee and filled the tanks with gas—just here two shells hit across the street, so I was interrupted. To resume, while we were filling the tanks with gas, some Bosch airplanes bombed us and wounded a man. At two o'clock, having heard nothing, we sent out a patrol of three tanks to find out what was doing. They were attacked and we sent five more tanks and chased the Bosch to ____ over the Hindenburg Line, capturing a battery of 77[mm] guns and 8 machine guns. The men tried to tie the guns to the back of the tanks, but got hit by shrapnel and two officers and two men were wounded, so they came back, and finding that the division had withdrawn, and that the tanks were 2 miles ahead of our own lines, we returned. But at ____ we were 8 kilometers ahead of the fastest advance of the rest of the troops. . . .

Total losses for 3 days, 4 men killed, 4 men and 4 officers wounded. Two tanks smashed.

George S. Patton Jr., letter to his father, September 20, 1918 (Patton Papers, Box 8, Folder 16)

Dear Papa,

We have all been in one fine fight and it was not half so exciting as I had hoped, not as exciting as affairs in Mexico, because there was so much company. When the shelling first started I had some doubts about the advisability of sticking my head over the parapet, but it is just like taking a cold bath, once you get in, it is all right. And I soon got out and sat on the parapet. At seven o'clock I moved forward and passed some dead and wounded. I saw one fellow in a shell hole holding his rifle and sitting down. I thought he was hiding and went to cuss him out; he had a bullet over his right eye and was dead. As my telephone wire ran out at this point, I left the adjutant there and went forward with a lieutenant and four runners to find the tanks. The whole country was alive with them crawling over trenches and into woods. It was fine, but I could not see my right battalion, so went to look for it. In doing so, we passed through several towns under shell fire, but none did more than throw dust on us. I admit that I wanted to duck and probably did at first, but soon saw the futility of dodging fate; besides, I was the only officer around who had left on his shoulder straps and I had to live up to them. It was much easier than you would think and the feeling, foolish probably, of being admired by the men lying down is a great stimulus. I walked right along the firing line of one brigade. They were all in shell holes except the general (Douglas MacArthur) who was standing on a little hill. I joined him and the creeping barrage came along toward us, but it was very thin and not dangerous. I think each one wanted to leave, but each hated to say so, so we let it come over us. The infantry were held up at a town, so I happened to find some tanks and sent them through it. I walked behind and some Bosch surrendered to me. At the next town all but one tank was out of sight and as the infantry would not go in, I got on top of the tank to hearten the driver and we went in. That was most exciting as there were plenty of Bosch; we took thirty. On leaving the town I was still sitting sidewise on top of the tank with my legs hanging down on the left side when all at once I noticed all the paint start to chip off the other side and at the same time I noticed machine guns. I dismounted in haste and got in a shell hole, which was none too large. Every time I started to get out the Bosch shot at me. I was on the point of getting scared as I was about 100 yards ahead of the infantry and all alone in the field.

If I went back the infantry would think I was running and there was no reason to go forward alone. All the time the infernal tank was going on alone as the men had not noticed my hurried departure. At last, the bright thought occurred to me that I could move across the front in an oblique direction and not appear to run, yet at the same time get back. This I did, listening for the machine guns with all my ears, and laying down in a great hurry when I heard them. In this manner I hoped to beat the bullets to me. Sometime I will figure the speed of sounds and bullets and see if I was right. It is the only use I know of that math has ever been to me. I found the major of the infantry and asked him if he would come on after the tank. He would not as the next battalion on his left had not come up (he was killed ten minutes later). Then I drew a long breath and went after the tank on foot, as I could not let it be going against a whole town alone. It is strange, but quite true, that at this time I was not the least scared, as I had the idea of getting the tank fixed in my head. I did not even fear the bullets, though I could see the guns spitting at me. I did, however, run like H____. On reaching the tank about 400 yards out in the field, I tapped on the back of the door with my stick, and thank God it was a long one.

The sergeant looked out and saluted and said, what do you want now colonel? I told him to turn and come back; he was much depressed. I walked just ahead of him on the return trip and was quite safe. We now got five tanks and decided to attack the town, but one of the tanks started shooting at our machine guns and I had to go out again and stop it. A third time I went out as the tanks were keeping too far to the right, but the last time was not bad, as the machine gunners were mostly dead or chased away by the tanks. We took the town, 4 field guns and 16 machine guns.

Then I walked along the battlefront to see how the left battalion had gotten on. It was a very long way and I had had no sleep for four nights and no food all the day as I lost my sack chasing a Bosch. I got some crackers off a dead one (he had not bled on them as in the Polk's story); they were very good, but I would have given a lot for a drink of the brandy I had had in my sack. The major [Sereno E. Brett] of the left battalion was crying because he had no more gas. He was very tired and had a bullet through his nose. I comforted him and started home alone to get some gas. It was most interesting over the battlefield like the books, but much less dramatic. The dead were about mostly hit in the head. There were a lot of our men stripping off buttons and other things, but they always covered the face of the dead in a nice way.

I saw one very amusing thing which I would have liked to have photographed. Right in the middle of a large field where there had never been a trench was a shell hole from a 9.7[-inch] gun. The hole was at least 8 feet deep and 15 across. On the edge of it was a dead rat, not a large healthy rat, but a small field rat, not over twice the size of a mouse. No wonder the war costs so much.

On the 13th we did nothing, but on the 14th the left battalion personally conducted by me, went to hunt for the enemy. We found the only place on the entire front where, for space of half a mile, there were no troops. We went through and were attacked by the Bosch. We drove them six miles, took a town, Joinville, on the Hindenburg Line, battery of field guns, 12 machine guns, but no prisoners. Then, finding that we were eight miles ahead of our line, and that all the cannon in that part of Germany were shooting at us, we withdrew with only four men hit. I was in at the start of this very fine feat of arms, but not at the finish, as I was ordered back just after the tanks started and before we knew the Bosch were there. We withdrew that night. Total losses 4 men killed, 4 officers, and 4 men wounded.

I am writing this in what was once a house, but what is now a sort of quay. The Bosch shell us at 7:30 each night. It is now that time so I will stop and put this in an envelope. This is a very egotistical letter, but interesting as it shows that vanity is stronger than fear and that in war as is now waged, there is little of the element of fear, it is too well organized and two stupendous. . . .

George S. Patton Jr., letter to his wife, Beatrice, September 26, 1918 (Patton Papers, Box 8, Folder 16)

Darling Beat:

Life is just one D____ thing after another. One whole battalion has failed to show up and I can't find it. The battalion commander spent the day looking for a house instead of getting his tanks. He is a fool, but I a greater one to trust him.

Still, I am reaping what I sowed. I spoon fed these hounds so much that they are helpless and run to me every time they ought to go to the W.C. [water closet] to see if it is all right. Sometimes I think I am not such a great commander after all, just a fighting animal. Still, I will improve in time, at least if one learns by mistakes I ought to be wise. I have made all there are.

I am getting on fine with the corps and the division, which is a comfort as things ought to be right somewhere.

One fine example of efficiency, nix, has just happened. 100,000 gallons of gas arrived in tank cars with no pump. Now we can't get it out except by dippers!!!

It is a good thing I have a cheerful disposition. I have, in spite of certain lapses that you know of.

But I have got a rotten staff and no mistake. Probably my own fault. I have done too much for them. Well, I will never do it again if I pull through this. But it is a big if. Hellish big. . . .

6. George S. Patton Jr., letter to his wife Beatrice, September 28, 1918 (Patton Papers, Box 8, Folder 16)

Darling Beat:

We went into our second fight on the morning of Sept. 26 at 5:30 a.m. It was terribly foggy and in addition they were shooting lots of smoke shells, so we could not see ten feet. I started forward at 6:30 to see what was doing, but could see little. Machine guns were going in every direction, in front, behind, and on both sides, but no one could tell who they belonged to. I had six men—runners—with me and a compass, so I collected all the soldiers I found who were lost and brought them along. At times I had several hundred.

About 9:30 we came to a town called Cheppy. I went past the infantry as we were supposed to have taken the place. All at once we got shot at from all sides, with machine gun and shell also, but still we could see nothing. Pretty soon some of our infantry came running back. So, as none of my men had any rifles, I went back with the infantry, but stopped before they did. Also, I stopped in a better place just back of a crest.

When we got here it began to clear up and we were shot at to beat hell with shells and machine guns. Twice the infantry started to run, but we hollered at them and called them all sorts of names so they stayed. But they were scared. Some acted badly; some put on gas masks; some covered their face with their hands, but none did a damn thing to kill Bosch. There were no officers there, but me, so I decided to do business. Some of my reserve tanks were stuck by some trenches, so I went back and made some Americans hiding in the trenches dig a passage. I think I killed one man [U.S. soldier] here.[1] He would not work so I hit him over the head with a shovel. It was exciting for they shot at us all the time, but I got mad and walked on the parapet. At last we got five tanks across and I started them forward and yelled and cussed waved my stick and said come on. About 150 doughboys started, but when we got to the crest of the hill the fire got fierce right along the ground. We all lay down. I saw that we must go forward or back and I could not go back, so I yelled, who comes with me. A lot of doughboys yelled, but only six of us started, my striker, me and four doughs. I hoped the rest would follow, but they would not. Soon there were only three, but we could see the machine guns right ahead, so we yelled to keep up our courage and went on. Then the third man went down and I felt a blow in the leg, but at first I could walk, so went about 40 feet when my leg gave way. My striker [Private First Class Joseph T. Angelo], the only man left, yelled, "and there ain't no one left." He helped me to a shell hole and we lay down and the Bosch shot over the top as fast as he could. He was very close. The tanks began getting him and in about an hour it was fairly clear.

Some of my men carried me under fire, which was not at all pleasant.

Finally, I got to a hospital at 3:30. I was hit at 11:15.

The bullet went into the front of my leg and came out just at the crack of my bottom about two inches to the left of my rectum. It was fired at about 50 meters, so made a hole about the size of the dollar where it came out.

It has hurt very little and I have slept fine. I will be out in 10 days. . . .

302d Tank Center

*"New Jersey Boy Bravest Man in American Army" (*Rockford Republic, *May 9, 1919, 3)*

[Private First Class Joseph T. Angelo—Headquarters, 302d Tank Center]

When Colonel George S. Patton Jr., commander of the 304th Tank Brigade, was wounded in action on 26 September 1918, at Clermont, France, his orderly, Private First Class John T. Angelo, dragged him to safety. Angelo later received the Distinguished Service Cross for saving his commander. Angelo gave the following interview to the press about the event:

You see, we went over the top at 6:30 in the morning. We had 150 tanks on the move and were plowing through a dense fog. As I was the colonel's orderly I accompanied him in the advance. We had 15 men and two first lieutenants in our party. The tanks followed us. I was walking by the side of the colonel, but when we came to a crossroad the colonel told me to remain there and be on the watch for Germans.

While I was on duty two American doughboys came along. I asked them what their mission was and they replied that they were "just mopping up."

"Well," I said, "if you don't get out of here you will get mopped up, as the Germans are pouring plenty of lead our way." When several high explosive shells burst the doughboys took refuge in a shack. A moment later a shell hit the shack. The doughboys were blown to atoms. A moment later I saw two German machine gunners from behind a bush and they fired on me. I returned the fire and killed one; the other one beat it.

The colonel, who was ahead of me, appeared on top of a knoll and shouted: "Joe, is that you shooting down there?" Then I thought sure hell had broken loose. Bullets from machine guns just naturally rained all around.

"Come on, we'll clean out these nests," shouted the colonel, and I followed him up the hill. The colonel was sore and couldn't understand why our boys couldn't break up those nests. Then he saw the tanks were not moving and sent me to see Captain [Math L.] English, in command of the Seventh [327th Tank Battalion] tanks, to find out the cause. The tanks were stuck in the mud.

The colonel ordered me to follow him and when he reached the tanks, almost hub deep in the mud, he grabbed a shovel and began digging the tanks free. Other men and I also got busy digging. The Germans were sending across a heavy artillery fire, but finally we got the tanks moving and took them over the hill.

The colonel here found some infantrymen who did not know what to do, as their officers had been killed. The colonel instructed me to place them with the tank detachment. Later the colonel told me to get around to the side and wipe out the machine gun nests. "Take 15 men with you," he ordered.

"I'm sorry," I told him, "but they have all been killed."

"My God! They are not all gone?" the colonel cried.

When I told him the infantrymen had been killed by machine guns he ordered me to accompany him, declaring he would clear them out. I thought the colonel had gone mad, and grabbed him. He grabbed me by the hair and shook me to my senses. Then I followed him. We went about 30 yards and the colonel fell with a bullet in his thigh.

I assisted the colonel into a shell hole, bandaged his wounds and took observations of our surroundings. Shells flew all about us. Two hours later the colonel revived and ordered me to go to Major [Sereno E.] Brett and instruct him to assume command of the tank corps. I found him and did so, then reported back to the colonel. A few moments later the colonel, with three tanks, one French and two American, camped about 20 yards from the shell hole.

"Jump out there," the colonel ordered, "and scatter those tanks or they will be blown up."

I rushed out, gave the order and came back again. The American tanks got away, but the French tank was shot to pieces and the men killed. The colonel then ordered me to get out on top of our shell hole and prevent any oncoming tanks from getting below us, the fire from the enemy being terribly heavy. Then the colonel said, "Joe, the Germans have been making this shell hole a living hell since you left. Get a tank and wipe out those nests." This was done and after that I found four infantrymen who carried the colonel to the rear.

344th Tank Battalion

*Excerpt from "Only One of Us Can Get Out—And Out You Go" (*Literary Digest *for March 29, 1919, 48)*

[Sergeant Virgil L. Morgan, Company A, 344th Tank Battalion, letter to John A. Roberts, the father of Corporal Harold W. Roberts, Company A, 344th Tank Battalion]

Corporal Harold W. Roberts, Company A, 344th Tank Battalion, United States Army, is the San Franciscan who will go down in history's pages as among the bravest of Uncle Sam's fighters. He was the son of John A. Roberts, of 1050 Green Street, with offices in the Humboldt Bank Building.

Corporal Roberts had just turned twenty-two when he made the supreme sacrifice. He enlisted at nineteen, following his graduation from the University of California. He was awarded the Congressional Medal of Honor, America's highest military decoration.

Sergeant Virgil L. Morgan, a comrade of "Bob," describes the death of young Roberts in the following letter to the elder Roberts, received here today. The letter reads in part:

"Bob, as we called him, came to our company early last summer. Almost at once he was liked by everyone in the company.

"He was in my platoon and by his good work was made corporal.

"Bob and I became very close friends, and when it became time for the sergeants to pick their tank-drivers, I picked Bob. But because he showed up so well as a tank driver, the lieutenant of our platoon took him away from me. So as the platoon leader tank-driver he went to the front and went through the St. Mihiel fight. There never proved a better soldier. There was not a minute that I did not try to get him back to my tank.

"Finally, Bob asked the lieutenant if he couldn't drive for me. We were two tickled boys when we got together again. Immediately we went to the Verdun front in the Argonne Forest sector. All through the drive until he was drowned we fought together in our little tank. Little did we both care. We were young, I being only nineteen. Our whole idea was to get Germans at any cost.

"It was on the morning of October 4 that he met his death. It was foggy. We were at the head of a new division in the line. After we left our point of departure and were in battle formation, shooting at everything that looked like a German, Bob looked up to me and smiled, saying:

"'Dink (which he always called me), I wouldn't miss this for a thousand dollars.'

"We went along in the fight for about a mile, when we saw on our left a tank standing still. A dough-boy came crawling along to our tank. Bob opened his door and the doughboy yelled that the tank on the left was struck and wanted protection from a German machine gun, pointing toward the trench woods.

"Off we darted amid bursting shells and the sound of machine bullets lighting on our tank. Thinking that the enemy was in the bushes ahead. Bob speeded up and we plowed right into it.

"In a moment we were turned over and water was rushing into the tank. The back door was the only way to get out because the other doors were buried in the mud.

"Bob's last words were: 'Only one of us can get out, so out you go,' and he gave me a push. I had to be the first out because there are the gunners' doors and the drivers' doors.

"Bob's doors were buried.

"When I came to the top of the water I waited and yelled for Bob, I was as helpless as a baby, because the tank was completely covered with water and I couldn't get back in after him, I cried like a baby and waited, but he didn't come.

"When I came to myself I found that we had gone into a tank trap. With the machine-gun fire increasing furiously, I had to fall back after waiting for twenty minutes."

*"Many Times over the Top in Tanks" (*Meyersdale [PA] Republican, *December 26, 1918, 1)*

[Corporal James O. Chambers, Company A, 344th Tank Battalion, letter to William S. Livengood]

The editor of The Republican has received the following letter from a former employee, James O. Chambers, a Meyersdale boy who has had many thrilling experiences in battle:

Langres, France, Nov. 26, 1918

Dear Mr. Livengood:

You may be a little surprised at hearing from me, because it is a long time since I left the old home town. I used to work for you during my last year in Meyersdale high school in 1912, but left there in 1913 and have been traveling around more or less since.

I made three voyages over here in 1916, two to France and one to Italy, when the submarines were getting in their dirty work. Visited at the ports of Le Havre, La Pallice and Bordeaux in France, and my other trip was to Genoa, Italy. Came over on the ship Madonna, with cargo of horses. My fourth trip over now in the service of Uncle Sam. Landed at Brest during January of this year, and was lucky enough to get into the tank corps when it was first organized. The American tank corps on this side of the water was first composed of men who volunteered for the "suicide outfit," as it was called, and got transferred from other outfits, and over half came from the 6th F.A.R.R. [Field Artillery Reserve Regiment], Col. [Frederick B.] Henessey [Hennessey] commanding. The most of the remainder transferred to the tanks from the 1st division and the 26th division.

At first, when we numbered but 200 men, it was tough work building our center and training the new men how to operate the tanks and repair them, but finally when our strength was two battalions and we got enough tanks, we went "over" at [the] St. Mihiel sector Sept. 12 (the first American tank corps over the top). About the 21st or 22d we pulled out of that sector and went "over" in the Argonne on the morning of the 26th. The St. Mihiel affair was more or less of a party, as our casualties were very light, but that Argonne was a battle, believe me. In every wood, ridge and town was a battle, and some of those d—d Boche wouldn't surrender. We had to ride right over them and their machine guns with the tanks. I felt a little bit queer the first one I smashed, but I got so wild when I thought of our own lads lying back on the ridge, that all I could think of was, "I hope I'll last long enough to get a few more of them before they get me." I don't think a fellow worries much about getting "bumped off" in the battle; that is, after he sees his pal "go west." I know that is how it was with me.

I could write volumes on things that happened, but I do not like to tire you with a long letter, for I know you are a busy man. I had quite a few narrow escapes, but the worst was when we were moving up one night to go "over" in the morning, at Charpentry, where Fritz had counter-attacked and held up our boys. Just as we entered the town he dropped a few shells on one of our ammunition dumps, and all I know is that I heard an awful explosion and at the same moment I felt myself going, and the next thing I knew I was picking myself up off the road. My tank was about fifteen feet behind me with the front doors wide open and the engine stalled. The fellows told me that the dump was blown up, but I was dazed so that I didn't know what had happened. The only way I can account for it is that my turret door was open and when the dump went up the rush of air from the explosion took me right out through the front. Went over just the same next morning and got in the way of one of Fritz's 77's, which took off our tread, but not before we put two of his machine gun nests out of action.

Was in the engagements at Dead Man's Hill [Le Morte Homme], Boureilles, Cheppy, Varennes, Montblainville, Epinonville and Exermont in the Argonne, and Seicheprey, Nonsard and Hattonchattel in [the] St. Mihiel sector. . . .

*"Hot Cakes, Hot Shot and a Hot Old Time Chasing the Huns out of Argonne Forest" (*Meyersdale [PA] Republican, *January 23, 1919, 1)*

[Corporal James O. Chambers, Company A, 344th Tank Battalion, letter to William S. Livengood]

Langres, Haute Marne, France,
December 28, 1918

Dear Mr. Livengood:

In my last letter I told you about the St. Mihiel offensive and a few things that happened there, as I remembered them. This time I'll try to tell you about the Meuse and Argonne drives.

After the return from the advance, we put in a week of hard work collecting and repairing the tanks and getting them ready for our next drive. There were about 300 of us there, and we all ate in the same mess, each company's cooks taking a day cooking for the crowd. Co. A cooks on duty one day, Co. B cooks the second day, and Co. C the third. It was about the third day, I guess, when our new rations came up, and there were several sacks of flour and a couple cases of syrup, so there was nothing to it but we just had to have hotcakes for breakfast the next morning. So we went to the mess sergeant and said to him: "Say Sarge, how about hotcakes tomorrow?"

"How about roast turkey, cranberry sauce and ice-cream?" says he, sarcastically. "How the hell can I make cakes without a griddle?"

So there we were up a tree—plenty of flour, plenty of syrup and everything except a griddle! Well, we argued for about an hour trying to plan how we could have the cakes, and finally a lad who hadn't said anything but had been doing a lot of thinking, speaks out:

"Say, boys, how about taking one of those side plates out of a busted tank? I've got an idea that would make a dandy griddle."

I don't know who that guy was, but he sure ought to have been awarded a medal, for he saved the day. That griddle was big enough to make 40 or more flapjacks at a time, and that gang of hungry tankers kept two cooks busy till nearly dinner-time next day. They mixed the batter in a couple of big G.I. cans, and I know that I went back for seconds and thirds and fourths.

It was about eleven o'clock and the mess sergeant was then making them. He had been relieving the cooks every once in a while since five o'clock in the morning. He said: "I bet that line of soldiers, if all strung out would reach from here to the Statue of Liberty. I believe I've fed the whole army. Well, I'm going to bake them until twelve o'clock, and then to the devil with you all; I've got to stop and get dinner ready."

We sure had enough hotcakes for once.

Well, that wasn't what I started to write about at all, but little incidents come back to me everytime I start to tell about something. A couple of days afterwards we got everything ready, so we drove the tanks to the rail-head, and there was no train, so nothing to do until the cars arrived. To make everything as miserable as possible it started to rain, which was nothing unusual, because it always rained when we moved. I've never seen it fail yet. So there was nothing to it but to find a place to get shelter until the train pulled in. We got to work and, with the aid of a few spare tarpaulins, which we used to cover the tanks, we managed to make a fairly comfortable rain-proof place to sleep in. We had just got settled when the cars came in. You should have heard the boys cuss!

Well, we finally got them all loaded and away we went. We arrived at Clermont the next evening, and about every five minutes a shell would come whistling over just to remind us that "Fritz" was very much alive in that sector. It certainly was hard work the next couple of days, for we cleaned the machinery and put in new spark plugs and oiled all the parts and looked over them again and again, because we knew it was going to be a tough scrap, and no one wanted his tank to fail him and stop at the wrong time.

Just after dark, on the night of Sept. 25, we moved up to the "jumping off" place, which is the place where we await the word to go over the top. We filled up with gasoline here and got a little rest. Then our barrage started, and the whole horizon was filled with flashes and the ground trembled with the roar of the guns. Soon afterward the word came down the line to "tune 'em up" and "get ready to go."

Then away we went in the darkness, and it sure was rough riding, because it was an awful country through which we had to go. All little hills and bumps and hollows and trenches, and a tank is a rough-riding machine on good land, so you can imagine what it was over that kind of ground.

Just a little after daybreak we came to the top of a ridge which was just lined with belts of barbed wire, but that doesn't bother a tank. They just roll over it, crushing it down and making a path for the infantry to get through. The fog was so thick one could almost cut it with a knife, which being favorable to us, was also useful to the "Fritzies." They couldn't see us and we couldn't see them, but the machine gun bullets began zipping around and ping-pinging on the sides of the tanks.

Then away we went down the hill, the leading tank searching the best trail to get through, and we came to the foot of a high bare hill. According to our charts we were supposed to go around at this point, but found out that we couldn't get there, so we filed up the slope to the left. This hill I learned later was called Dead Man's Hill [Le Morte Homme], for many a man had fallen there in desperate fights between the French and Germans earlier in the war.

We had just got about half way up when old "Jerry" began dropping them [artillery] all around, and I'll say there was sure some shrapnel flying, making things a bit unpleasant for awhile. About 20 Germans came out of a trench yelling the old familiar "Kamerad!" and they were quickly sent to the rear. . . .

You should have seen some of the tanks that came back that evening. A few of them had thousands of bullet nicks on them, and the packs were just cut to pieces. We tie our packs on the outside of the tank because there isn't much room inside the front half of a tank, in a space of about 4 × 6 feet, or maybe just a little larger, when you have two big ammunition racks, a gunner and a driver, and levers all jammed in together, besides the gun which takes up most of the turret, and the machinery takes up all the room in the back of the tank. . . .

"A Tanker's Experience in Clearing Hun Army out of Argonne Forest" (Meyersdale [PA] Republican, *January 30, 1919, 1, 4)*

[Corporal James O. Chambers, Company A, 344th Tank Battalion, letter to William S. Livengood]

Langres, France, Dec. 23, 1918

Dear Mr. Livengood:

I am still in camp here and don't know when we will be sent back to the good old U.S. but am hoping that it will be soon but we ought to know about the time the peace conference starts. I am well and feeling tip-top and ready to go after old Fritz again, if he should decide he hasn't had enough. But I can't say that I'll be so lucky and come through with a whole skin if hostilities should open again. We sure did give them hell. The reason was because we had worked so hard all summer, learning to drive and repair the tanks in the rain and mud, and were bawled out so much for our mistakes that we were fighting mad, and we just had to take our spite out on some one. Just couldn't help fighting.

I remembered our first drive. In fact I shall never forget it. A Co. had three towns to take the first day, and they were ours shortly after 1 p.m., and then we had lunch—corned Bill, Boston baked [beans] in a tin overcoat, jam, punk and old java, and believe me I did justice to it, because I had had no breakfast and we had attacked about 5 a.m. That afternoon we did a little patrolling, as most of us had run out of gasoline and we had to wait until it was brought up. There was very little resistance that afternoon, only an occasional shell coming over, but none dropping close enough to make things interesting. Our gas came up that night and the next morning off we went—infantry and tanks—and just drove thru town after town but only a few Fritzies showed any fight; but what chance they against the tanks with their machine guns? The bullets just rattled like hail on the sides of the tank and I didn't see any anti-tank rifles.

Only once that day did the game get interesting and that was when we were moving up the road in column and suddenly one of Jerry's planes dropped down out of the clouds, played a little with his typewriter, spraying the road with bullets and then opened his tail-gate and dropped five bombs, and got away without any one getting a shot at him. I've got to hand it to some of those "birds." They sure have the "guts." It certainly makes a fellow feel queer when the planes get on his trail. I guess it's about the same feeling a German infantryman has when a tank comes toward him. I know I would rather be the hunter than the hunted, and I've had both sensations.

But neither compares to that feeling when you run into a battery of Jerry 77's on which our own artillery didn't register, and they get point blank range on you. You look out the side slits and old Fritz registers on that tank. You look out the other side and another gets a hit. You think then, "Will I ever get close enough to get one good shot at them?"

The tank seems barely to crawl, although going at fourth speed. Well, I came through, but I hope I never again have to go up against the same hell.

I seem to be getting off my story. It was about my first drive, and this last incident happened during the second. We hit the railroad at Hattonchatel and followed the road running parallel with it. In the towns along here the Germans had factories in which they employed the civilian population, who were forced to work. The factories were all burning when we entered the towns, and they had driven off all the stock and carried the women with them. Some old folks that we met told us about it with tears streaming down their faces. This was my first evidence of "kultur."

Two towns further on we got a German canteen and among the stores in it were found tobacco and cigarettes of very poor grade, and jam and several cases of little cookies, which sure went fine with wine that we found in the cellar of the German officers' headquarters.

The next day we moved ahead a few towns and noticed the same conditions. The towns were uninhabited except for a few old people. All the rest had been carried away or had fled because the people not knowing whether we were hostile or not, and having been in captivity for more than four years, were afraid to come out from their places of refuge.

Some French units moved up that evening and we started back. You should have seen the tanks and men. Every tank had one or more German helmets tied to it, and every "tanker" had souvenirs, such as Mauser pistols and Lugers, trench knives and mirrors and a great assortment of other articles. One of the boys had a bicycle, another a German motorcycle, and two more rode horses and wore high-top German cavalry boots. It certainly was a picturesque outfit that returned from that drive. The characters in the book "Treasure Island" of Morgan's buccaneers didn't have anything on us. We drove all night and next morning arrived at one of the towns that was captured in the first day of the drive and camped there and repairing the tanks that were out of commission. . . .

*"Plunging Onward toward Victory" (*Meyersdale [PA] Republican, *January 30, 1919, 1)*

[Corporal James O. Chambers, Company A, 344th Tank Battalion, letter to William S. Livengood]

Langres, France, Jan. 1, 1919

Dear Mr. Livengood:

In my last letter I told you about the first day of the Argonne offensive. Well, the second day was worse than the first. . . .

The next few days were uneventful, only a shell coming my way once in a while, but none near enough to do any damage so a few days later I found myself back at Varennes for repairs for the tank. In the meantime Cpl. Harper with whom I had started out the last time, was sent out with another bunch of tanks, so I had to find a new partner. Sgt. White came in that night and his driver was sick, so I took his place.

That night we were ordered out so we went and looked over our tank and tuned it up and started out. I felt funny that night. Something seemed to tell me that we were going into a real scrap the next morning, and sure enough when we got near Charpentry, business opened up with a rush, when Fritz started shelling the road. He started them over about two a minute, and he wasn't missing the road very often by the number of times pieces of shrapnel rattled on the tank.

We halted just near the top of the ridge and a sentry stationed there told us there was gas in the valley, so we moved down the road at second speed and wore our gas masks. It's bad enough to see with a mask on, let alone drive a tank. If I could have had my way I would have thrown it into fourth speed and rushed thru the fire, but orders are orders. Sgt. White got out of the turret by the back doors and was guiding me, for the night was almost as black as pitch, and I could just dimly make out the outline of the tank ahead. I wasn't worrying about myself, because I knew that only a direct hit would put me out of the game, but there was "Whitey" outside and I was a little afraid for him, but every time a shell burst, he would get behind the tank ahead which sheltered him. Once when one landed pretty close, a shower of dirt and rock was thrown over us and "Whitey" got one right between the shoulders, and I saw him stagger.

Everything went all right from there, but I could scarcely make out the road and I fell behind. Pretty soon I passed what seemed to be the outline of a building and then old Fritz wakened up in earnest, because about a dozen shells came over all at once, and then I thought I heard an awful roar and I felt myself lifted and I seemed to be flying. After that I don't know what happened, but when I came to, lights were flashing in all directions and it seemed to me that thousands of machine guns were firing at once. I went up the road running part way and crawling part way and came up to the other tanks. I didn't realized what happened at the time, but when they asked me where my tank was I didn't know.

"I was driving it and then something happened and I found myself lying in the road."

"Yes, something did happen, the ammunition dump blew up," they told me. I went back shortly after and found my tank all right, only all doors were wide open. The concussion of the explosion must have come right through the back doors of the tank, which had been left open when "Whitey" got out, and just carried me right through the front.

Just after I had caught up with the rest of the gang, some fellow came up and reported that one tank got blown up on the road back there, and that he saw a man flying through the air. I said: "yes, that was me."

The shells then started coming over in bunches because the burning ammunition dump made everything almost as light as day. Then we moved on and turned up a small valley to the right where we joined another bunch of tanks.

We tried to get a little sleep after we filled the tank with gas and water, but that was impossible for the small arms ammunition kept cracking as the fire reached it, and Fritz kept sending over some big stuff which kept us awake all night.

The next morning, we went "over" in the fog. It was awful. We had a long hill to climb and as our tank had just been repaired the day before, we could show our heels to any of them when it came to speed. I passed tank after tank going up that hill, and when I got over the top of it, we got into the worst of the shelling. I had been in plenty of shelling before but never anything like that. Shells just rained all around, and there was just a continual roar and scream, but I couldn't see anything but shells dropping. Not a man in sight, so I shoved her into fourth [gear] and away we went. How I came thru that I don't know, and then I spied the two Germans on the road, but I couldn't stop, so rolled right over them. One of them seemed to rise half up before I hit them, and then we went on.

Soon I came to a trench and saw Capt. English of C Company, who stopped me and asked who I was. I yelled out "A Company, under Lt. Seoul [Thomas W. Saul]. Came up with the reserve last night!"

"Go to the right," so I turned out to the right.

After that everything seems like a bad dream. We chased out a bunch of Fritzies and then I slipped a tread and went out of action. We got out and jumped into a shell hole, because there was almost a barrage coming over and we figured we were safer on the ground than in the tank. There was a line of brush along here and a bank behind it, which formed a natural protection and we dug in there. Old Fritz could drop shells within twenty feet of us, but couldn't touch us. I have dug plenty of holes, but never did I get out of sight so soon as I did that time.

And then the fog began clearing away and he sent over aeroplanes which dropped a few bombs around us. Then we could see our boys coming over. They took the town that day but had a hard battle on the hills behind, and I couldn't get into it. I was stuck there with that tank and couldn't get it repaired, because all my tools had been shot off. We lay there two days in that hell, with the shells bursting around. I never expected to get out of that place alive.

There were some queer sights here, but it would take too long to tell about all of them. One strange sight happened when the cavalry went in. They were coming over the hill and Jerry got the range on them and commenced firing. A shell landed right beneath a horse and exploded. The rider was blown about fifteen feet in the air. He came down in a sitting position and then got up, brushing the seat of his breeches and walked away. The horse was blown almost in half and all that happened to the rider was a little shaking up.

At last we saw that there wasn't much chance of getting our tank repaired out there, and one of our mechanics came up and told us to report back to Charpentry. . . .

"A Hero of the Tanks" (Treat 'Em Rough, December 1918, 43)

[Lieutenant John W. Castles Jr., Company B, 344th Tank Battalion, letter to his mother, Mrs. John W. Castles, New York City]

I was wounded about one o'clock on the first day of the Argonne battle. The first hour of the battle we had a hard time, as the fog and mist were thick, but when it cleared off we went ahead in fine style. It was the same old story of thousands of machine guns all placed in echelon and we had a long morning cleaning them out. We had a Pennsylvania division with us and they were fine, following us up close and helping us across trenches, etc., when necessary, regardless of heavy machine gun and shell fire. We cleaned out one town, Goureilles [Boureilles], quite a strong point, without much trouble, and breezed on. We hit Vereaues [Varennes] about eleven o'clock, found it a strong point, with much resistance there, but the tanks got through and drove Fritz out on the run, and we did plenty of execution when we got him in the open. Up to that time I had been sometimes in my tank, sometimes on foot, in order to see more and be able to communicate better with the other tanks. In an open field I met my Waterloo. I was hunting for Boche machine guns that were cutting up the doughboys, when "crack!" the lights blazed up for second and then went out. A 77 shell hit my turret and tore it half off.

*"Lieut. Arthur Snyder Aims to Make Army Life Career" (*Washington Evening Star*, December 23, 1918, 9)*

[Lieutenant Arthur Snyder, Company C, 344th Tank Battalion]

After rumor had killed him in action—a rumor which did not reach Washington—Second Lieutenant Arthur Snyder of the 344th Battalion Tank Corps, son of Rev. Dr. William Taylor Snyder, rector of the Church of the Incarnation, writes:

"I was wounded in the head by splinters from machine gun bullets hitting the tank. It was very slight and the worst of it was a mild case of shell shock. But even that is a thing of the past, and I believe my nerves can now stand again the racket of the front."

A letter of a late date from a colonel whose name is withheld states that Lieutenant Snyder was in the battles at the St. Mihiel salient, September 12–15, and of the Aisne, September 26 to October 4.

"His work, I am sure, would have won him the distinguished service medal in any other corps than the tanks. His officers described to me the heroic action of a tank which, disabled and surrounded by the enemy, refused to surrender. Only the other day I found that he was commanding that tank. You may well be proud of him."

Lieutenant Snyder, after referring to the fact that he had finally received his commission as an officer after working 13 months for it, all of which except two were spent in a foreign country, says, "If I be allowed to hold my commission after the war, I intend to make it my lifetime occupation."

"I am trying to get sent back to duty from here," he continued, "but maybe I can't work it, and I may have to be sent to another base hospital and thence to a replacement camp, then back to my outfit, or what is left of it, for my captain (Capt. [Math L.] English) and several of my pals have 'gone west,' while others are crippled for life. Sixty percent of the company was lost in casualties, but, of course, this means slight wounds, gas and everything. But it was sure bad, believe me.

"Only one officer of the four was left when I was sent to the rear. Only a few tanks left, too, when I got mine. I was the last tank of our platoon (five tanks), and it was not the tank I had started the day in, for when we had jumped off that morning there were two tanks, a [Second] Lieutenant [Harlow A.] Wood commanding one and I the other. This was on the Argonne front, in front of the little shelled town of Exermont. We had only been in action a few minutes and were trying to put out some machine gun nests concealed in an orchard when I saw Lieutenant Wood suddenly turn to the rear. I thought I had best communicate with him, not knowing the sector myself, so I turned and had not gone 50 yards when a German 77 burst right under one of my treads and snapped it off, of course putting it out of action for the day. The driver and I got out and got to the lieutenant's tank without the dense machine gun fire getting us. There I found Lieutenant Wood wounded about the eyes from splinters, but the blood ruined his vision, so I got in his tank with the orders and a map and started for the day's objective—Fleville.

"I had then 'Kid' [Horatio R.] Rogers for a driver. He is 17 years old, comes from Evanston, Illinois, and his father is a rector of one of our churches there. He is some kid—full of pluck.

"We went back to the same orchard and then the early morning fog had lifted, also the dense smoke of our own barrage. There, on the edge of the orchard, I could hardly believe my eyes. In an enormous shell hole were at least 20 Huns, with three machine guns. As I came up firing as fast as I could with my 37-one-pounder, they began getting uneasy and some were putting on their clumsy packs. I wish they were all doing the same, for their fire was perfect hell—the worst I've yet to experience. We were in upon the devils so close that they were throwing 'potato mashers' (Boche grenades) at us. Then Rogers got wounded slightly about the eyes, just like the lieutenant, and I had to turn back for a new driver. I went on the party where I 'got mine,' but the nest was taken."

Lieutenant Snyder was breaking broncos in Montana, on the Tongue River, when he enlisted in Captain [Dean] Hudnutt's battery, 6th Field Artillery. After two months he went abroad as stable sergeant, but was afterward transferred to the Tank Corps, where he won his second lieutenancy.

Arthur Snyder, "The Five of Hearts at Exermont" (1939, Fort George G. Meade Museum, Fort George G. Meade, Maryland)

[Lieutenant Arthur Snyder, Company C, 344th Tank Battalion]

The French (light) Renault tank, weighing six tons, which now stands in front of the 66th Infantry Headquarters building at Fort George G. Meade, Maryland, was part of the tank complement of Company "C" 344th Battalion, Tank Corps, U.S.A., during the World War, 1917–1918.

This tank's serial number was 1516, and it carried a symbol thus: five of hearts.

It participated in the St. Mihiel offensive, the Toul defensive, and the Meuse-Argonne offensive.

The organization of an American light tank company during the World War consisted of four platoons with five tanks to a platoon.

I vividly remember seeing the infantry of the First Division, on September 30, 1918, marching to its positions in the Meuse-Argonne. We, in the Tank Corps, cheered with much feeling as we watched this gallant division come into the line for we had supported it at St. Mihiel. We were well aware of its efficiency as a fighting unit, and there existed "a bond of comradeship that inspired mutual confidence and admiration," as the *History of the First Division* phrases it.[2]

Late in the afternoon of October 3rd, at our tank rendezvous at Charpentry, my company commander, Captain [Math L.] English, gathered his officers and senior noncoms together for instructions for the attack to take place the following day. He had a map spread out on a tractor of one of the tanks, and as we were gathered about it a German shell exploded far enough up the valley that none of us "hit the dirt." However, a small fragment of the shell landed on our map, cutting through it and lodging in the mud on one of the tread plates. Captain English calmly picked it out, carefully examined it—it still being hot—and said, "Well, I must admit that their shells have beautiful fragmentation."

The following day it was a similar shell fragment that penetrated Captain English's trench coat and other clothing, and piercing his heart, killed him instantly. Captain English always reminded me of the officer that Donald Hankey must have had in mind when he wrote that beautiful chapter, "The Beloved Captain," in his book, *A Student in Arms*.[3] It is with profound feeling that I recall that one of the streets at Fort George Meade is named after my old company commander.

On October 4th as we left Charpentry for the Exermont-Fleville attack, we did not have a full complement of tanks because of material casualties in previous engagements. The jump-off -line was south of Exermont, and as we proceeded to it we lost a tank in my platoon. I doubt if more than three tanks in this particular platoon made the attack. The *History of the First Division* cites that Company "C" had 16 tanks engaged—this seems to bear out my supposition. I was a sergeant at the time in command of the tank, but not the "Five of Hearts" at the beginning of the attack, although in the same platoon with it. [Second] Lieutenant [Harlow A.] Wood, our platoon leader, was in the "Five of Hearts" and had Corporal Horatio Rogers as a driver. I do not remember the symbol of the tank I was commanding—due to tank casualties we all had to switch from one tank to another during the Meuse-Argonne offensive—but I distinctly remember having a Corporal Kelly from Texas as a driver.

It was planned that we would not jump off ahead of the infantry because of the absence of preliminary artillery fire, which would tend to neutralize the noise of the tanks as they moved up to the line of departure. The elements of surprise were maintained as much as possible. At 5:25 a.m. a barrage was dropped in front of the jump-off-line, and the attack started five minutes later. Enemy resistance was very stubborn even at the initial stage of the attack, and we immediately found the 16th Infantry engaged, but being held up by heavy machine gun fire, and not a little artillery fire.

Lieutenant Wood was on my right proceeding along a hedgerow from which the Germans were producing a severe machine gun flank fire. My orders were to keep strict liaison with Lieutenant Wood's tank, and when I saw it change direction I did likewise. If we had had radios, this would not have happened, because Lieutenant Wood had been wounded and his driver, Corporal Rogers, was taking him behind the infantry assault line.

Then Rogers, who was only a kid in his teens, under great danger to himself, crawled beyond the assault wave, endeavoring to signal me to proceed on in the attack. Just at this time a German shell exploded under the right tractor of my tank, severing it in two—like a knife cutting a piece of string. Of course the tank could then go only in circles. Kelly got it facing our lines. We got out through the driver's door, and had a crawling race to the rear of our infantry assault line. Here we found Lieutenant Wood and Rogers, and their tank, the "Five of Hearts." I took command of it and using Rogers as my driver returned to the attack.

The enemy machine guns in the hedgerow had been partially silenced, but the infantry could make little progress because of heavy frontal machine gun fire. The mist and fog of the early morning, plus the smoke from the artillery barrage, made visibility poor. As we proceeded in a frontal direction from the jump off-line we suddenly encountered at close quarters an extremely large machine gun nest, that was well concealed in a big shell crater. The position had undoubtedly been improved by field fortification methods, and it contained at least three machine guns and maybe more. We were fortunate that the position was not supported by artillery accompanying piece, because we were practically on it before observing it. I saw a German raise a "potato masher" [grenade] to throw at us. If he let it go, it did no harm, and we were causing confusion and damage in that machine gun nest with our 37-mm fire.

The armor plate on those old French Renaults was good, but when you came to close quarters the splinters from bullets, hitting around the vision slits and gun sights, did considerable damage to our personnel. Lieutenant Wood got wounded in this way. As Rogers and I were trying to get around the right flank of that big machine gun nest, he was hit about his eyes with splinters. He fell forward in his driver's seat, but fortunately did not stall the motor, which was an easy thing to do with those old tanks.

I knelt behind Rogers, cautioning him as to the use of the foot throttle, and reaching forward to the two steering levers, steered the tank back to our line. The blood from Rogers's wounds was blinding him, and when I left him at a dressing station, it was obvious that he was no longer fit for duty. I took his .45 pistol so that the "Five of Hearts" would be sure to have a full complement of weapons, and then I looked around for another tank mate. I was in the process of trying to get an infantryman when I saw a runner wearing the Tank Corps armband. I found that he was from the 345th Battalion, and that he had become lost from his organization. He told me he had graduated from our driver school at the tank center at Langres so I immediately pressed him into service as my third driver for the day.[4]

We at once returned to the attack and found that the big machine gun position had been taken. Some of its personnel were being taken to the rear as prisoners. We proceeded down into the Exermont ravine. At the bottom of this ravine is a stream, and to the west of Exermont was a stone bridge that spanned it. Orders had been issued not to use this bridge because of it being mined. When approaching the stream and looking for a place to cross, I discovered that there were machine guns well concealed on the other side. They fired little in our direction so as not to expose their positions, and their commander was undoubtedly aware that we would find difficulty fording the stream because of its banks being boggy. While trying to locate a safe place to cross, I saw a German noncommissioned officer taking cover from behind one tree to another. He undoubtedly was going to the different machine gun positions, but his technique was so excellent that he did not expose them. I admired his ability, calmness and courage as he went about his business, although I tried to lay the crosshairs of the telescope site on him more than once, but without success.

It was obvious that we were accomplishing nothing here, so we turned back toward Exermont hoping to find a suitable stream crossing. When we reached a place that afforded protection from enemy fire, we stopped in order to fill up the radiator tank. There was a marked lull in the fighting, so we also went to work on our fuel rations. I poured several canvas buckets full of water into the tank, but the thirst of the "Five of Hearts" showed no signs of being quenched. I looked under the tank and found that all of our water toting had been for naught. I inspected the engine chamber and found that a German antitank bullet had cut the ribs of the radiator. We did not notice it before trying to fill the tank, but the holes from that were plainly visible in the armor plates.

There was no other tank near us, nor any other Tank Corps personnel. This is not surprising when you consider the following taken from the *History of the First Division*: "Five of them" (meaning tanks) "reached the stream in the Exermont ravine, where they were destroyed by direct hits. Only three remained at the end of the day, and casualties amounted to eighty-four percent of personnel."

My driver and I were just getting ready to reconnoiter for a stream crossing when I was approached by a captain from the 16th Infantry. He informed me that his company was being held up by machine gun fire on the other side of the ravine. I told him that we would support his company as soon as I could locate a place to ford the stream. He asked why I did not use the stone bridge, and I explained about the orders. He mentioned having received similar ones, but had discovered that if the bridge was mined, it was no longer so. He asked me where my officers were, and I told him about my platoon leader having been wounded early in the morning. I did not know where any of the Tank Corps were as the "Five of Hearts" was covering the whole company front. I was unaware of my captain's death, and also of the fact that I myself had been commissioned two days before. I told the infantry officer that I would be glad to cross the bridge, under the existing circumstances, if he so ordered. This he did with a smile, and the "Five of Hearts" crossed the bridge safely.

Upon gaining the heights on the north side of the Exermont ravine, we immediately contacted the enemy. The outpost gave way rapidly, and machine guns were abandoned. I have little doubt in my own mind, that the enthusiasm to follow in pursuit made me go too far ahead of our infantry. The terrain flattened out and there was little cover available, and though the going was rough, it afforded a rare opportunity to fire at moving targets. I fear that the backs of those Germans with their packs and heavy overcoats were impressing me more in keeping liaison with our infantry. However, the party was not to last long for when cover was reached we met with enemy resistance. Upon being fired on at close range, my driver was shot in the throat, and at the same instant our engine stalled. I made many attempts to crank it from the gunner's compartment, but to no avail. This was undoubtedly due to engine trouble caused by the damaged radiator.

We were much in the same condition as a disabled man-of-war. Our mobility was gone, and with it all chance of maneuver and ability to seek cover. Our firepower was not far from zero because little effective fire could be produced now that the "Five of Hearts" had become a besieged fort. The cradle of our 37-mm gun was jammed with bullets fired at the tank at close quarters during the day. Several times I had put my entire weight on the breach so as to elevate the piece, but now this had become ineffective. Our projectiles would hit the ground only a few yards from the tank. Fortunately we had ample ammunition, and a large portion of it was high explosive. The turret could not be rotated because it was also jammed with bullets.

To our left and about 25 yards away was an enemy accompanying field piece—a German 77-mm. There was plenty of ammunition besides its trail. The breech block had been removed when the gun was abandoned, but now the Germans began to reappear. It was a local counterattack.

My wounded driver kept filling pistol clips, and I produced as much fire as possible with our pistols and crippled 37-mm. I paid more attention to the volume of fire than its accuracy, for I feared that the enemy would close in if the volume ever diminished. As it was, three machine guns were set up at very close range, but just out of range of our piece with its limited elevation. The fragmentation from our shells did afford some protective fire, but I could not train this fire on the German field piece. This caused me no little concern, for I knew what to expect if the breech block was returned to that gun.

The constant hammering from these machine guns at such close range, about 40 yards, was terrific. The hinges on the doors could not stand up under it long, but it was the mushroom turret that gave way. I was hit in the back of my head with fragments of it and bullet splinters. Fortunately, I remained conscious and was able to keep on firing. The Germans made no attempt to close in; on the contrary, they began to give way and then fled.

I have seen many marvelous sights of troops in action and on parade, but I have never seen nor do I ever expect to see a more glorious sight than our infantry advancing at the high port.

The "Five of Hearts" and her crew had done their job, and our colors were not struck until relief came to us. I took my driver to the rear, and I judge that I was none too clear in my head, for I wandered aimlessly until some staff officer directed me to a dressing station. Here I left a gallant soldier, whom I never saw before that day, and whom I never saw again. From various accounts, it has always been assumed that he died of his wounds, because no search in 345th Battalion could later locate the man. Maybe he told me his name and because of being hit in my head I failed to remember it, and maybe during that eventful day we did not bother about such trifles.

"Steering a Baby Tank" (Los Angeles Times, *May 18, 1919, sec. III, 35)*

[Private Alfred Truitt, Company C, 344th Battalion]

Private Alfred Truitt joined Tank Corps in April, served at Chateau Thierry and St. Mihiel and Argonne. At the Argonne:

"We went over early in the morning and I was driving a baby tank with one pal who worked the 37-mm gun, which our machine carried. We advanced about 200 yards ahead of the infantry, who were holding the front line trenches, when all of a sudden our 'fort' went out of commission, and there we were, right in no man's land, left flat, with the Huns trying to blow us into eternity with their artillery and machine guns.

"To stay in that tank meant certain death for both of us, so we climbed out of the 'can' and started to crawl back to our own line, keeping the crippled tank between ourselves and the 'Jerries' as much as we could. Well, we hadn't got very far when we ran right into a German machine gun nest, which we had somehow failed to get on our outward trip. Four 'Heinies' were working away for dear life, peppering our front lines with their old typewriter, and we were right on top of them with our revolvers before they saw us. We finished off the Dutchmen in short order, yanked up the gun and dragged it back to our own trenches. That's all there was to it."

The life of a tanker is just one thrill after another in the opinion of Private Truitt. Besides dodging enemy shells, the driver of the tank has to watch out for mines and pitfalls which are cunningly constructed by the enemy. The Germans had a favorite trick of digging a hole about 25 feet deep, covering it over so that anything but a tank could cross the trap without injury. The weight of one of these huge machines, however, caused the planking to give way, and the tank and its crew were often plunged through into about 12 feet of water. Mines were placed in the ground by the Germans, but Truitt declares that these were easy to dodge, because they were visible and look like little boxes about a foot high.

Very few tanks were lost in this manner. Direct hits were sometimes scored by the Hun artillerymen, and these always prove fatal to the tank and its brave crew. Truitt saw one tank, carrying two men, 37-mm gun and a big load of ammunition struck twice by direct hits. The ammunition exploded in the tank and its men were blown to atoms.

"No, I never was in a tank when 'Jerry' scored a bull's-eye," said Truitt, "but one machine that I was in was hit twice, both times glancing blows. If they had been center shots I wouldn't be here today."

*"U.S. Tank Corps Did Good Work in Every Big Fight" (*St. Louis Post-Dispatch, *April 17, 1919, 15)*

[344th Tank Battalion]

The American tank battalion made its initial bow at the St. Mihiel offensive September 12, 1918, the first American offensive. Into that action went 174 American tanks. . . .

The artillery preparation had already started. The night was reverberating with the roar and flash of guns. The infantry was to go over at five a.m. and in order to get into their position in the front these tanks had to cover eight miles over a road jammed with traffic and then cross the American trenches.

"Colonel, make them wait! Make them wait! We must get there on time," the young officer commanding the last section urged Lieutenant Colonel [George S.] Patton [Jr].

"Keep moving. If they start ahead of you, catch up," was the only consolation the colonel could give them. The tanks got there.

That first action of the American tank corps formed a large part of the correspondence cables the following day. Two tanks captured the town of Pannes, full of Germans and supplies. Lieutenant Colonel Patton went into one town riding outside on the tail end of the tank. In the subsequent engagement in the Argonne he was wounded in the leg.

Lieutenant Julian K. Morrison, of Louisiana, was wounded three times in the left hand on the first day of the St. Mihiel drive. The battalion commander that night ordered him to the rear. He had his hand dressed, but instead of staying at the rear was at the front again at midnight. The next day his hand was so swollen that the general commanding the brigade ordered him to the rear again.

He pleaded so hard with Lieutenant Colonel Patton against being ruled out of the fight that the latter said, though he must go to the rear as ordered, he could return if he would bring up 10 tanks which were there. The joker in this promise was that the roads were believed impassable and bringing up 10 or any other number of tanks was considered an impossibility. However, before noon Morrison was back in Woel with the 10 tanks and his wounded hand. That time he was permitted to stay. Later he was decorated with a D.S.C. [Distinguished Service Cross]

A couple of days after, a squad of 50 tanks was working its way along the road toward the front when they met Brigadier General D. S. Nolan, head of the intelligence section of the expedition.

"Where is the First Division, sir?" asked the officer commanding the tanks.

"You've passed it," said General Nolan.

"Well, we're looking for a fight. I guess we'll get it ahead," replied the optimistic officer, his string rattling into motion again.

About the same time, Lieutenant Colonel Patton, who at one a.m. had sent Lieutenant [Edwin A.] McCluer of Arizona, from Woel with three tanks and five runners to reconnoiter, received the following message from him:[5]

"Have been attacked by one battery 77s. One machine gun company, one battalion of infantry. Am now counter-attacking."

Five more tanks under Captain Gordon M. Grant, Long Island, N.Y., were sent to his support and they chased the Germans into Joinville, on the Hindenburg line, the first Americans to arrive on that defense barrier. However, as a tank at its best makes eight kilometers an hour, usually only one when in action, they are not hard to run away from.

A tank in which Captain H. H. Semmes, of Washington, and a noncommissioned officer were attempting to cross the little stream known as the Rupt de Mad was hit by an enemy shell and stalled in the water. The captain crawled out through the top and, with enemy machine gun bullets splashing around him, swam to the shore. Then he discovered that the man with him had not followed, probably being unconscious from the gas which filled the tank. He swam back under fire, pulled the driver out and brought him to shore.

Chances of surviving for two occupants in the tank were small if it received a direct hit. However, Captain John Castle, a former Yale halfback, was in a tank when its top was smashed by a 77 shell and escaped with his life. Bullets did not make an impression on a tank nor could a tank do much with a German concrete pillbox, one of those miniature forts which were everyplace along their trenches. In one instance where a tank was sent out to silence a pillbox, the two spit at each other for half an hour, the bullets splashing harmlessly against each other's sides. Then the tank commander had a bright idea. He waddled his tank right up to the pillbox and leaned its side against the opening in the concrete wall. The Germans could not fire after that and a couple of minutes later the pillbox was surrounded and a grenade dropped inside.

345th Tank Battalion

*"Brave under Fire: Lieutenant Guy R. Chamberlin Never Flinched in Face of Danger" (*Burlington [VT] Free Press, *December 24, 1918, 5)*

[Lieutenant Arthur N. Chamberlin about Lieutenant Guy R. Chamberlin, HQ, 345th Tank Battalion]

A former Free Press associate of Lieutenant Arthur N. Chamberlin has received from him a personal letter containing an account of how his brother, Lieutenant Guy R. Chamberlin, met death on a French battlefield. The dead officer leaves so many warm friends in Burlington who will be interested to learn of his gallant service that the Free Press takes the liberty of printing the following paragraphs from the surviving brother's letter:

4th Section, General Staff,
A.P.G., 717,
Dec. 4, 1918.

Guy did splendid work as a reconnaissance officer during the St. Mihiel drive and was cited in the brigade orders for it. He had been ordered back to the tank school at Langres as an instructor, but before he left St. Mihiel, the Argonne push started. A call was sent out for the best men of the tank corps and he was ordered to that front as reconnaissance officer for the 345th Battalion of the 1st tank brigade.

The Argonne, as you know, was our hardest fight of the war. It is a dense forest, swampy underfoot, and the Germans had fortified every inch of it with barbed wire and machine gun nests. Our artillery could do little toward demolishing these defenses, so when our infantry attacked they were unable to advance and the tanks were ordered in to clean out the machine guns. The 345th Battalion led the tanks and Guy led the 345th.

There was a dense fog on the morning of September 26th, and the tanks, which are blind creatures at best, the driver having only a very narrow slit through which to peer, were helpless. In such a case, some officer has to lead the tanks one at a time, marching a short distance ahead of them and signaling the driver by arm motions.

Guy had been reconnoitering the previous night and knew the ground. Under heavy fire from six machine guns, situated in a pillbox but a couple of hundred yards away, he led the five tanks of a company of the 345th, one at a time, across a sunken road. Just as he got the fifth tank across, a machine gun bullet struck him in the mouth, penetrating his brain.

Capt. [John T.] Cole, a classmate of his at West Point, who was bringing up the company, saw him fall. Cole reached his side, and Guy smiled at him and said, "Well, old man, it's hard trying to cover your whole body with only one tin hat," and then the light flickered out of his eyes, and I am sure that the gallant boys who had preceded him were giving him glad welcome on the other shore.

Even in the midst of the fight, the officers and men of the battalion paused long enough to bury him with military honors. He is buried almost where he fell, about 500 yards to the left of the town of Varennes, which is near Verdun. The camp at the tank training school at Langres has been named Camp Chamberlin in his honor, as he was the first officer of the American tank corps to be killed. Officers who were with him in the battle told me he was the bravest man under fire that they ever saw. . . .

Light Tank Battalions

*C. H. Claudy, "Story of the Tank Man" (*Boston Globe, *May 11, 1919, Editorial and New Feature sec., 3)*

[Unnamed soldier from a light tank battalion]

We started in with 216 tanks. They cost about $10,000 each. Yes, motor not unlike a good automobile motor; four-cylinder, about 40 horsepower. Indeed, the tank has a lot of automobile mechanism about it.

These Renaults have four speeds forward and reverse; two levers. If you want to go to the right, pull the right-hand lever. That disconnects the right-hand tread and lets it run free. The left-hand one, still engaged, pulls the left side of the tank around faster and you turn to the right. Pull the lever still further and the right-hand tread is locked. Then you spin around in your own length. It's astonishing how fast those little tanks can turn when they have to. Fast enough to cut a man in two if he's in the way.

Yes, it happened more than once. Some Boche had an idea they could do something to a Renault with a hand grenade and tried it at close quarters. Might just as well have thrown eggs at us, unless some splinters got in the slits.

And if they were close enough and we whirled her around they were out of luck sure—broken legs, you know, or mashed ribs.

No, the Boche anti-tank gun never hurt us to amount to anything. Ever see one? It weighs about 50 pounds and shoots a whale of a bullet, but unless it strikes sharp at right angles it doesn't get through. Pretty hard steel, you know, that tank armor.

What did stop us, when we were stopped was the 77[mm field gun]. Even that took a direct hit. A 77 could go right beside us and would hardly know it. But if it made a direct hit—well, you don't expect to run a war without any casualties, of course.

Of course there are places a tank can't go. You read a lot about how a tank loves mud. Don't you believe it. The tank can slither around in mud just like an automobile. Of course it can go, but can't climb at the same angle on mud as on dry ground and somehow we always did fight in the mud.

France is a great place for mud; if you can sell it France wouldn't have any national debt at all. Mud didn't stop us of course, but it made it more difficult. On dry ground we can climb 45 degrees, and 51 degrees in reverse.

You hear a lot about the way a tank can crawl over trenches. But that's the big heavy tank. The little fellow can't run over a trench the way it can down and up a shell crater. The Renault is tail heavy, you see.

It gets its nose across a trench all right, but if the trench is a little too wide the heavy tail drops back into it. Then you have to get out and dig out or get another tank to come and pull you out. That's why two tanks together are worth four separately. They can jam themselves up and still get along by doing the brother act with chains.

Once that I know of, a tank got stuck and the second tank couldn't pull it out so the officer outside signals another tank and it comes up—all this under fire,—and he hooks that on, too, and the two of them pull the helpless one up and over. He got the D.S.C. [Distinguished Service Cross] for it, that officer.

It's not nice when you're stalled, you know. As long as you can move around, the 77 has a hard time getting you. But if you get stuck somewhere it doesn't take a Boche gunner so very long to get your range. That's why we were so anxious to have self-starters put on the American tanks, when we thought we were going to have American tanks. If there had been any self-starters on our Renaults, we'd probably be shy about 20 casualties. No, they didn't put the self-starters on. Don't ask me why; I don't know.

Sure, the American tanks were good tanks. We never used them in action that I know of. Those I saw got to France, or got where they might have been used, after the armistice. But they were sure American all over—too much American, if you know what I mean.

There was so much ingenuity about those tanks there wasn't always room for the crew. For instance, machine gun belts. When you use them they are rolled up and in a carrier. Some wise tank builder decided all the ammunition in a machine gun tank ought to be in carriers, rolled up ready for use.

When he got through there wasn't any room inside for the crew! No sense to it, of course; the same amount of ammunition stores flat, and leaves plenty of room, and it only takes a few seconds to roll up a belt and put it in a carrier.

Then there was the compass. Someone must have read that British tanks carry compasses. So they did, until the tank crew could throw it away. So our American tanks came over with the handsomest compasses inside you ever saw—regular ship affairs, gimbels and all!

Now, of course, that's all foolishness. In the first place there wasn't room for the compass and the crew. In the second place, when you start the engine, the compass does a foxtrot and keeps on whirling. It's no good as a compass.

And if it was, there wouldn't be any sense in it. There's a map stuck up right under your nose, and that's all you need, not to mention a few officers with flags telling you where to go, if they are not sitting on top going with you.

Then there was the speedometer. Why anyone should imagine a tank crew needed the speedometer I don't know. Maybe they thought, down in Washington, we were going to establish a tank speed record or something.

And the hook—I mustn't forget the hook. It's so typically American. To put a hook in at the top of the tank meant at least two hours' time. In 100 tanks that was almost 200 hours or 26 working days, slowing up production.

The idea of the hook was that it would be so convenient when a crane had to lift the tank. Now the average tank gets lifted by a crane just four or six times; on a car at the factory, off the car, on the ship, off the ship, and maybe on and off a car again.

So to save the six or 12 minutes it would take a crew to slip a chain around the tank, they put a hook at the top, because it was efficient!

Oh, well I oughtn't to grouch. We never used the tanks. And no one that I know minds much. Those Renault tanks were little dandies. You have no idea how easily they run. You can crawl over a telegraph pole and hardly feel it, so well worked out has been the spring suspension and relation of rollers, chariots and treads.

And they didn't go in for any fancy touches, the Renaults. No armor for the guns nor fancy locks on the floor to keep someone from crawling up and throwing a grenade inside, nor deflection armor at odd angles which never did anything but stop bullets and make splinters that otherwise would never have endangered anyone's eyes.

We had about 44 percent casualties, and that covers 22 actions. Ten percent of the casualties were deaths. But I don't recall many men dying without doing something first.

I recall that there was one tank got stuck in a trench and nobody handy to rescue it. Captured of course. Well, we captured it back two days later. Every round of ammunition was fired. Every pistol cartridge had been fired. And both men had been wounded long before they were killed. They must have put up a beautiful scrap. Americans don't like to surrender, somehow.

*"Life in Tank Corps Not for Mollycoddles but It Has Many Attractions, Nevertheless: Sergt. Joseph A. W. Appleby and His Pet, Ermentrude" (*Seattle Daily Times, *July 27, 1919, 11)*

[Sergeant Joseph A. W. Appleby, unnamed light tank battalion]

Right here I might explain something of the difference between the light tank and the heavy.

The light tank weighs six-and-a-half tons, carries one 37-mm gun—a one pounder—and is manned by a crew of two, having a speed of eight miles an hour. The heavy weighs some 45 tons, carries two 3-inch, six-pounder guns, and eight machine guns; is manned by from nine to 15 soldiers, and has a speed of about three miles an hour.

The heavy can go through obstructions that the light one has to go around, and it carries much heavier armament. But, on the other hand, the light tank is much faster and, because of this and its lack of bulk, is not as easily hit. Neither tank can be stopped by anything less than a direct hit by a shell—machine gun and armor piercing bullets mean nothing in the life of a tank.

The light tank corps of the United States Army was organized in France in February, 1918, a call being issued by General Headquarters for volunteers. Each man had to have some special qualifications. He had to be an auto mechanic, a machinist, and expert gunner, or a first-class signalman. In addition, he had to be physically fit. For the Tank Corps man in battle gets about every kind of hard knock that can be imagined and he's got to be in trim to stand the gaffe. The tank treats the enemy rough, but also treats its friends none too gently when it is in action.

There was a great response to the call from every division in France, but only a few were lucky enough to be accepted. Our maximum strength for two battalions was 700, and at first we only had one company.

The first volunteers were put to work building the tank center, a sort of the gigantic garage. When we had that completed the training worked again.

Probably no soldiers in the world have as strenuous training as the tankers. Driving the tank, gunner, signaling, mapmaking—these are but a few of the subjects drilled into the pupil, and in addition there are long hours of tactical problems. Before a man is allowed to go into battle with a tank, he must be able to maneuver into and out of every conceivable position short of riding upside down—and he must have banished fear from his heart.

I might mention that there seems to be a general misconception regarding the use of the tank. Almost everybody seems to think that its sole mission is physical destruction—smashing of pillboxes, machine gun nests, wire entanglements and the like. Equally as great, if not greater, is its psychological use—the breaking of the morale of the enemy. And as its function is to spread terror, the driver has to be without fear.

The fact that we were learning and the fact that we soon would be allowed to go up against the Hun were what kept us going in those days of training. We were billeted in French barns—and no one who has ever seen a French barn can imagine what it was like. I was quartered in a billet directly over a pigpen and I had to tread lightly over the floor or fall down with the pigs.

"C'est la guerre [It is war]," said the French soldiers who visited us, with good-natured grimaces, but I think it would have been more to the point to say "C'est sont les cochins! [It is all disgusting!]"

Finally, we were ready for action, the 326th and 327th light tank battalions of the First Tank Corps Brigade (later our names were changed to the 344th and 345th), and late in August, 1918, we moved up into action.

Never have I seen a sight that thrilled me so as the sight of 150 tanks lumbering out to battle. I have seen infantry charges. I have seen lines of super dreadnoughts drawn up in battle array. I have seen duels in the air, and nearly every other form of modern battle—but the tank has it on all of them.

A long, bending, squirming line we were, stretching out as far on both sides as I could see. Some of the tanks dropped out of sight as they went into shell holes, then reappeared as they came out again. Some crawled, crab like, around obstructions, some kept a straight course, deviating neither to the right or left, and tearing down what chanced to be before them.

Every machine seemed to be a living, breathing thing, each with a mind of its own, each pursuing a different course, but all going forward. Now and then there would be a direct hit, a rending explosion, and one of the tanks would burst into flames, careen wildly, and it was good night tank. A queer thing, isn't it, to think of a tank, a creature of solid metal, burning up? But that was an all too frequent occurrence. A shell in the gasoline tank, the tank flooding with flaming petrol, the explosion of the ammunition—and two more of our comrades had gone west.

This battle was in the St. Mihiel drive, on September 12. My outfit, going ahead of the 1st Division, took Mt. Sec, the same Mt. Sec where the French lost 30,000 men in 45 minutes—and we took it in three hours with only 2,000 casualties. The tanks and infantry went ahead so fast that the artillery had to keep on the move day and night to keep up, and finally after three or four days, we found ourselves miles ahead of the infantry—patrolling behind the Hindenburg line! The war experts all say the tanks can't hold ground unsupported, but we did for 24 hours, while waiting for the doughboys to come up.

Our losses in this drive were extremely light. Our souvenir booty was great, and when we came back we looked like Germans, we had so many helmets and other trophies.

As soon as we were relieved we were shipped by rail to the Argonne, without any pause for rest.

On September 26, we went over the top again, in Clermont Woods. There we caught it hot and heavy. At St. Mihiel the Germans evidently had not been prepared for tanks, and it had been quick work, for we seemed to terrify the Heinies before we reached them. But here it was different. The most careful preparation had been made for our reception and the Germans turned everything they had loose on us. Special antitank guns and tank mines were used and they had built many tank traps.

These were great holes with perpendicular sides, and filled with water, so that if a tank went in and couldn't get out its occupants would be drowned. Only one of our machines was caught in one of these, for the simple reason that the tanks didn't play fair. They refused to be caught; down they would go, and up again, climbing up the sides like a fly on the wall. The only casualty was caused by the water getting into the engine and stalling it.

Still, for four days it was a touch and go proposition. We were going forward—but, slowly. Our gains were hardly perceptible, and we began to grow discouraged; then, all of a sudden, we started advancing and there was no stopping us. We took part in 18 distinct battles in as many days, and we had the Germans utterly demoralized. True our losses were heavy—terribly heavy.

In November, of our original 150 tanks, there were but 25 in line and 10 of these were useless, they had been smashed around so badly. Yet, if it hadn't been for the armistice, I believe those 15 useless tanks—one of which I am proud to say, I piloted—would have smashed right on through to Berlin.

We had the Germans so badly terrified that they came to look on us as something supernatural. Impossible deeds were ascribed to us by them, in spite of the fact that the things we actually achieved were unusual enough for anyone.

I remember one German major we captured—a rather decent fellow as Germans go, who spoke university English.

I realize that I am a prisoner, gentlemen, he said, and as such entitled to no privileges. But, as one soldier to another, I want to ask you a favor. Show me one of those 75-mm machine guns that your heavy tanks use.

We had been firing our guns so fast that he thought we carried machine guns with a 3-inch caliber! Needless to say, there never has been such a thing, and probably never will be.

For this service—covering only a scant two months—we received 11 citations, one signed by President Wilson himself. Yet the public doesn't seem to know much about it.

301st Tank Battalion

*"Riding a Tank into Mouths of Machine Guns Is Real Sport" (*Muncie [IN] Morning Star, *January 6, 1919, 12)*

[Second Lieutenant Paul S. Haimbaugh, Company B, 301st Tank Battalion]

Telling the purpose of, and describing the manner of attack of the big tanks, which he said were the last word in modern warfare, Lieut. Paul Haimbaugh, of the tank service, has written interestingly to his father, Postmaster F. D. Haimbaugh. The operations of these monster machines have been among the most interesting of the entire Army, and the letter which follows gives a splendid idea of the "modus operandi":

St. Pol, France, Nov. 29, 1918

"Dear Dad:—. . . . Your calling my attention to the tanks, reminds me that I recall seeing pictures of the tanks in the "Stars and Stripes," but they were the small French tanks which our Americans used in the light battalions; really they were quite small compared with our monsters. When one sees the giant English tanks moving over the field they remind one of some ungainly prehistoric monster seeking out some quarry with which to fill his capacious maw. Our tanks are 32 feet long, 6 feet wide and 8 feet high and weigh 40 tons. With these modern engines of destruction we could smash houses and barns and ride down good-sized trees. The tank is really the last word in modern warfare.

"My tank was known as a 'male' by the reason of the armament of two six-pound guns, about two-and-a-half inch bore and in addition had four machine guns, quite a formidable opponent for the Hun, at least he thought that way. They are armored with half-inch plate, making them safe from machine gun and rifle fire. But the Hun had an anti-tank rifle and armor piercing machine bullets, which could penetrate the armor and raise Cain with the crew and machinery. Of course he had his larger guns, the light artillery which could put a tank out in short order. We lost quite a number of tanks by direct hits with shells. The Germans would place a number of their 77-mm guns well up in front to act as defense against tanks. We would be following up the barrage ahead of the infantry and find some German guns firing away at us. Would have to dodge around and put these guns out of action with our six pounders.

"The primary purpose of the tank is to put the enemy machine guns out of action. When the infantry goes up against machine gun fire they usually lose heavily. When tanks are operating they search out the machine gun nests and destroy them. It would be fun if there were no artillery or anti-tank rifle shooting at you. We would "jump off" at the zero hour, still rather dark, and rumble toward the Germans. Up ahead our barrage would be laid down. Of course the Germans would lay low until the barrage would lift and then they would bring up their machine guns. Leading the procession we would get properly shot at. The machine gun bullets would make a noisy tattoo on the wall of the tank, not much danger though save that the splashes of the molten metal would come in the little cracks and burn the face and hands. The machine gun nests of the enemy must be located and put out. Consequently the tank commander must look around through the peepholes and sometimes stick his head out of the top of the tank. Having spotted the nest he points out the target for the gunner. He then steers a course for the guns. The tank guns and machine guns pepper away and there soon is a bunch of German guns that will not hold up the infantry. That is the way we go. Each commander of the tank has a definite sector in every attack, covering this and nosing out machine guns, looking for batteries, shooting down dugouts and raising the devil with the Dutch. The infantry certainly like tanks—gives them confidence to have a big machine up ahead clearing the way for them. We seemed irresistible. But I have seen tanks pretty well broken up when a shell gets them.

"I am still thanking my lucky stars that I am here, alive and kicking. One of our officers is just back from the hospital to get his stuff, preparing to leave for the States. He lost an eye and will be discharged from the service. He was using one of the peepholes when a shell fragment came in.

"You were right in your surmise when you thought I was in the fight on September 29th, when the Hindenburg line was stormed. I was also in three more major operations. October 8th, 17th and 23rd—got enough action in these four fights to furnish the materiel for stories to last a lifetime. We operated one time with American troops, the 29th and 30th divisions. General Haig cited these two divisions in a special order, commending them highly.[6] It is a real compliment to receive citations such as that. In addition our tank battalion established a record for continuous service in the line and for the number and character of the fights engaged in during that period and we were the last tanks withdrawn from the line. Not a bad record, is it?

"I had good luck in all my fights but one. On that occasion I got stuck in the river Selle in the midst of a German barrage. I had nearly reached my objective anyway, but I could not get the darn thing out and in the meantime a German trench mortar on a hill in front of us kept annoying us.

"Incidentally I might mention that we frequently would run into gas. It is difficult to distinguish gas when in action. The engine would give off fumes, this with powder and gasoline fumes made it difficult to distinguish the gas of the enemy, so we just went ahead and would encounter the gas.

"Tank work is very fatiguing. The heat and fumes and inadequate ventilation made a combination that would exhaust a man in four or five hours. After an action of from six to eight hours a tank crew was generally all in and greatly in need of a rest.

"Well, I think that I was pretty lucky in getting in early, went to the front with the first and was in the only battalion of heavy tanks that saw action. Only three battalions of tanks got into the fight, ours and two light tank outfits. But I think this is quite enough about tanks. Hope before many months to give you the real details in person."

"Decorated Vet Recalls Tank Battles on Hindenburg Line More Than Half Century Ago" (Gettysburg [PA] Times, *July 21, 1972, 3, 5)*

[Sergeant Carl E. Rosenhagen, Company C, 301st Tank Battalion]

Sgt. Carl Rosenhagen, World War I tanker now from Dayton, Ohio, and National Tank Corps commander Don Warner, are among the tankers here for their 54th reunion, and are swapping stories at the Holiday Inn.

Rosenhagen, who won a British military decoration and the Military Medal, recalled today a special Friday evening in the experiences of the 301st Heavy Tank Corps. They had gone to England in March 1918, ahead of the men from Camp Colt.

Rosenhagen's recollections follow:

"Friday evening, it was still daylight: three of our boys from the 13th crew, 'C' Co. took a walk through the woods where our tanks were hidden and camouflaged. In a little while they came back, one of them carrying a black cat in his arms that they came upon in the woods. Jokingly the remarks were: Well a black cat on a Friday night for the 13th crew, sure portends good luck for the 13th crew.

"The next day we started out to take our place in the battle lineup. We stopped at a tank park or repair center and the English mechanics mounted large fascines, or a large octagonal squirrel cage about eight feet in height, made of very heavy timbers and metal facings on our 29-foot-long tanks being used in this engagement. These tanks could not cross the 12-foot anti-tank trench the Germans had at the point where we were to go over the top. The 35-foot tanks could not be stopped by any trench; but the 29-foot tanks would nose down into the trench or against the other side of the trench and there was no way for it to crawl out.[7] By dropping this large fascine or squirrel cage into the trench, the front end of the tank would not get below the ground level, and could get across any trench.

"While we were at this repair center awaiting the tanks to be rigged with all the necessary equipment, a firing squad shot a German spy dressed as an English officer, and an English sergeant who had been caught robbing the dead.

"I drove the tank after we left the repair center, and after dark we got into a couple of bad mustard gas attacks. It was sure a hardship driving with a gas mask on for the manual labor required to drive a tank over rough territory with the heat of the motor and confined space inside, made you perspire profusely. With both hands and feet working, it was next to impossible to keep the nose clips from slipping off, and the gas burned terribly around your face and eyes; and to breathe through the mouthpiece and see where you were going was really brutal punishment. It was impossible for the driver not to breathe in a part of the gas.

"We finally came to a halt to load up with gasoline, or petrol as it was called. Aviation gas was used and it was passed in two-gallon tins, man to man in a line to the back end of the tank, and the gas put outside in armored fuel tanks. The refueling area was within a short distance from the front lines, and artillery and machine gun fire was heavy, and well illuminated by German flares causing several deaths and others being wounded in our battalion. After fueling we were briefed. Then it was time to go.

"Zero Hour was 5:55 a.m. The artillery of both sides sounded like the end of the world was here besides the chattering of machine guns. We had a hermaphrodite tank, which is machine guns on one side and a six-pounder Hotchkiss gun on the left side. I had turned the driving over to Sgt. Barnard of Kokomo, Ind., and I was standing in the observation tower standing on a platform over the transmission picking out targets for the gunners. Before we came to the antitank trench, we ran into about 20 machine guns corralled together; and they were firing against the right side of the tank.

"The fire from all those machine guns firing every other bullet on this front, an armor piercing bullet, the whole inside of the tank seemed to be on fire from the sparks of the armor piercing bullets around the gun slots; and through the other slots the gunners had to see their targets. It was so intense one gunner laid back away from his gun, and jumped down and took his place.

"Pvt. Adams (Wooden shoe Adams), he was called, from Indianapolis, I believe, looked up from the gun he was on, and his face was a mass of blood. Seeing we could not cope with these machine guns, I pounded on the motor cowling, which is how we attracted the driver's attention, and put up my fist for a left turn. He must have had his window flap wide open, and he turned to the right, right into those machine guns, and was badly hit. They hollered for first aid and I jumped to him and said, 'For God's sake Barney keep on driving until we get through this mess.'

"And brave Barney did, turning the tank around where we were able to knock out the machine guns. We got Barney out of the driver's seat then, and I resumed driving. This happened I believe, in the first 30 or 40 minutes, or shortly after 6:00 a.m. We were in a bad fog and smoke screen; and I remember seeing a fascine get knocked off or flying to pieces by a direct hit on one of our tanks, and I thought, those boys are in a bad way for that anti-tank trench.

"Our six-pounder gun was manned by Corporal Gagnon and Private Evans. They made short work of the machine gun nest, firing case shot out of the muzzle of the gun, as the Germans were not more than 30 or 40 feet away from us.

"The artillery fire on both sides was terrific, and from what some English officers told us, it was the worst since the first battle of the Somme, which had been the world's greatest artillery engagement on record then.

"By this time the smoke screen and fog had really worsened. There were some dummy tanks, made of paper mache and wood, which had a donkey inside them. These were used to draw anti-tank fire so that our observers could spot enemy anti-tank guns.

"I headed into a trench at an angle and we bogged into the side of a trench. I worked and worked stabbing into the side of the trench, and dirt and stones and everything just kept rolling on top, making it seem that getting the tank out would be an impossible job. The German infantry made it even tougher on our right side without a six-pounder gun there. Being down in the trench I guess, saved us from their artillery.

"Having torn so much of the top of the trench away, we finally came out on a bias; as I swear we were tilted sideways at a 45 degree angle. I was looking for the tank to turn over on its left side but we lurched out, how, I do not know. Before we had gotten to the anti-tank trench, we had trouble with the infantry, our American 27th Division, men were running in front of our tank, cutting us off from helping them against the German machine guns. Smoke and fog were so heavy now, we could not even see any of our infantry anymore; but as we had a timetable to get to Le Catelet, we continued on.

"We got to the outskirts of Le Catelet and it was lighter here, but we saw no supporting infantry. We stopped at the edge of the crossroads, and the boys opened the doors to let some fresh air in. Second Lieutenant Earle Dunning and I were looking at the map we spread between us, when I looked up and in the gloom could make out some men running toward us. I thought they could be our own men, and when Lt. Dunning grabbed the machine gun between us, I grabbed his hand saying, 'Don't fire, they are Englishmen,' but I was mistaken. When Dunning went to fire the gun, it jammed; not even a shot came out. A German pushed his rifle into the front window on Dunning's side and shot a piece out of his nostril.

"I dropped into gear and gave the tank a leap, as Dunning used his Colt automatic. I had in the meantime, hollered to the men in the back to close the doors, even though I thought they were not Germans. We had a little commotion for a few minutes, swinging the tank around to get the Germans off the side machine guns so that our six-pounder could get to them. Our six-pounder crew was really good and made short work of them.

"After this we drove the reverse direction, opposite the way we came by compass, taking a south westerly course, hoping and watching for our infantry. We followed along a bank until the terrain changed. Then a shell hit us on the right rear and tore a hole in our back end, bursting our main water line running up to the motor. In no time, steam filled the tank so bad, I don't know how any of the rear crew lived through it; as we had our front windows open gasping for air.

"We came to the bottom of a ridge 10 to 15 feet high and tried to climb it, but the motor conked and knocked so bad and would not pull anything.

"There were two terrific explosions outside of the tank, and then a shell hit us on top. I believe the motor casing saved us.

"We caught fire and the tank seemed to be on fire. I climbed though Lt. Dunning's seat, the only way I could get out. I slid out. Lt. Dunning got his face burned getting out of the tank. I was lucky, and only lost some hair from my head.

"The four of us ran for some small trenches we could see ahead, and while in there; the largest German I had ever seen made a running jump over us in the trench. I don't know whether he was a runner carrying a message, or if he had started to go to Berlin. German machine guns were firing a barrage; and we lay there concealed by the fog and smoke, seeing only the fire coming out of the barrels of the machine guns. We jumped into some shell holes. We could then make out our tank eight or nine hundred feet away. Lt. Dunning and I were in the same shell hole, not very big. Didn't see the other two boys until later that night.

"Our tank was burning and blowing up all afternoon with smoke belching out. German planes were flying right over our heads, but they must not have seen us lying below. I think the Germans figured we never got out of the tank, as the door through which we fled was near the side of the ridge mentioned earlier; so they could not tell what had happened.

"There was a battery of German five- or six-inch guns lined up on the top of that ridge, and that afternoon our artillery was trying to blast them out. About two o'clock that afternoon our artillery started a box barrage laying it where we were, no doubt intending to get the battery of guns on the ridge. We were right in the middle of it! The box barrage was constant for an hour or more and they were dropping all big shells every 40 or 50 feet apart. All we could do was to push our heads against the sides of the shell hole. Lt. Dunning got hit in the hand by a piece of shell. I pulled a big piece of shell away between my arm and body; but it hadn't got me. Lt. Dunning was in great pain, what with his burns, his nose, and now the hit on his hand. We had nothing to help us medically.

"About six o'clock it began to get dark, but our own artillery started throwing a line of shrapnel about six or eight hundred feet south of us, on the other side of a canal. Just as we were ready to start out on the only alternate way, six or eight Germans from the gun crews were walking only 50 or 60 feet to the side of us. We then had to go toward the shrapnel barrage. We got up and started walking to where we thought our buddies were killed, and they popped up as we neared them.

"We walked on to the Canal du Nord, and crept along its bank. We continued to crawl then through the underbrush, and could hear men talking and mess kits rattling. We crawled very slowly. Lt. Dunning and I stopped at a path through the bushes, and someone walked in front of me. I reached up and grabbed him by the neck, shoving my gun in his face, wondering what to do with him. I heard him mumbling, as he was on his knees then; and I looked into his face and saw it was Daley, our big Irish crewman.

"We came to a bunch of quonset huts about 50 feet ahead of us. Two Germans came from the right of us and stopped at a clump of bushes and started smoking a cigarette. I could have reached out and touched the shoe of one as he passed us. Flares lit up everything and they were hunting for us.

"I heard someone say, 'How many of there are you?' Then I heard crewman Daley say, 'Two of us.' This German spoke good English. They took two of our men away. There were about six Germans that captured Daley and [Corporal Richard J.] Capstick.

"I was at the edge of the left side of a road when someone said, 'What are you going to do?' It was Lt. Dunning. We continued down that road together. We saw a woods on the right and went into it, but there was nothing but real big shell holes filled with stagnant water.

"We had no real sense of direction.

"Two Germans had come to the edge of the woods and were looking for us. I swear one of them saw us; and as he raised up his rifle I could hear him as he moved the bolt of his rifle and brought it up to his shoulder. He held it there, peering through the gloom, and after a couple of minutes he lowered his rifle. They walked around a little, and we watched them go into the woods.

"While with an English tank company for experience, an English officer, commander of that tank company; taught me how to read directions by the stars, using the big dipper.

"I began looking for the big dipper. As we lay there, I prayed for God to show me, or just let me see that seventh star of the big dipper. Do you know, it was not very long, and my prayer was answered; and we knew which way to go!

"Machine gun bullets were over us, too close to stand or walk. The strange thing was that we were going correctly, but we did not know before this time. It at least was assurance to us that we had not gone deeper into the German lines.

"I will never forget waiting for a glimpse of the tail of the big dipper.

"We got to the top of the ridge and below us we could see by the light of the flares and star shells, the territory ahead of us was trenches and barbed wire. We were back at the front lines again.

"We moved ahead, encountering the bodies of many German dead.

"A German machine gunner, less than 100 feet from our right, would reel off a belt of ammunition to keep any of our patrols away, or to let them know they were still in the fight. We found some boards across the trench, about four or five feet above the bottom of the trench. German infantry were under the boards, keeping dry, as it was raining and drizzling all the time."

*"Rosenhagen, Dunning Won Decorations from British in Field for Tank Exploits" (*Gettysburg [PA] Times, *July 22, 1972, 5)*

[Sergeant Carl E. Rosenhagen, Company C, 301st Tank Battalion]

In the reminiscences of Sgt. Carl E. Rosenhagen, of Dayton, O., begun Friday in the *Gettysburg Times,* he was recounting the efforts he and Lt. Dunning made to make their way through a rain drenched No Man's Land to their own lines after their tank had been blown up and set afire by German artillery.

The incidents involved the 301st Heavy Tank Corps on the Hindenburg Line more than a half century ago.

In Friday's account Rosenhagen and Dunning had come upon a German trench with boards across it under which German soldiers were talking shelter from the rain.

"We jumped down into the trench and I boosted Lt. Dunning up and he crawled over it and reached down. Somehow I also got out of the trench and we both ran ahead and flopped down, as machine guns started shooting up the ground all around us. We had slid into very small shell holes. Flares went up and they really lit things up, but due to the rain I do not think they knew just what was the matter.

"We started to crawl again and get through the barbed wire, in front of us, when they picked us up again and really tore the ground up around us. How we lived through that I do not know. God had to be helping us!

"We picked our way through several more wire barriers, and it was starting to break daylight. We had gone through one trench when we found loads of potato mashers, 'German Grenades,' so we turned away from there.

"We got into a trench, with dead machine gunners in it. A terrific shell or shrapnel fire had started, and we were caught in both German and our own shell fire. As we started up a dirt emplacement at the top of this trench, a shrapnel shell hit directly in front of me and exploded in the dirt. It really knocked me off my feet.

"I thought my legs were blown off and Lt. Dunning ran to me but I was OK after a couple of minutes, just badly shaken up and my leggings and pants legs torn up.

"The next thing I know or saw was an English soldier, rather five or six of them, and one of them was pulling on Dunning's foot, hollering 'Yanks! Yanks!' Were we glad to see them!! I saw two German machine gunners strapped or bound to their machine guns, both of them killed by shell fire.

"The English soldiers took us down into a big dugout, where they had set up a headquarters of some sort, and they gave us each a big glass of Scotch and a mutton sandwich before they started to question us. After giving them any information we could, they showed us how to go, and we went to the rear to an English dressing station.

"We finally found what was left of Co. 'C.' I'll never forget, [First] Lt. Ramah E. Cole grabbed me and hugged me and gave me a bacon sandwich he had in his hand. Before this, a Lt. General Reid, I believe of the 27th Yank Division, shook our hands and complimented us on what a great job our tanks had done.[8] We then went to Major [Roger B.] Harrison's headquarters and told what we knew. Lt. Dunning had big patches of white hair, as it had turned over night. They took him to the hospital, and wanted me to go, but I said I was OK. Two days later they took me to the hospital anyhow, as I could not sleep. It took me another three days before I could walk again.

"Got back to St. Emily about the 8th of October, the day of the next show. Was back up again for the next one on October 18.

"Lt. Dunning came back to us shortly after that, and about the 3rd of November, he came to me and asked if I would volunteer for a night attack, taking the King's Own Infantry over the top. I agreed and he told me to pick out the tank I wanted; but to save room for our First Sgt. Carnter, and to leave place for two six-pounder gunners from 'A' or 'B' Co.

"The tank I picked out was the J-23. It was a male Mark V, 35 foot long tank, and had never been able to get over the top. Always developed mechanical troubles for the English and for us. I could never understand it, as to me it was the sweetest running tank then of 'C' Company.

"I got our crew lined up, we went over the motor, tuning it up; and on November 6 at 1:20 a.m., we went over the top again in a night attack leading the King's Own Infantry Regiment.[9] We ran into a very deep fog not long after we passed the end of the tape that had been laid to guide us to our correct positions. We ran into terrific shrapnel fire, and the Germans' timing was very good; shells exploding 50 to 75 feet over the tanks. One of the crew was wounded by the shrapnel. We went through heavy phosgene gas concentrations, which made some of the crew very sick, vomiting and retching.

"The Germans were also throwing chlorine gas shells that were very deadly. About eight or nine o'clock that morning we came back a little way to let out the sick crew members, and pick up replacements.

"We went back, mopping machine gun nests. We also found a battery of German field pieces behind an elevated railroad track. They were trying to knock us out, but they were not able to. One of two Germans never missed, a perfect performance (with a potato masher), and hit the edge of the window opening on our right side. I saw him throw it and I ducked down, keeping myself from falling by holding onto one of the handles placed around the tower. I got hit in the left hand, nothing severe, just skin lacerations and a piece of grenade in my middle finger.

"We also encountered a lot of anti-tank rifle fire, and one of our magnetos was shot off, but because of the double ignition system, we were still running on all six cylinders when we finished that night about 6 p.m. The anti-tank rifles were bad actors sometimes, as they would come through our heaviest armor plate. The 'J-23' performed beautifully and was able to lose the name of the 'Jinx.'

"When we looked the tank over the next day, you could see where we had many hits that night by the shrapnel shells, knocking out our semaphore and tearing up our ditching beam guide rails. We were told that our volunteer night was highly successful. All twelve tanks came back okay. Our motor had actually been running for about 26 hours without shutting it off, never missed, a perfect performance. . . .

"Major Ralph I. Sasse was our battalion commander from the La Selle River attack until we arrived back in Fort Meade.

"Colonel Patton (his title then), came up to our front several times, as he and Major Sasse were working on a wireless communications system then. I got acquainted with Colonel Patton then, and met him again at Langres where we stopped for delousing and clothing, before we went to Marseilles for embarkation to the USA.

"Lieutenant Dunning was awarded the British Military Cross for officers only, and I received the British Military Medal. These were immediate awards and were given in the field under the hand of General [Sir Henry S.] Rawlinson, commander of the British 4th Army.

"Also received a certificate from the British Tank Corps, and a brown, red and green 'whistle cord'; which represented the green field of Flanders, the mud in Flanders, and the red, the blood shed in Flanders field. The awards were for our September 29 action.

"We came back to Camp Meade in March 1919, and I was sent to Camp Zachery Taylor at Louisville, Kentucky, for discharge April 16, 1919."

The National in the World War *([Cleveland, OH: General Electric Company, 1920], 47–52)*

[First Lieutenant William M. Rosborough, Company C, 301st Tank Battalion]

William McLure Rosborough, when the United States declared war with Germany, was southern manager for the Shelby Division [of the National Lamp Works of the General Electric Company] and had his office in Atlanta, Georgia.

Rosborough applied for a commission in the Engineer Reserve Corps and was granted a 1st lieutenancy. He was called to active duty on September 2nd, 1917, and was ordered to the Second Engineers' Training Camp at American University, D.C., where he remained on duty six weeks. He was then assigned to the General Engineer Depot, Washington, D.C. In February, 1918, while he was acting as assistant to Col. W. H. Rose, Commanding Officer, he was allowed to transfer to the 65th Engineers (the Tank Detachment of the Engineers). After a month in Washington where he was on duty with Colonel H. B. Ferguson, Tank Corps organizer, he was ordered to Company C, 301st Battalion, Tank Corps. He joined his organization at Camp Meade and one month later was on his way to the other side.

The 301st arrived in England early in April. The entire outfit was detailed under British instruction at Wareham, England, until August, moving from that center to the port of debarkation at Havre, France. Here they remained but a few days before entraining for the front. At Bapaume they took over and added to the equipment of the 10th Battalion, British Tank Corps, until it had reached a strength of forty-eight of the heavy tanks known as English Mark 5 and Mark 5-Star.

"Rosie" went into action in the Second Battle of Cambrai on the morning of Sunday, September 29th, 1918, experiencing in this engagement the thrills of action, wounds, capture, escape and all the lurid thoughts and fears which must necessarily possess the mind of one who, alone on hostile terrain and without means of protection, roams and suffers for two days and two nights.

The army objective in this drive was the tunneled portion of the St. Quentin Canal midway between Cambrai and St. Quentin. It was a four-mile stretch and was strongly fortified, being a part of the renowned and "unbreakable" (?) Hindenburg Line. The American line at this date was approximately four kilometers west of this point. According to the plan of advance, Rosie's platoon of five tanks, posted near the town of Ronssoy, was directed to form a part of the second wave of the attack, following up and assisting the infantry of the 27th Division of the American troops.

At zero hour (5:40 a.m.), Lieutenant Rosborough gave the tank commanders the order to advance. Due to darkness and climatic conditions the attack was not carried out as organized and before seven o'clock, after advancing a distance of less than two miles, the tank in which Rosie was riding became separated from the other four tanks of his platoon and got considerably in advance of the infantry as well.

Besides Lieutenant Rosborough, the tank on which our interest centers contained a second lieutenant and ten enlisted men, one of whom was killed shortly after the advance was begun, being struck by an anti-tank rifle bullet which had penetrated the tank.

The terrain in this vicinity was moderately hilly and from a depression down which the huge caterpillar was crawling, it was possible to observe the enemy trenches as they zig-zagged away up the slopes. Some of them contained only a few men and the machine gunners fired on these as their tank crossed over. But finally, as one trench was approached, it was seen that it was strongly held by German machine gunners farther up the hillside. So the tank crossed it and began nosing along behind it, meanwhile pouring machine gun and six-pounder fire into the enemy. At this point a German field piece, concealed in a hedge at the crest of the slope, took a hand in the game and scored a hit, but got it down in the running gear where it did no material damage. The crew recognized the danger, and immediately turned their attention to this more formidable enemy, but he was so located that he got in another shot before those in the tank could maneuver into a position from which to fire upon him effectively. This last shot was well aimed. It penetrated the tank armor at the front of the machine and exploded in the midst of the crew. The engine was put out of commission and five men were killed. The remaining six were all wounded but were able to get out of the tank and into a shell hole. Rosie, besides being wounded in the right wrist and left shoulder was badly burned on the hands and face by a gasoline blaze. They removed the large first-aid kit from the tank as well as two machine guns with which to protect themselves should the enemy attack, and lay in waiting all that day, giving one another first aid and wondering what their fate was to be.

Their position was serious because the trench which they had been firing upon was only about three hundred yards away and was between them and their own troops. Rosie decided that the safety of his men depended upon getting back to the American lines and summoning help. Starting out alone, he crept from shell-hole to shell-hole, taking a roundabout course in order to avoid detection. Finally, having gone as far as was prudent in daylight, he waited for darkness and then started again. Soon afterwards he came upon a group of wounded Yanks who informed him that an American machine gun crew had set out a short time before in the direction of the tank. Desirous of overtaking this party and of effecting the rescue of his men, Rosie turned back again.

In the darkness it was hard to distinguish friend from foe, and the machine gun that he was headed for was firing spasmodically as temporary halts were made. Obviously, he was in no little danger of being mistaken for an enemy. At last, edging his way around an angle in the trench to which he had trailed the machine gun, he saw faintly silhouetted against the sky, two unmistakably German helmets. Thinking that possibly he had not been observed, Rosie slipped into a small ammunition dug-out to await developments.

These came only too soon. He had barely hidden himself when a third German filed past, said a few words to the other two, and then retraced his steps. When directly in front of Lieutenant Rosborough, he stopped and drew his pistol. Realizing that resistance was worse than useless, and believing his only hope for safety depended upon giving himself up and feigning injuries more serious than they were, Rosborough stood up, explaining to his captor that he was in dire need of aid.

Unheeding his plea and making no effort to search him for possible weapons or valuables, the three Germans started to march Rosie off in the direction of their rear. His only hope lay in attempting to break away and escape in the darkness.

The Hun who led the way was short of stature and Rosie, as if unable to advance unaided, placed his left hand upon the German's left shoulder. The German did not resent this, so he brought his right hand to his captor's right shoulder, meanwhile watching for a place where some friendly shell had battered down the side of the trench sufficiently to help him get away quickly. He had not gone far when the opportunity came. Giving the leading Boche a sudden thrust forward, he jumped over the parados [rear side of trench] and was swallowed up by the night before his enraged captors could make a move to stop him.

Hours elapsed. Finally, after much wandering about between the German lines, Rosie succeeded in getting back to his tank, only to find the second lieutenant and his men gone.

Weary, and unprotected from the rain which had been falling all night, Lieutenant Rosborough secured rations from the tank and in the early hours of Monday morning dug himself in under the battle-scarred old hulk. Here he rested all that day and the next night, hoping that on Tuesday he would be sufficiently recuperated to make his way to the American lines.

He was awakened Tuesday morning by voices coming from the direction of a plane, which had been shot down not far from the tank. Still weak and slightly shell-shocked from his experiences of the past two days and nights, he crawled out and got up into the wreck of his Juggernaut. He could see the strangers but was unable to tell positively whether they were friends or foes. They wore the helmet-covering and the blouse peculiar to the Australians but still Rosie was not firmly convinced that he should show himself. He did not know that pressure on each side of his position had made the Germans evacuate the whole area, and he did not propose to take chances on being captured again.

Once more summoning his strength, he left the tank and crept from shell-hole to shell-hole until within hearing distance of the group. Meanwhile, a few of the onlookers had rambled off in the direction of the tank and as they were retracing their steps passed the shell-hole in which Rosie lay. Convinced that he was in friendly hands, Lieutenant Rosborough made himself known to a surprised and welcoming group of Australians who gave him medical attention and brought him to an American first-aid station.

He was removed to a hospital at Rouen, where he met his second lieutenant. The latter and his men had given Rosie up for dead and had set out to work their way through the German lines. Fortunately, they had escaped capture and had arrived within the American lines early Monday morning.

From Rouen, Rosie was removed to a hospital in London where he was under treatment until December 1st, 1918, when he rejoined his battalion in France. He returned to the United States in March, going to Walter Reed Hospital in Washington, D.C., to have shrapnel removed from his left shoulder. Upon being discharged in July, 1919, he joined the Engineering Department.

*"8 Vessels Bring in 12,000 U.S. Troops" (*New York Sun, *March 14, 1919, 10)*

[Lieutenant Earle B. Dunning, Company C, 301st Tank Battalion]

Lieut. Earle Bogart Dunning of Los Angeles:

"We were with the 27th Division as everybody knows. On the morning of September 29 we started with O'Ryan's men to smash the Hindenburg line. I was attached to the platoon of Lieutenant R. E. Cole of 45 West 11th Street, New York, and with me in my tank I had a sergeant and six men. Under hellish barrage we got about two miles, shooting down Germans with our eight machine guns and our six-pounders. As we ambled along, clambering over trenches and brushing aside wire, we got beyond the village of Bony, across the St. Quentin Canal tunnel to Catelet.

"At eleven o'clock that morning our tank was struck by a shell which set fire to the tank.

"The majority were badly burned, but we crawled out and carried our machine guns with us, for we were in enemy territory. We sought shelter in shell holes and fought off those who tried to get us. Night came and mighty welcome it was too. We started to crawl back through the German lines. Six of my men were captured and this left Sergeant Rosenhagen of Indianapolis, who was badly burned and myself.

"We wriggled into a trench, and at seven o'clock in the morning the British took the trench and we were taken to a hospital. I was pretty badly burned and had a shrapnel wound in my hand. The sergeant was worse off. We stayed in hospital two weeks and then rejoined the battalion. I was wounded again on October 17 near Molian and St. Souplet, but I soon got over that."

The British gave Lieut. Dunning the British Military Cross, Sgt. Rosenhagen the British Military Medal.

The British gave Major [Ralph I.] Sasse the Distinguished Service Order, while Military Crosses went to Capt. Theodore C. Neadale [Naedele] of Hartford, Yale end on the 1908 team; Lieut. E. F. Kusner of Gary, Indiana, and Lieut. Elliott P. Frost of Waltham, Mass., captain of the Yale varsity crew 1911.

*"Tomcat of the Tanks Wins 3 War Crosses" (*Portland Oregonian, *March 16, 1919, 16)*

[Lieutenant Earle B. Dunning, Company C, 301st Tank Battalion, letter to his mother]

We were shooting down the Hun with our eight machine guns and our six-pounders as we ambled along, clambering over trenches, crushing the foe under the tractors and brushing aside the thick barb wire entanglements. . . .

As we broke that old Hindenburg line I was in the front wave that went over, but the Huns were putting up the fight of their lives and made a great deal of trouble for us but not so much as we made for them. I literally ran over dozens of them at a time.

The order was to go to a certain place and I got there after four hours of hard scrapping. I was the only one to get through and then my tank was knocked out by the artillery and blew up. I succeeded in getting my crew out, some of whom were wounded, and then dropped into a shell hole. When I looked around I was in the middle of a German position with the Huns on all sides of me.

I stayed there until night, then crawled back through the main German lines on my hands and knees. One man and myself returned, the rest being captured. Then I crawled into a dugout toward the morning to hide during the day and fell asleep—I was awakened by someone pulling at my leg and yelling to come out and surrender. Everything was O.K. though for they were British Tommies who had captured that trench. We were given food and they carried me back to the first aid post, for I was about all in.

"American Heavies in France" (Miami Herald, *July 20, 1919, 8)*

[301st Tank Battalion, from Stars and Stripes]

"Treat 'em rough" and did we do it? Ask Mr. Hindenburg what happened on September 29 when we led the 27th Division into and through the Hindenburg line. If he is doubtful about that, ask him about October 9th when we strolled into Brancourt with the 30th Division and asked him to vacate, and, if he is still unconvinced, you might ask about their swimming party in the Selle River on the morning of October 17th when we all paid him a morning call. Oh, yes, and then there was that moonlight stroll when we went over the top with the sixth British division and rolled up east of Le Cateau. That is a brief summary of what one of the smallest but best fighting units in the A.E.F.—the 301st American tank battalion—did while it was gaining its gold [wound] chevrons.

The battalion, which was the beginning of the American heavy tanks, was organized in March 1918, and landed in England—the birthplace of the rolling fort which lives on barbed wire, machine guns and Huns—early in April for training in the British schools. Here we spent five months learning the fine points of the game after which we were attached to the British Tank Corps and sent out to France, to show what we could do.

We arrived just as the British were completing their big August drive, and were forced to wait nearly a month before we could join in the game, but our assignment more than repaid us for our delay. We were to lead the 27th Division, which at that time, was in the Second Corps and attached to the fourth British army, in the attack on the Hindenburg line, and we knew that our christening was to be a real one. Everybody knows the Hindenburg line—the backbone of the Hun defense on the western front—with its broad, deep trenches, concrete dugouts; miles of barbed wire; thousands of machine guns; backed by masses of artillery, and we knew that we had a real job ahead of us and made our preparations accordingly.

One minor incident in our preparation was typical of the allied ability to outguess the Huns. Tanks have difficulty in crossing exceptionally wide and deep trenches as the front wall of the trench is very liable to give way, under the enormous weight of the heavy tank (forty tons) thus causing the nose of the tank to stick into the back wall of the trench and making it impossible for the tank to go forward or backward. This difficulty was foreseen in the Hindenburg line with the result that each tank that went over the top on the morning of September 29 carried its own bridge nicely balanced on its nose, all ready to drop into the Hindenburg line when it arrived there.

Our fight on the 29th started for us about 10 p.m. On the 28th, when each tank took a slight sip of gasoline or petrol as our British friends call it, 75 gallons, and rumbled out of the woods where they had spent the day to investigate why Hindenburg thought that his line could not be broken. If the Huns could have seen that line of monsters headed their way, crawling in and out of shell holes, across ditches, and pushing over an occasional tree that was unfortunate enough to be in their paths, they would have known that the next day was to be a very busy as well as a very sad one for them. Six o'clock found us at the start lines, and ten minutes later we were engaged in one of the hardest fought and decisive battles of the war.

When the sun went down that evening Hindenburg was a sadder but wiser man, and the world knew that the Hindenburg line was a thing of the past and we had helped to finish it. All day the tanks smashed through the wire, breaking paths for the infantry to follow, and crushed the machine guns whose bullets, so deadly to the infantry, merely tickled their steel hides.

It was a hard fight and we paid the price for our success, but it made everybody more determined to give the Hun a good clean cut licking to "get our own back," and this opportunity was given us on the 9th of October, when we went over with the 30th division and informed the Huns that they would have to move out of Brancourt.

That was a wonderful day for us, and all the tanks had a glorious banquet of Huns and machine guns, and one tank even thought itself long enough to put out a whole battery of field guns. There were machine guns everywhere, and many a doughboy who is growling to come home today was saved by those crawling monsters who crush machine guns as easily as eggshells.

The chief of the British Tank Corps was aware of our vow to get our own back, and sent the following note:

> Advance Headquarters, Tank Corps, October 9. A note to congratulate you and your fellows on the splendid results obtained today. I am more glad than I can say that you have had the opportunity of getting your own back on the filthy Hun.
>
> Yours sincerely,
> Hugh Elles.

After this engagement we had a short rest which was spent in tuning up the engines and getting the tanks ready to continue our march to Berlin, which was resumed on the morning of October 23, when we crossed the Selle River with the 27th and 30th divisions and chased the Hun out of his position there. This was the same old story of machine guns, but we had the added difficulty of a dense fog which was a very great handicap. All steering had to be done by compass, and this gave one lieutenant a right to pose as a rival of Christopher Columbus. His compass was damaged by a shell, and as a result he crossed the Selle River three times thinking each time that he crossed a different stream and getting angrier each time because he had been told that there was but one river to cross.

Our next engagement was a minor attack to straighten the line and to cover the flank of a major attack on our left. We went over the top in the moonlight and everybody was back eating breakfast by 10 a. m. after having taken all of our objectives without having lost a man or a tank. After this fighting we were placed in reserve and the Hun did his final Kamerad before we had another opportunity to meet him.

From the time of their first appearance on the western front the tanks proved their worth and were a wonderful aid morally, tactically, financially, and what is more important, in saving the lives of the infantry who followed them. British statistics show that the losses were ten percent less in the offensives where the tanks were used than those in which the tanks were not used.

Tanks were used in many attacks without the preliminary bombardments so necessary without them, thus saving artillery ammunition and in the first battle of Cambrai, where tanks were used instead of a bombardment the value of the artillery ammunition saved was equal to the total cost of building, equipping and training of the entire British Tank Corps to that date.

Tanks are the only logical weapon to combat machine guns, and are one of the products of the great war that have come to stay, and it does not take too vivid an imagination to picture the future wars as a combat between the "land navies" of the contending forces.

*"Tank Corps Men Suffered Heavily from Artillery" (*Brooklyn Daily Eagle, *March 18, 1919, 4)*

[Private Frank Halvey, 301st Tank Battalion]

Camp Mills, L.I., March 18—Life in most units of the Tank Corps, that war-baby unit of the American forces, turned out to be a work shop affair, with the mechanics far removed from the battle lines, studying engines, cleaning oily axles and performing other dirty and unromantic work. Only one unit of heavy tanks, the 301st Battalion, actually saw a real action, and in that unit, Private

Frank Halvey, 329 42d St., found a life of thrilling adventures and exciting experiences. His company of engineers which had been trained at Camp Meade, had the good or bad fortune, depending upon whether one views it from Frank Halvey's angle or that of some more cautious person, to be immediately sent across as a tank company and to participate in four "shows" before the end of the war.

"I wouldn't call going over the top in a tank much more dangerous than as a doughboy," he said yesterday upon his battalion's arrival at Camp Mills.

"Of course, we must look out for mines and airplanes and anti-tank rifles. There is no use looking out for direct hits from the enemy's artillery, because if they come, they've just got you, that's all. Mined fields are unusual and antitank guns are scarce and airplanes have to keep an equally sharp lookout for antiaircraft rifles, so there is some relief from them after all. Direct hits from artillery should be rare. I say they should be rare on account of the difficulties of obtaining them on a moving target like tanks. But we suffered heavily from artillery firing on this scattered target, miles away and unable to see us, but good gunnery and a lot of luck helped them to nick a large hole in our tanks.

"The 301st Battalion was unfortunate in running across nearly all of those dangers. Our first 'show' carried us across a field mined by the British months before, when they were retreating and of which no warning had been given. We lost heavily and so did the British tanks with whom we went into action. I've seen a German airplane sweep down within 25 feet of the ground and drop a bomb on a tank wrecking it, but that is unusual too. When an airplane showed up near a tank camp, nearly every gun in sight was turned on it, rifles, pistols, machine guns and antiaircraft guns.

"When we landed in England in March 1918, we were sent to a British tank camp near Dorset, where we were trained in handling British tanks. In August we landed in France with the British tank brigade and were given 48 tanks to take up to the front lines. On September 29, we saw our first action, on the Cambrai–St. Quentin front, moving ahead of the 27th Division, and flanked on both sides by British tanks. The 30 first tanks were given Ronssoy as their 'jumping off' place, and Bony, the French town that figured so prominently in the 27th Division campaign, as their objective.

"The barrage opened at 6:30 o'clock in the morning and it was our first hearing of real big guns opening up. Our tanks had been removed from the freight cars and were lined up at intervals of about 30 yards along the front of about a mile-and-a-half. We climbed in, eight men in each tank and started the big 'Recordeer' engine.[10] From then on, or about three hours, we experienced the sensation of going into battle for the first time.

"Tanks are small and hot. Eight men are carried, but there is no place where men can stand straight up. Inside everything is painted immaculately white, and kept as clean as an operating room. On one side is a six pound gun for pillboxes and concrete structures. On the other side are eight machine guns for nests and individuals. There is no ventilation, only the pinpoint peepholes for the gunners. An electric fan stirs the hot air a little and electricity generated from our motor gives light. The 150 horsepower motor drowns all talk; the machine guns, eight of them in that close place, are continually pattering. The enemy machine guns patter on the sides, so you can imagine the noise in our ears. Gas from the machine gun chambers and burning powder from the six pounder dim the light until we can barely see. We are stripped to the waist, so hot is it in there, and sometimes we wear gas masks, although we'd never realize gas was there until some man keeled over.

"It's all mighty romantic, this tank business, and it is the greatest branch of the service and all that, but the three hours spent in those Turkish baths would come near knocking any man out," said Halvey.

"But there is a kind of consolation to it. As long as we stick in that 'bus' we are pretty safe. Machine guns just knocked the paint off the sides. The Germans know it, so as soon as a tank comes into view it's 'Kamerad' [surrender]. Does them no good, though. The tanks have orders to take no prisoners. They used to trick the British that way, surrender, and head back to their lines, and as soon as they passed the tank, surround and capture it. So, we don't take chances anymore. Sometimes a German manages to climb on top of a tank, but we never mind him. He cannot get in and he is merely wasting his time trying.

"One Fritz who tried to surrender with his platoon attempted a plucky act to keep his men from being killed. He tried to surrender with about 40 of his men. Nothing doing. We turned the gun on him and let fly. He sprang forward, grabbed the gun in his hands and tried to turn it away. Of course he was shaken off in a second and the gun righted again, but some infantry came up at that time and saved the men from being wiped out.

"The other dangers of a tank life? Sometimes a gunner from a pillbox would damage our sprockets and so stop the caterpillar tread. If our infantry was behind we remained there until it came and then brought up the salvage crew to repair it. In some cases where the infantry was far back the tank and its crew were compelled to surrender and the German salvaged the tank. The Germans were not much on tanks. We never had an opportunity to mix with them. Their tanks are lighter than ours and their tread is so arranged that it is comparatively easy to get out of order. High pay and a lot of advantages are offered, but the prisoners told us that there were not many applicants for the jobs.

"Then there is the motor. Sometimes a score of tanks would start into action and on account of the motor stalling and failing to pull the 45 tons of steel only one would reach its objective. They were required to make eight miles an hour, but considering the kind of ground it was forced to travel, trenches, shell holes and shallow streams, it was a hard task. The motor used was an English Recorder, six cylinders and 150 horsepower."

Private Halvey will probably move with his battalion to Camp Meade this week. The battalion has received orders not to be mustered out at once and will parade with three brigades of tank men in Washington.

Of the 500 men who were with the battalion at the beginning of its fighting, about 135 were killed. The battalion participated in the captures of Bony, Serain, Busigny and La Selle River, where the 27th's action stopped. On November 4, La Cateau was named as objective, but the armistice stopped them. All of their fighting was done with the 27th and 30th divisions except at La Cateau. The 301st was in the field, actually fighting, longer than any British battalion. The 14 tanks, all that was left of the 48 first drawn, and many others drawn later, are waiting shipment to New York at St. Nazaire.

*H. J. Buxton, "Daredevils of War" (*Detroit Free Press, *November 24, 1918, C4)*

[Sergeant Hugh J. Follette, 301st Tank Battalion]

Sergeant Hugh Follette of the Tank Corps gives a thrilling description of the onrush of the "Iron Horses" into German territory. He was wounded, but in a few days will be able to again take his place with the "Iron Horse Brigade."

"When the order came to go and get 'em meaning the dirty Huns, we started up our engines, and the tanks charged ahead in a good formation.

"The tanks went at it as if they were human—they seemed to enjoy this awful game of destruction.

"But the Huns didn't lay down in the fighting—they fought us tooth and nail and then some. We crashed into a group of 100 or more of them, and they swarmed over our iron horses like so many hornets, hunting for openings through which to paste us with their automatics. But some of our infantry boys came along in the nick of time and cleaned them up with the bayonet.

"Everything was fine in my tank until the Boche artillery got our range, and then hell broke loose. First Fritz shot all our periscopes off, then two portholes were opened up by the rivets being shot off. One could imagine it was hailing by the way the bullets came through. Next a shell landed alongside of us, exploded, and tore a portion of our top off. The stream of bullets poured into the jagged opening. It was then that I sure thought the United States government would lose $10,000 for the opening was just over my head.[11] A couple of seconds later a carburetor was smashed, and about 15 minutes later our magneto was hit and the old boy stopped. Just then a shell came through the right side of the tank and caught me in the leg just below the hip and went right through, carrying about five pieces of tank along with it. Everyone evacuated the tank and sought refuge in a trench, the boys carrying me along with them."

V

Unofficial Tank Corps Operational Summaries

"Tanks Stood Gaff from Belgium to Argonne Battle" (*Stars and Stripes*, June 13, 1919, 1, 8)

[301st, 344th, and 345th Tank Battalions]

The functions, wonderfully combined, of cavalry, infantry, artillery and perambulating fortifications gave to that primarily British invention, the tank, in the early days of its use a prominence out of proportion, no doubt, to the numbers of men who were identified with the operations of these uncouth contrivances, but certainly not out of proportion to the results which they achieved, either in the British or the French armies. On the contrary, the Tank Corps of the American Expeditionary Forces, although it never attained to anything like the proportions which it would have reached had the end of the war not come so suddenly, seems hardly to have received the commendation to which it was justly entitled, in view of the brilliant success with which its units functioned on the occasions when they had opportunity for action.

It would be quite impossible within the limits of a single article even to outline the work of the various units of American tanks, for though comparatively few in number, they were exceedingly active. But it may be possible, by telling something of the battles of a few typical units, to shadow forth in a degree the sort of difficulties and dangers which they all confronted and the splendid spirit of heroism with which they met dangers which were not only often, but ordinarily, even greater than those encountered by the men of other branches of the service on the battlefront.

In describing some weeks ago the operations of the 27th and 30th United States divisions of the Second United States Army Corps against the Scheldt canal tunnel sector of the Hindenburg Line between Le Catelet and Bellicourt, the fact was mentioned that with the American divisions fought a number of tanks including the 301st Battalion of the American Tank Corps, the only unit of American heavy tanks on the Western Front. The 301st Battalion, commanded by Major R. I. Sasse, functioned under the brigade command of the

2nd United States Tank Brigade, which included the 1st and 4th Tank Supply Company, also British. For the attack of September 29th the whole brigade was allotted to the Australian corps with which the Second U.S. Corps was affiliated, the 1st Tank Battalion attacking with the 30th US Division and the 301st with the 27th Division.

Several days of careful reconnaissance and consultation with the infantry commanders preceded the attack, and when the plans for the operation were fully developed the three companies of the 301st Battalion were assigned—Company C, with 15 tanks, to the 108th Infantry, which was to attack on the right of the division sector; Company A, with 15 tanks, to the 107th Infantry, which was to attack on the left and Company B, with 10 tanks to the 105th Infantry, which was to follow up and after crossing the German trenches, deploy facing north to protect the left flank of the division. The seven remaining tanks of the battalion were held in Australian corps reserve.

Careful study was made of aerial photographs and all other information available bearing upon the nature of the ground in front, and all obstacles, trenches and enemy works that could be located were noted on record maps for the use of the tank commanders. The advance of the C Company tanks was to be directed upon both sides of Bony, particularly to the south of it, that of A Company upon Le Catelet and the area immediately north of it, and that of B Company upon the area east of Vendhuille and the north entrance of the canal tunnel.

The "tankdrome" of the battalion was located at Manancourt, about 15 kilometers behind the front line, and the battalion started from there on the night of September 27–28 and went to Villers-Faucon, where the supply dump had been placed. Thence they moved to the front, distant about eight kilometers, on the night of September 28–29.

The noise of their advance to the start line as zero hour—5:50 a.m.—approached was to have been drowned by airplanes flying overhead. Only one airplane made its appearance but the noise of the approaching tanks was, nevertheless, quite effectually deadened to the enemy by the roar of the artillery preparation fire. Following paths which for the last 3,000 yards, had already been taped out by pioneers, of whom one was killed and two were wounded in the performance of this hazardous mission, the majority of the tanks went over the line on time and in touch with the infantry.

The ground was dry enough to make good going, and the mist which covered the ground at zero hour had cleared away by 7 a.m. But the dense obscurity of the smoke barrage and the exploding shells took the place of the mist, and soon most of the tank pilots could see nothing ahead, sometimes not even the noses of their own machines, and had to rely wholly upon their compasses for maintaining the right direction. The tank commanders spent much of their time on the ground, moving ahead of their machines and guiding them, but the main difficulties did not arise in crossing the trenches, which most of the machines negotiated successfully, though a few had to be dug out with shovels, while one was unditched by stretching a wire cable across two opposite spuds on each caterpillar track. The constant and terrible peril was the fire of the German artillery and anti-tank rifles. The moment the tank came into view, it was made the center of a concentration of artillery fire, and many machines were demolished or compelled to retire from action by direct hits. Machines on the right, with the 108th Infantry, were able to keep contact with infantry and to cooperate directly. Those with the 107th Infantry, on the left, could not do so.

It will be remembered that two days before the main assault, the 106th Infantry had made a preliminary attack to conquer the intended jumping off line in the advance trenches of the old British front about the Knoll and Guillemont farm. This attack had been completely successful; consequently, the 107th Infantry, in jumping off for the main attack, virtually did so 1,000 yards west of the line intended and was considerably behind the front of the rest of the division and behind its own barrage during the advance. Its accompanying tanks, on the other hand, were ahead. In going down the small and narrow Macquincourt Valley, between the Knoll and Guillemont farm, they suffered a misfortune which should have been avoidable by running over an old antitank mine field which had been laid by the British the previous spring, when the German drive on Amiens was impending. The tank command had not been notified of the existence of this minefield and two American and several British tanks were blown up. Nevertheless, a number of the tanks of this flank went through the Hindenburg Line, in spite of all the mines and trenches and the artillery and anti-tank rifle fire, and ambled about behind it, carrying terror and destruction among the German infantry and machine gunners with the fusillade of their Hotchkiss [machine] guns and six-pounders [cannons].

Similar conditions prevailed with the B Company tanks, which could not keep in touch with their infantry, but which went ahead, nevertheless, and did much damage to the enemy. One tank of one of these units crossed the Scheldt River at Le Catelet by using its “crib” for getting over, though the cribs were not found necessary in crossing trenches. A German battery in Richmont Quarry, east of Vendhuille, was particularly destructive to the tanks on the left flank and one antitank fort was encountered in Le Catelet. The prowling about inside the enemy’s lines without infantry support was exceedingly dangerous business, and the crews of several tanks were taken prisoners after their machines had been knocked out and were unable to proceed or to retreat.

At the end of the day’s heroic work, the casualties among the personnel of the 10 tanks of the 301st Battalion which had been in action amounted to 112, of whom three officers and 20 enlisted men were killed, seven officers and 55 enlisted men severely wounded and eight officers and 15 enlisted men slightly wounded, and one officer and six enlisted men missing. Of the tanks engaged not more than 25 percent escaped without more or less serious injuries, but they had accomplished a great deal of damage to the enemy, not merely in a material sense, but in breaking the morale of his troops.

The 301st Tank Battalion did further excellent service in the operations on October 8, when the 30th Division took Brancourt, the tanks attacking this town from the northern and southern flanks. One tank captured a German battery by approaching it from the rear. On the 17th they again assisted the advance east of St. Souplet and on the 23rd such tanks as still remained serviceable supported the attack of the six divisions toward the Sambar River, north of Chatillon.

It would be interesting to follow in some detail the notable activities of the tanks with the First American army in the St. Mihiel operation. Perhaps, particularly those of the 344th and 345th battalions of the 1st American Tank Brigade, which went across the front lines, respectively, near Xivray and Seicheprey, crossed the Rupt de Mad and worked freely through the woods and open country around Lahayville, Nonsard and Heudicourt and around Essey, Pannes and Beney. The brigade was under command of Lieutenant Colonel G. S. Patton Jr., and its two battalions embraced 144 light Renault tanks, while the American army had also with it, operating in other sectors, a large number of French tanks, consisting of a group of 18 medium Schneider tanks, under Commandant Chanione; the 1st (French) Tank Brigade, under Colonel Wahl, containing two groups of St. Chamond medium tanks, and the 50th Regiment, consisting of 225 light tanks divided into three battalions.

The American battalions and Commandant Chanoine's French tanks operated with the 42nd and 1st U.S. divisions and the 39th French colonial division, and Colonel Wahl's command operated with the 90th, 5th and 2nd U.S. divisions on the right of the attack, working toward Remenanville, Vieville-en-Haye, Thiacourt, etc. It will, perhaps, be better, however, to tell a little of the even less well-known operations and some of the tank units in the Meuse-Argonne offensive.

The First American Army had for this offensive the 1st American Tank Brigade, under Lieutenant Colonel George S. Patton Jr., who was wounded early the first day and was succeeded in command by Major Sereno E. Brett; and the 13th and 14th battalions of the 505th French Tank Regiment. The two battalions last mentioned operated on September 26th in front of the 37th Division, the tanks under command of Captain Gaitan Liaras doing particularly heroic work in forcing their way across the ravine between the Bois de Malancourt and the Bois de Cuisy, clearing out the machine gun nests ahead of the infantry and attacking the German trenches south of Montfaucon, all under intense artillery fire. Major Brett's brigade consisted of the 344th and 345th battalions of American tanks, embracing 141 tanks and the 14th and 17th groups of French tanks. The scene of its operations was on both banks of the Aire River, just east of the Argonne masiff, in the sectors of the 35th and 28th divisions.

The 1st Brigade was disposed for the assault with one company of the 344th Battalion west of the Aire and two companies east of that river, between it and the Baunthe River; the 345th Battalion in support with its companies arranged similarly to those of the leading battalion, and the 14th and 17th groups in reserve east of the Aire and 2,000 meters in rear of the leading battalion.

On moving forward to the attack, immediate and very severe artillery and machine gun resistance was encountered, but the tanks continued advancing, outdistancing the infantry and proceeding along the edge of the Argonne Forest, and into the towns of Cheppy and Varennes. The town last named was entered by tanks at 9:30 a.m. and by infantry at 1:30 p.m. After the day's fighting, the tanks west of the Aire that could move assembled at Boureilles and those east of the river in the woods southwest of Cheppy, but the severity of the struggle which they had been through was evidenced by the fact that 43 of them were out of action from more or less severe injuries.

Next day, 11 tanks supported the 28th Division's advance along the edge of the Argonne, fighting all day against the great number of German pillboxes in that region. East of the river, two platoons supported an infantry attack on the plateau north of Very, and at 5 p.m. the 12 tanks of the French group advanced to the road from Charpentry to Serieux Farm and entered Charpentry, but the infantry did not follow them. The Germans, being fully aware now of the tank strength in front of them had developed by September 28th very strong defense methods against this form of attack and the tanks suffered the heaviest casualties of any single day during the offensive, 41 officers and men being killed or wounded among the personnel of the 83 American and 12 French tanks in action.

West of Aire, the tanks took the town of Apremont five successive times before the infantry succeeded in consolidating the position, while the French group again did find work in and around Charpentry.

Only 55 American tanks were able to engage on the morning of the 29th and during the day the French group was withdrawn by the First Army. The 15 tanks with the 28th Division worked all day in the vicinity of Apremont under severe artillery fire from the edges of the Argonne Forest, while the 40 machines with the 35th Division aided, late in the afternoon in resisting a counterattack from the Montrebeau Woods, north of Baulny, holding and patrolling a line between Baulny and Eclisfontaine until the infantry could organize upon it.

About 5:30 on the morning of October 1st, the enemy made a violent counterattack on the 28th Division just north of Apremont. The Americans themselves were preparing to jump an attack over at six o'clock and eight tanks were in position to assist. Their fire into the closely massed ranks of the assaulting Germans produced terrible execution and the First Army Corps headquarters declared officially after the action that prisoners of the II Landwehr Division state that in the counterattack north of Apremont they were completely demoralized by our tanks, as most of the soldiers as well as most of the officers had never seen tanks before. Tanks did very effective work, and after having gone through the lines turned around and came back at them again, the same time inflicting casualties. During all the fighting of the day the tanks themselves suffered only 16 casualties, of whom none were killed.

On October 4th came the second general attack along the whole front of the First American Army. By repair and salvage work on disabled machines, 89 tanks had been made ready for action again, of which one company was assigned to the 28th Division and two companies were assigned to the 1st Division, which had relieved the 35th. The remaining tanks stayed in brigade reserve. The tank commanders with the 1st Division found excellent support from the infantry, and they assisted against bitter resistance in the capture of Hill 240, north of Exermont, while those with the 28th Division pressed the fighting along the edges of the Argonne.

The most direct testimony to the severity of the work which they all underwent is found in the figures: 30 tanks were ready for action October 5th out of the 89 which had been fit the day before. The rest had been destroyed or disabled, and 28 officers and enlisted men had been killed or wounded during the day.

Moreover, mechanical difficulties, due to long and terribly severe usage were daily becoming more troublesome, while an epidemic of influenza had caused many men to be evacuated and, wrote Major Brett in a report, "the nightly gassing on the positions around Charpentry has caused a little sickness and inconvenience." Nevertheless, he added, "the men and officers are in good spirits!" It would seem that only confirmed optimists occupied positions in the Tank Corps.

It was not until October 7th that any machines were called into action again, and then the eight which were fit for duty on the west side of the Aire went in to assist the attack of the 28th Division that morning on the heights of Chatel-Chehery. One of the tanks struck a mine and was disabled, but the remaining seven continued in the battle, which was a very severe and important one, throughout the day, being engaged chiefly in patrol work. After the engagement there was no particularly important tank activity for a week and during that time the remaining tanks were reorganized in a provisional company under Captain Courtney Barnard. The strength of this company was 10 officers and 149 enlisted men and it had 24 tanks at its disposal.

On October 14th the Provisional Company was loaned by the First Corps to the Fifth Corps to participate in an operation of the 42nd Division on the morning of the 15th against the Kriemhilde-Stellung positions between Landres-et-St. Georges and St. Georges. The tanks had to make a long night run from Exermont to the jumping off positions and were obliged to make such speed that many of them broke down and only 10 arrived, just in time to go over at H-hour.

These machines, however, advanced into the enemy's immensely strong positions and across his trenches, where they trundled into what appeared to be the formation of a counterattack. Their own supporting infantry was undergoing such a terrific fire in front of the German wire belts that it would not come up, so the tanks contented themselves with dispersing the concentration of German infantry, and then retired. Fifteen machines repeated the attack in this vicinity on November 1st, in support of the 2nd Division, one platoon being directed against the town of St. Georges and the wire in front of it and two platoons against Landres-et-Georges and the wire there. In both places excellent results were achieved, and with very few casualties to the attacking tankers.

The tanks were not called upon again to participate in action before the armistice, as the fighting after November 1st assumed the character of open warfare in which their services were not so necessary as in the attack of strongly entrenched positions. During the course of the Meuse-Argonne battles, tank units of the first brigade had lost three officers and 16 enlisted men killed, and 21 officers and 131 enlisted men wounded. These losses were suffered in 18 separate engagements, in many of which some of the French tanks also participated, these engagements occurring in the course of supporting different divisions, including, besides those already mentioned, the 77th, the 82nd and the 91st.

Eighteen of the 141 American tanks were totally demolished by enemy fire and one tank disappeared entirely and was never found, the theory being that it was either disabled and captured by the enemy or that it fell into the Aire River and was completely submerged. The dangers of tank service were many and among them oddly enough, that of drowning was not negligible.

Major General John F. O'Ryan, *The Story of the 27th Division* ([New York: Wynkoop Hallenbeck Crawford, 1921]: 334–37)

[301st Tank Battalion]

The 301st Tank Battalion, commanded by Major Roger Harrison, was assigned to the division to the attack of September 29th. It consisted of three companies: Company A, with 15 tanks, commanded by Captain Kit Varney, who was killed on September 29th; Company B, consisting of 10 tanks, commanded by Captain Victor L. Ralli; and Company C, commanded by Captain Ralph Clark, consisting of 15 tanks. The seven remaining tanks were held in reserve. The signal tank was in charge of Captain C. Reynell. Company A was assigned to the 108th Infantry on the right, Company B to the 105th Infantry in support, and Company C to the 107th Infantry on the left. The tanks were guided to their positions with the various companies of the attacking battalions by guides furnished by the infantry companies.

Each tank commander took into action with him necessary map showing roads to be followed, obstacles to be encountered, barrage table with objective drawn upon it, and a number of oblique photographs of the relevant terrain. Opportunity had been afforded tank officers for several days prior to the attack to reconnoiter the approaches to their start positions and to study the maps and data available.

The tank equipment is shown in the following table:

	Mark V Star *Male*	Mark V Star *Female*	Mark V Star *Composite*	Mark V *Male*	Mark V *Female*	Mark V *Composite*	Total
Company A	9	2	4				15
Company B	7	2		3	1	3	16
Company C				7		9	16

Note.—All Mark V tanks carried cribs.

In addition, one Renault tank was issued to battalion headquarters, but due to a broken track, damaged shortly before the battle, it was never used.

On September 25th all tank officers of the battalion attended the conference at Division Headquarters, at which all available information was given them. Upon the completion of the conference they conferred with the brigade commander, who approved the details of the plan of operations for the tanks. From September 25th until the 29th, company and section commanders conferred daily with the infantry commanders with whom their units were to be associated.

The report of the tank commander shows that on September 29th, Company A cooperated with the 108th Infantry, but Company C never gained contact with the 107th Infantry on the left. The tanks of Company B were knocked out before they could render any service. In cases where tanks were ditched in trenches and sunken roads, the cause as stated by the tank commander was that the smoke through which the tanks traveled was so thick that the obstacles could not be seen. He reports the tanks lost their way in the smoke immediately after leaving the tape and had nothing to depend upon except the compass. Some of the tank officers reported their compasses defective and that they were seriously handicapped in consequence. Some of the crews reported difficulties with the Hotchkiss [machine] guns and belts, but no difficulty with the six pounders [cannons]. All tank crews reported that the tanks drew concentrated fire. Nearly all crews were handicapped by lack of pistols. Incidents were reported were tank crews were taken prisoner in consequence of lack of arms, after evacuating their tanks.

Two tanks ran on ground mines which were later reported to have been laid by the British when they occupied the area prior to the German offensive of March, 1918, and information concerning which had not been given to American troops. Most of the casualties to tanks were caused by direct hits from enemy artillery fire. A number of tanks continued in action after being hit a number of times by armor-piercing bullets.

The tank crews report much help derived from the use of the ampule ammonia which had been furnished by the Medical Corps.

The casualties in the tank battalion were three officers and 17 enlisted men killed, seven officers and 55 enlisted men wounded and seven enlisted men missing.

Two tanks under [second] lieutenants [John R.] Webb and [Clarence J.] Hartt of Company A were reported to have crossed the Hindenburg line and return safely. In Company B one tank under [Second] Lieutenant [Foster] Ellingwood reached the Hindenburg line, but was stopped on account of mechanical trouble. In Company C one tank commanded by [Second] Lieutenant [Earle B.] Dunning went through, across the Hindenburg line and the tunnel, but on its return was put out of action by a direct hit. The writer on the morning of October 1st reached Bony in making an inspection of the field and saw the track of one of our tanks which crossed the Hindenburg line several hundred yards south of Bony. The track was plainly visible. Where it crossed the main trench one of the treads ran upon and partially crushed the wooden cover of a pit sunk into the parados of the trench. The track could be seen leading to the spoil over the tunnel a short distance beyond. It could not be followed farther because of shell fire.

Appendix A

The following description of the Mark IV tank, produced in 1916, is from "General Parks' Address at the Tank Corps Dinner Saturday," *Gettysburg (PA) Times*, August 30, 1954, 7.

The Mark IV tank weighed about 30 tons, was 32.5 feet long, 11 feet wide, and had a maximum speed of 3.7 miles per hour, with a gas tank capacity of 53 gallons, which gave it a 12 mile range.

The following description of British Mark V through Mark IX series tanks is from *The Encyclopedia Britannica, The New Volumes,* vol. 22 (London: Encyclopedia Britannica Company, 1922), 688.

The Mark V tank was in design and size the same as Mark IV, but was superior to it in the following particulars: the engine, a six-cylinder Ricardo engine 150 H.P., was more powerful and was expressly designed for the tank. The maneuvering powers were improved by one-man control and an epicyclic gear. The means of observation were improved. The unditching gear could be worked from inside the machine. Better means of clearing the tracks of mud were provided. The design for this was begun in October 1917 after the experiences of Messines and the third battle of Ypres, and was to meet the requirements as then known. Some of these machines reached France in time for the attack on Hamel on July 4, 1918, and this tank was the principal machine of all subsequent fighting. In all, 403 were made.

The Mark V, Star tank was the same as the Mark V machine, with six feet added to the middle of its length. It could cross wider trenches (14 feet) than the Mark V machine and could carry about 20 men in addition to the crew. The design was not started till February 1918, 32 machines being made, of which some were delivered in time for the battle of Amiens. The tank was too long to be very handy.

The Mark V, Two-Star tank was the same as the Mark V, Star, but, with a 225 H.P. Ricardo engine. Design was started in May 1918, with one being made but not delivered before the Armistice.

The Mark VI tank was intended to be the same size as the Mark IV, with an improved transmission (the Williams-Janny variable speed gear), but did not get beyond the design stage.

The Mark VII tank, was 3 feet, 6 inches longer than the Mark IV and Mark V. It had a 150 H. P. Ricardo engine and a variable speed gear. Seven were made, but none was used in the field.

The Mark VIII tank was commenced in December 1917; seven machines were made, but none was employed in the field. It was larger (34 feet, 2 1/2 inches) than any other tank, and was designed so as to be made up of parts manufactured in England and the United States, and was to be engined either with the American 300 H.P. Liberty, or the British 300 H.P. Rolls-Royce engine. The engine room was separated from the fighting chamber by a bulkhead and the ventilation was improved.

The Mark IX (infantry) tank was begun in September 1917. Thirty-five machines were made, but none was actually used. It was a long machine with space in the center to carry 50 infantry or 10 tons of stores.

Appendix B

Tank Corps Organization Chart, *Order of Battle, The United States Land Forces in the World War, Zone of the Interior: Directory of Troops*, vol. 3, pt. 3

(Washington, D.C., U.S. Army Center of Military History, 1988): 1542–47.

TANK CORPS

TANK CENTERS

Unit designation and redesignation	Organization		Stations in United States		Overseas		Demobilization		Remarks
	Month and year	Place	Month and year	Place	From—	To—	Month and year	Place	
1st Light Tank Center	February 1918	A. E. F.							
a. 311th Center	June 1918	Do.							
b. 302d (II) Center	September 1918	do	April 1919	Cp. Merritt, N. J.		April 1919.			
			do	Cp. Meade, Md.					Active through 1919. G.H.Q. troops.
2d Heavy Tank Center	March 1918	Do.							
a. 302d (I) Center	do	Do.							
b. 301st Center	June 1918	do	March 1919	Cp. Mills, N. Y.		March 1919	April 1919	Cp. Meade, Md.	G.H.Q. troops.
3d to 300th Tank Centers.									Never orgzd.
301st Tank Center									See 2d Hv. Tk. Center.
302d Tank Center									See 1st L. Tk. and 2d Hv. Tk. Centers.
303 Tank Center									See 304th and 314th Tank Centers.
304th Tank Center	September 1918	Cp. Colt, Pa.	October 1918	Cp. Mills, N. Y.					
			do	P. of E., Hoboken.	October 1918.				
a. 303d (II) Center	November 1918	A. E. F.	May 1919	Cp. Stuart, Va.		May 1919	May 1919	Cp. Meade, Md.	G.H.Q. troops.
305th to 308th Tank Centers.									Never orgzd.
309th Tank Center	October 1918	Cp. Colt, Pa.					December 1918	Cp. Dix, N. J.	
310th Tank Center	do	do					do	Do.	
311th Tank Center									See 1st L. Tk. Center.
312th and 313th Tank Centers.									Never orgzd.
314th Tank Center	June 1918	Cp. Colt, Pa.							
a. 303d (I) Center	July 1918	do	September 1918	Cp. Tobyhanna, Pa.					
			do	P. of E., Hoboken.	September 1918.				
b. 303d Center Hq. Company.	October 1918	A. E. F.							Redes. Hq. Co. 307th Brig. November 6, 1918.

TANK BRIGADES

1st Provisional Tank Brigade.	August 1918	A. E. F.							
a. 304th Tank Brigade.	November 1918	do	March 1919	Cp. Mills, N. Y		March 1919.			
			do	Cp. Meade, Md					Active through 1919. G. H. Q. troops.
2d Provisional Tank Brigade.	October 1918	Do.							
a. 305th Tank Brigade.	November 1918	do	do	Cp. Mills, N. Y		March 1919.			
			do	Cp. Meade, Md					Active through 1919.
3d Provisional Tank Brigade.	October 1918	Do.							
a. 306th Tank Brigade.	November 1918	do	do	Cp. Upton, N. Y		March 1919.			
			do	Cp. Meade, Md			September 1919	Cp. Meade, Md.	
4th Provisional Tank Brigade.	October 1918	Do.							
a. 307th Tank Brigade.	November 1918	do	May 1919	Cp. Stuart, Va		May 1919	May 1919	do	G.H.Q. troops.

TANK BATTALIONS

1st Separate Battalion, Heavy Tank Service, 65th Engineers.	February 1918	Cp. Upton, N. Y.							
a. 1st Heavy Battalion, Tank Service.	March 1918	do	March 1918	Cp. Merritt, N. J.					
			do	P. of E., Hoboken	March 1918.				
b. 301st Battalion, Tank Corps.	April 1918	A. E. F	March 1919	Cp. Mills, N. Y		March 1919.			
			do	Cp. Meade, Md					G.H.Q. troops Active through 1919.

TANK BATTALIONS—Continued

Unit designation and redesignation	Organization		Stations in United States		Overseas		Demobilization		Remarks
	Month and year	Place	Month and year	Place	From—	To—	Month and year	Place	
1st Battalion, Light Tanl Service, 65th Engineers.	February 1918	Cp. Upton, N. Y.							
a. 1st Light Battalion, Tank Service.	March 1918	do	March 1918	Cp. Colt, Pa.					
b. 326th (I) Battalion, Tank Corps.	April 1918	Cp. Colt, Pa.	July 1918	Cp. Summerall, Pa					
			September 1918	P. of E., Hoboken	September 1918.				
			May 1919	Cp. Stuart, Va.		May 1919	May 1919	Cp. Meade, Md.	G.H.Q. troops.
2d Battalion, Light Tank Service, 65th Engineers.	February 1918	Cp. Upton, N. Y.							
a. 2d Light Battalion, Tank Service.	March 1918	do	March 1918	Cp. Colt, Pa.					
b. 327th (I) Battalion, Tank Corps.	April 1918	Cp. Colt, Pa.	September 1918	Cp. Summerall, Pa					
			do	P. of E., Hoboken	September 1918.				
			May 1919	Cp. Stuart, Va.		do	do	do	Do.
Co. D, 2d Battalion, Heavy Tank Service, 65th Engineers.	February 1918	Cp. Meade, Md.							
a. 2d Heavy Battalion, Tank Service.	March 1918	do	March 1918	Cp. Colt, Pa.					
b. 302d (I) Tank Battalion.	April 1918	Cp. Colt, Pa.	July 1918	Cp. Summerall, Pa					
			September 1918	P. of E., Hoboken	September 1918.				
			May 1919	Cp. Stuart, Va.		do	do	do	Do.
3d to 300th Tank Battalions.									Never orgzd.
301st Tank Battalion									See 1st Sep. Bn., Hv. Tk. Serv.,

302d (I) Tank Battalion									65th Engrs. See 2d Bn., Hv. Tk. Serv., 65th Engrs.
302d (II) Tank Battalion	June 1918	A. E. F.							
a. 302d Provisional Battalion.	September 1918	do.							Redes. 306th Tk. Bn. October 1918.
303d Tank Battalion	May 1918	Cp. Colt, Pa.	August 1918 March 1919 do.	P. of E., Hoboken Cp. Mills, N. Y. Cp. Meade, Md.	August 1918.	March 1919.			Active through 1919. G. H. Q. troops.
304th Tank Battalion	do.	do.	October 1918 May 1919	P. of E., Hoboken Cp. Mills, N. Y.	October 1918.	May 1919	May 1919	Cp. Meade, Md.	G.H.Q. troops.
305th Tank Battalion	June 1918	do.	September 1918 do.	Method, N. C. Cp. Polk, N. C.			December 1918	Cp. Greene, N. C.	
306th Tank Battalion	October 1918	A. E. F.	March 1919 do.	Cp. Upton, N. Y. Cp. Meade, Md.		March 1919.	October 1919	Cp. Meade, Md.	Do.
307th Tank Battalion	do.	Cp. Polk, N. C.					December 1918	Cp. Greene, N. C.	
308th Tank Battalion	November 1918	do.					do.	Do.	
309th to 325th Tank Battalions.									Never orgzd.
326th (I) Tank Battalion									See 1st Bn. L. Tk. Serv., 65th Engrs.
326th (II) Tank Battalion.	June 1918	A. E. F.							
a. 344th Tank Battalion.	September 1918	do.	March 1919 do.	Cp. Mills, N. Y. Cp. Meade, Md.		March 1919.			Active through 1919. G. H. Q. troops.
327th (I) Tank Battalion									See 2d Bn. L. Tk. Serv., 65th Engrs.
327th (II) Tank Battalion.	June 1918	A. E. F.							
a. 345th Tank Battalion.	September 1918	do.	March 1919 do.	Cp. Upton, N. Y. Cp. Meade, Md.		March 1919.			Active through 1919.

TANK BATTALIONS—Continued

Unit designation and redesignation	Organization		Stations in United States		Overseas		Demobilization		Remarks
	Month and year	Place	Month and year	Place	From—	To—	Month and year	Place	
328th Tank Battalion	April 1918	Cp. Colt, Pa.	August 1918	P. of E., Hoboken	August 1918.				
			March 1919	Cp. Mills, N. Y.		March 1919.			
			do.	Cp. Meade, Md.					Active through 1919. G. H. Q. troops.
329th Tank Battalion	May 1918	do.	August 1918	P. of E., Hoboken	August 1918.				
			March 1919	Cp. Mills, N. Y.		March 1919.			
			do.	Cp. Meade, Md.					Do.
330th Tank Battalion	do.	do.	August 1918	P. of E., Hoboken	August 1918.				
			March 1919	Cp. Mills, N. Y.		March 1919.			
			do.	Cp. Meade, Md.			October 1919	Cp. Meade, Md.	G.H.Q. troops.
331st Tank Battalion	June 1918	do.	August 1918	P. of E., Hoboken	September 1918.				
			March 1919	Cp. Upton, N. Y.		March 1919.			
			do.	Cp. Meade, Md.			do.	Do.	
332d Tank Battalion	do.	do.	September 1918	Cp. Summerall, Pa.					
			do.	P. of E., Hoboken	September 1918.				
			May 1919	Cp. Mills, N. Y.		May 1919	May 1919	do.	Do.
333d Tank Battalion	do.	do.					December 1918	Cp. Dix, N. J.	
334th Tank Battalion	August 1918	do.					do.	Do.	
335th Tank Battalion	September 1918	do.	October 1918	P. of E., Hoboken	October 1918.				
			May 1919	Cp. Mills, N. Y.		May 1919	May 1919	Cp. Meade, Md.	Do.
336th Tank Battalion	do.	do.	October 1918	P. of E., Hoboken	October 1918.				
			May 1919	Cp. Mills, N. Y.		do.	do.	do.	Do.
337th Tank Battalion	do.	do.	October 1918	P. of E., Hoboken	October 1918.				
			May 1919	Cp. Mills, N. Y.		do.	do.	do.	Do.
338th Tank Battalion	do.	do.					December 1918	Cp. Dix, N. J.	
339th Tank Battalion	October 1918	do.					do.	Do.	
340th Tank Battalion	November 1918	Cp. Polk, N. C.					do.	Cp. Greene, N. C.	
341st Tank Battalion	do.	do.					do.	Do.	
342d Tank Battalion	do.	do.					do.	Do.	
343d Tank Battalion	do.	do.					do.	Do.	
344th Tank Battalion									See 326th (II) T.Bn.
345th Tank Battalion									See 327th (II) T.Bn.
346th Tank Battalion	October 1918	Cp. Colt, Pa.					December 1918	Cp. Dix, N. J.	

Appendix C

Tank Corps Organization, July–November 1918, *Order of Battle, The United States Land Forces in the World War, Zone of the Interior: Directory of Troops,* vol. 3, pt. 1

(Washington, D.C.: U. S. Army Center of Military History, 1988): 495–96.

Tank Corps Organization as of 29 July 1918

Authorized	Organized in		Not yet organized
	United States	Overseas	
General Tank Headquarters			1
General Light Tank Headquarters			1
General Heavy Tank Headquarters			1
8 Tank Centers	1	2	5
8 Repair and Salvage Cos	2	1	5
3 Training and Replacement Cos. (H.)		2	1
10 Training and Replacement Cos. (L.)	4	4	2
1 Depot Company	1		
15 Heavy Companies	12	3	
5 Heavy Battalion Headquarters	1	2	2
60 Light Companies	24	6	30
20 Light Battalion Headquarters	1	2	17

On 29 August 1918, to provide training organizations in the United States, the following additional units were authorized: two heavy tank battalions, six light tank battalions, one tank repair and salvage company, and one heavy tank repair and salvage company.

On 12 and 27 September 1918, further authorizations provided for the following overseas organizations:

General headquarters	1
Army tank headquarters	2
Brigade and center headquarters	13
Repair and salvage headquarters	13
Heavy battalion headquarters	10
Heavy companies	30
Light battalion headquarters	20
Light companies	60
Training and replacement companies, heavy	6
Training and replacement companies, light	12
Depot companies	2

On 30 September 1918, training and replacement units in the United States were ordered increased by two training centers, one training and replacement company (light), and one headquarters.

In addition, to provide personnel for depots, schools, and the Office of the Director of the Tank Corps, an increase of 151 officers and 588 enlisted men was granted.

At the date of the armistice, the Tank Corps had a strength of 1,090 officers and 14,870 enlisted men. Of this total, 47 percent were in the AEF or on route, and 53 percent were in the United States.

Appendix D

The St. Mihiel Offensive, September 12–16, 1918, where the 344th and 345th Tank Battalions supported the 1st and 42d Infantry Divisions in the attack.

(John J. Pershing, *My Experiences in the World War*, vol. 2 [New York: Stokes, 1931], 270)

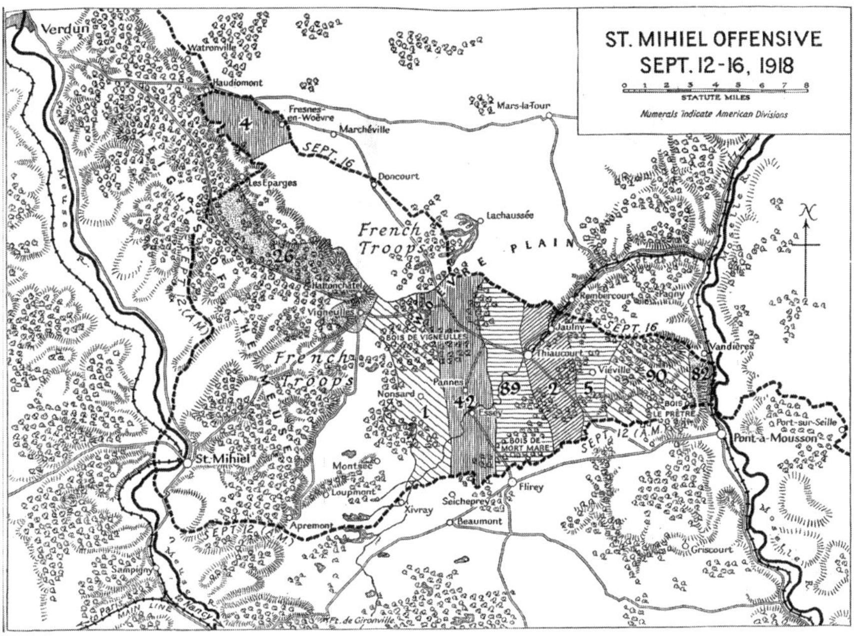

Appendix E

The Meuse-Argonne Offensive, which began on September 26, 1918, where the 344th and 345th Tank Battalions supported the 28th and 35th Infantry Divisions in the attack.

(John J. Pershing, *My Experiences in the World War*, vol. 2 [New York: Stokes, 1931], 352)

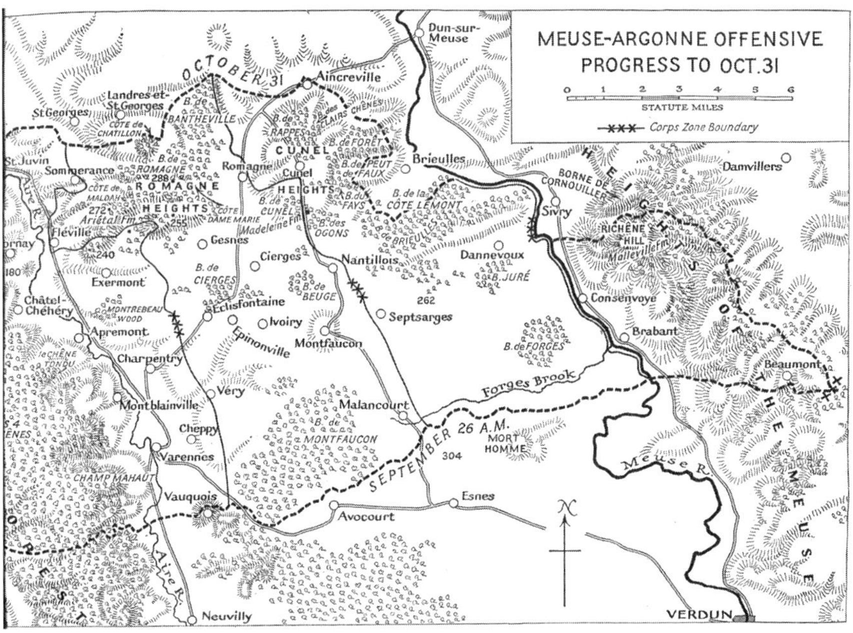

Appendix F

The 27th and 30th Infantry Divisions in the Somme Offensive, September 29, 1918, where the 301st Tank Battalion supported the 27th Infantry Division opposite the Bellicourt Tunnel, with the village of Bony as its objective.

(John J. Pershing, *My Experiences in the World War*, vol. 2 [New York: Stokes, 1931], 305)

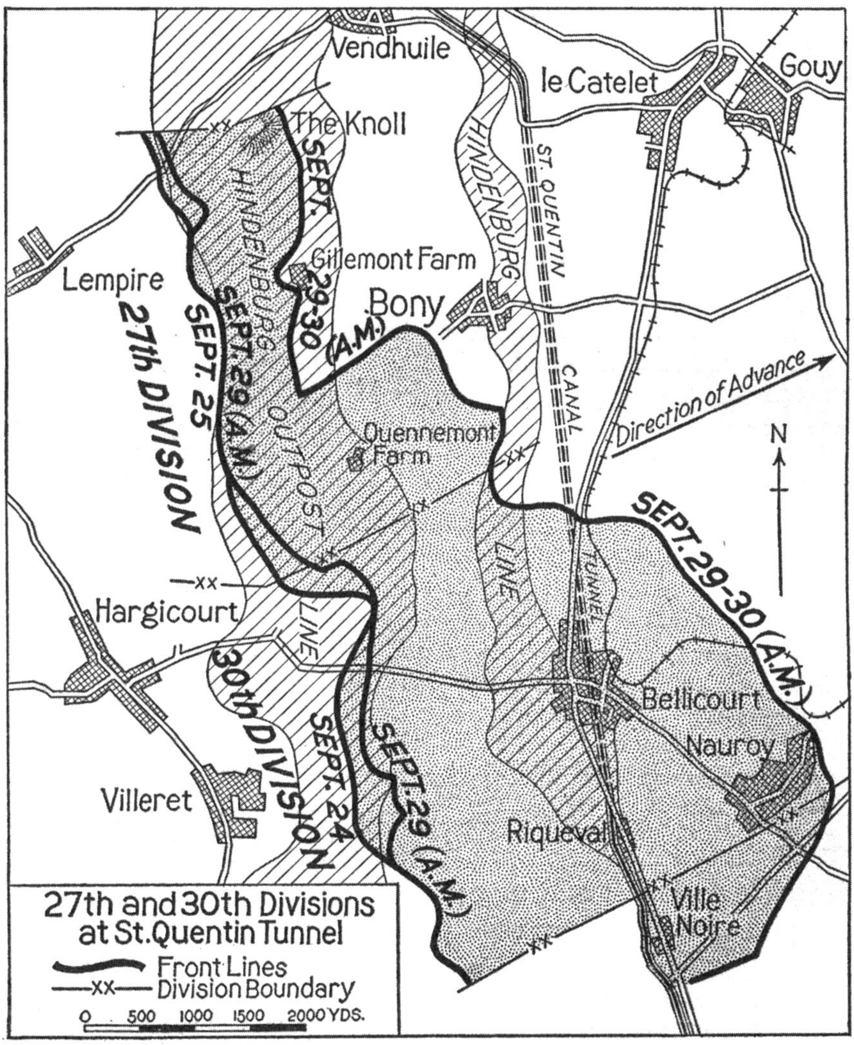

Appendix G

The 27th and 30th Infantry Divisions in the Somme Offensive, October 6–21, 1918, where the 301st Tank Battalion first supported the 30th Infantry Division at Brancourt and then the 27th and 30th Infantry Divisions at St. Souplet.

(American Battle Monuments Commission, *American Armies and Battlefields in Europe* [Washington, DC: Government Printing Office, 1938], 389)

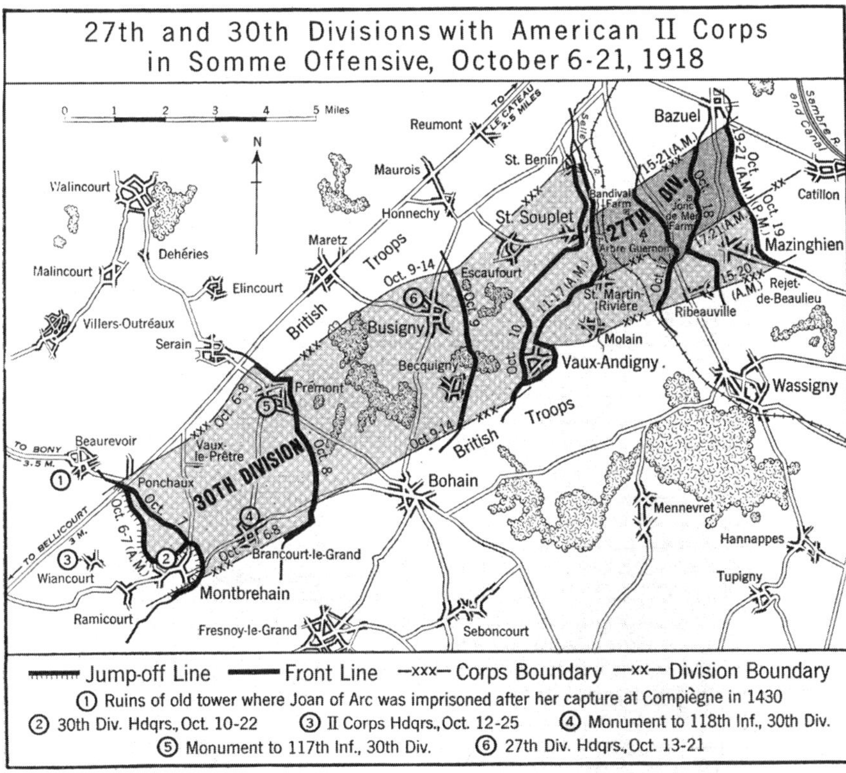

Appendix H

The British advance in the Somme Offensive (shown by white line) by October 23, 1918.

("Closeup of the Field Where Maubeuge Is the Goal," *Wichita Beacon*, October 26, 1918, 4)

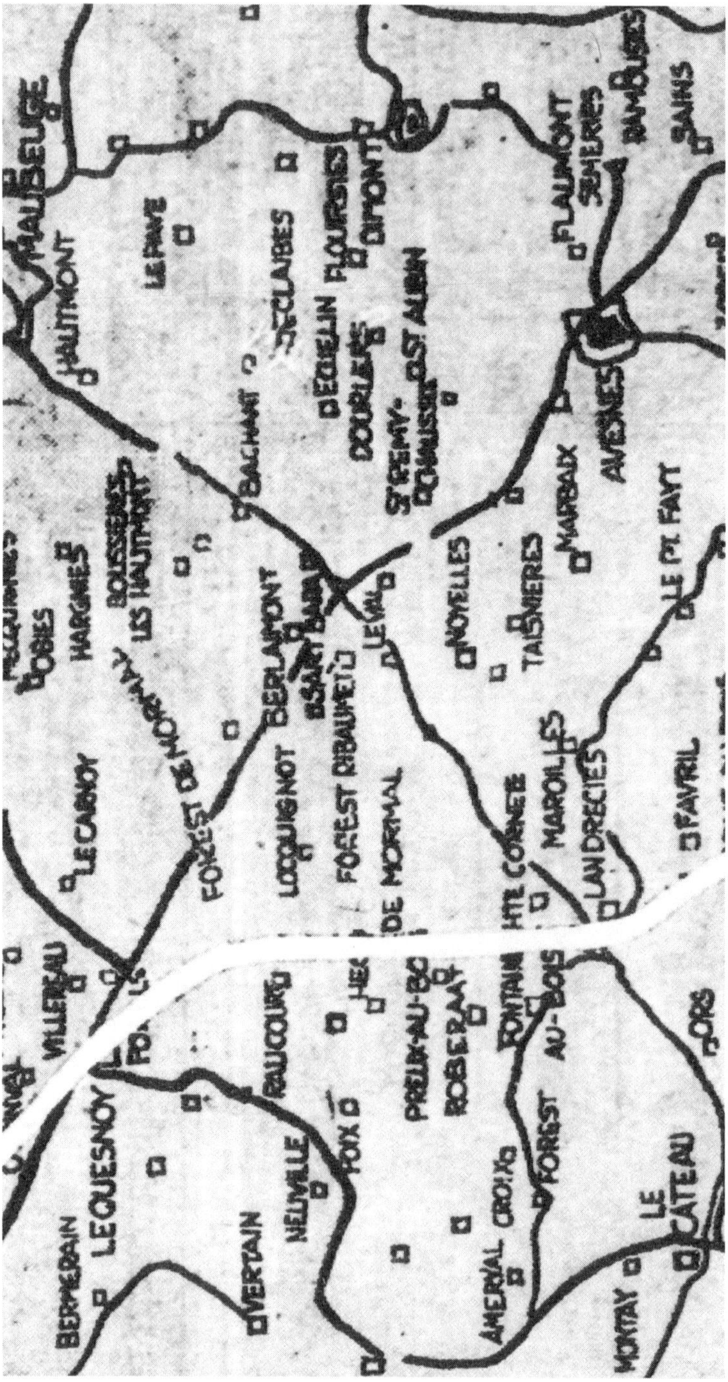
MAUBEUGE
HAUTMONT
LE PAVE
ECLAIBES
FLOURSIES
DIMONT
FLAUMONT
SEMERIES
SAINS
BACHANT
ECCLES
DOURLERS
ST AUBIN
ST REMY-CHAUSSEE
AVESNES
MARBAIX
LE PT. FAYT
NOYELLES
TAISNIERES
HARGNIES
BOUSSIERES
LES HAUTMONT
OBIES
BERLAIMONT
LEVAL
FOREST RIBAUMET
LOCQUIGNOL
FOREST DE MORMAL
LE CARNOY
VILLEREAU
HTE CORNETE
MAROILLES
LANDRECIES
FAVRIL
LE QUESNOY
BERMERAIN
VERTAIN
NEUVILLE
RAUCOURT
POIX
PREUX-AU-BOIS
ROBERSART
FONTAINE AU BOIS
FOREST
CROIX
AMERVAL
ORS
LE CATEAU
MONTAY

Appendix I

The following chart, "United States' Tank Program in Progress Just Before War Ended" (*Chicago Tribune,* February 2, 1919, D8) highlights the type and number of tanks the US Army planned to procure during the war.

UNITED STATES' TANK PROGRAM IN PROGRESS JUST BEFORE WAR ENDED

TYPE.	NUMBER ORDERED.	TYPE OF GUN.	REMARKS.
Six ton Special Model 1917	4,440 Maxwell Motor Co., Dayton, O. Best Foundry Co., Bedford, O. Van Dorn Iron Works, Cleveland.	Marlin or Browning machine gun or 37 mm. field type gun.	These are the Americanized Renault with Buda or Hudson motor and all other parts duplicate of Renault tank.
Six ton special Mark II. Alden design	1,000 Hudson Motor Car Co., Detroit.	Marlin or Browning machine gun or 37 mm. Puteaux field type gun.	These are the Renault with Hudson motor, transmission, fans, and clutches. Otherwise duplicates of Americanized Renault.
Mark I.	1,000 Ford Motor Co., Detroit.	One Browning and one 37 mm. Puteaux.	This is the new combination 3 ton and 6 ton, 3 man tank with two guns. Hudson engine. Ford tractor transmission, and worm drives.
Three ton.	15,000 Ford Motor Co. Detroit.	One Browning machine gun.	This is the small machine 2 men, one gun. Two passenger car Ford engine and transmission and truck worm drive.
Mark VIII. A. A.	1,500.	7 Hotchkiss machine guns, and two 6 pounders.	This is the Anglo-American program of component parts. England furnished armor plate and guns. Assembly to be at Chateau Boux, France.
Mark VIII. U. S.	1,450.	7 Browning machine guns and two 6 pounders.	These to be made complete in the U. S. except 6 pounders.

Notes

Editor's Introduction

1. The Hindenburg Line was a German defensive position on the Western Front from Arras to Laffaux, near Soissons on the Aisne River.

2. Memorandum, General Headquarters, American Expeditionary Forces, Office of the Chief of Tank Corps, Subject: Personal Experience Reports, 4 December 1918, Record Group 120, Entry 1298, World War I Organization Records, Tank Corps, Tank Corps Headquarters General Orders, Box 15A, 270/32/2600, National Archives and Records Administration, College Park, Maryland.

I. Historical Summary of US Army Tank Corps Operations

1. The previous summary is based in part on an undated article written at the US Army Tank School at Fort Meade, Maryland, in the 1920s in the George S. Patton, Jr., Papers, Library of Congress, Washington, D.C.; and the narrative from a US Army Center of Military History Lineage Series volume: Mary Lee Stubs and Stanley Russell Connor, *Armor-Cavalry, Part I: Regular Army and Army Reserve* (Washington, D.C.: Office of the Chief of Military History, United States Army: 1969), 40–48.

II. Tank Corps Senior Leader Commentary

1. General John J. Pershing was the commander in chief of the American Expeditionary Forces.

2. Colonel George S. Patton Jr. commanded the 304th Tank Brigade, and Colonel Henry E. Mitchell commanded the 305th Tank Brigade.

3. The attack at the St. Mihiel Salient was the first operation in the war carried out by a complete American army under the independent control of its own commander in chief, General Pershing. The plan was to reduce the salient as a preliminary to more decisive operation in the same vicinity. Marshall Ferdinand Foch, the Allied commander in chief, had plans for a convergent movement of Allied forces against the Germans. Under these plans, Pershing's AEF was to advance northward between the Meuse River and the Argonne Forest, supported on its left by French forces west of the Argonne.

4. Shrapnel rounds were antipersonnel artillery munitions designed to air-burst over the intended target, showering the area with dozens of small metal balls.

5. The Aviation Service was established as an independent, but temporary, wartime branch on May 19, 1918.

6. A Chinese copy is in reference to a Chinese tradition of reproducing Western made items.

III. Official Tank Corps Personal-Experience Reports

1. George S. Patton Jr. received a promotion to major on January 26, 1918, a promotion to lieutenant colonel in April, and a promotion to colonel on October 17, 1918. He

organized the Light Tank School at Langres in December 1917. He subsequently organized and commanded the 302d Tank Center at Bourg and commanded the 304th Tank Brigade.

2. Camp Chamberlin was named in honor of Second Lieutenant Guy R. Chamberlin, who was the first Tank Corps officer killed in action.

3. The SS *Appeles* was an ex-German ship that was renamed and fitted out by the US Navy for the US Shipping Board Emergency Fleet Corporation.

4. The Tank Corps shoulder sleeve insignia was a triangular patch divided into equal colors of the three combat arms: blue for infantry; red for artillery; and yellow for cavalry.

5. Maurice H. Knowles, later promoted to captain, was a first lieutenant at the time.

6. "Splash" were metal splinters dislodged inside the tank caused from external fire against its hull.

7. A German Mauser 1918 T-Gewehr 13.2mm anti-tank bullet reportedly could penetrate thirteen-sixteenths of steel armor at 220 yards (see "French Tanks Aid Yanks," *Washington Post,* September 1, 1918, 6).

8. Sergeant Nichols received the Distinguished Service Cross for extraordinary heroism near Charpentry, France, on October 4, 1918.

9. "Top Kicker" is a slang term for a first sergeant.

10. A crib, which was used on a Mark V tank, was a hexagonal-shaped framework of timber braced with steel, five feet wide and ten feet long, which weighed approximately 1,300 pounds, and was carried on the front of the tank to be dropped in a trench to provide better traction in crossing.

11. The tanks were named after playing cards.

12. The phrase "trays beanser" refers to the French term "*tres bien,*" which means "very well."

13. Major Harrison used the following sources in writing his narrative: A notebook he kept as the battalion commander of the 301st Tank Battalion; H. W. Warden Jr., *Acotank* (Philadelphia: E. A. Wright, n.d.); E. A. Montgomery, *Story of the Fourth Army in Battles of the 100 Days, August 8th to November 11th, 1918* (London: Hodder & Stoughton, 1920); J. F. O'Ryan, *The Story of the 27th Division* (New York: Wynkoop Hallenbeck Crawford, 1921); and Jack Price, *Tank Actions* (Kansas City: n.p., n.d.).

14. Price, *Tank Actions,* 27.

15. In this sentence, the German word *Kultur* is a reference to Germany.

16. Reference to Major General William T. Sherman, American Civil War.

17. The reference to "Blighty" signified getting evacuated to England due to a wound.

18. "Z" night is a designation for the initiation of a combat attack or operation.

19. A tank-drome was a tank park.

20. The Mark V series "male" tank was armed with 6-pounder cannons; the "female" version was armed with Hotchkiss machine guns; and the "morphodite" version was armed with both cannon and machine guns.

21. The term "bus" was a nickname for a tank.

22. The tank referred to was most likely named after Admiral of the Fleet, Sir John R. Jellicoe.

IV. Unofficial Personal Accounts

1. Assaulting or killing a soldier in such a manner would have been a court martial-offense if it had been reported.

2. The Society of the First Division, *History of the First Division during the World War, 1917–1919* (Philadelphia: John C. Winston, 1922).

3. Donald Hankey, *A Student in Arms* (New York: Dutton, 1917) was a British officer's essays about the British volunteer army.

4. Snyder is mistaken about the soldier belonging to the 345th Tank Battalion. He identified the soldier as Private Hadley from the 344th Tank Battalion in his official personal-experience report.

5. Lieutenant McCluer was from Virginia, not Arizona.

6. Field Marshal Douglas Haig commanded the British Expeditionary Force on the Western Front from late 1915 until the end of the war.

7. Rosenhagen is mistaken about the lengths of the tanks. The Mark IV tank was 26.5 feet in length, and the Mark V Star tank was 32.5 feet in length.

8. Rosenhagen is mistaken about the general. It was Major General George E. Read, U.S. II Corps.

9. Rosenhagen is mistaken about the date. The 301st Tank Battalion concluded combat operations on November 4.

10. Reference to the 150 horsepower Ricardo engine.

11. The $10,000 reference is to a U.S. government life insurance policy.

Index